FALLING POMEGRANATE SEEDS

THE DUTY OF DAUGHTERS

BOOK ONE OF THE
KATHERINE OF ARAGON STORY

Falling
Pomegranate Seeds

The Duty of
Daughters

WENDY J. DUNN

POESY QUILL PUBLISHING

Poesy Quill Publishing

poesyquill.com

First published 2019

ISBN 978-0-6487152-0-7

This title is also available as an ebook.

Cover Image

Catherine of Aragon as the Magda
Sittow, Michiel (1469-1525)

Credit: Detroit Institute of Arts, USA Founders Society
General Membership Fund/Bridgeman Images.

Those who know, do.

Those that understand, teach.

~ Aristotle

I dedicate this novel to my first born, my beloved son, James. I am so proud and happy you now walk the same road I started walking so many years ago. May you discover what I have learnt – that teaching is a true privilege and calling, where our students teach us more than we can ever teach them.

SCHOLAR

I cradle the books that found me.
Tonight, I prop them on my knees
one by one; each offering up
a lesson I must timely absorb.

The rain speaks of days like these,
in dim light, with only my wit as guide.
No feat of voluptuousness;
of womanhood, shall aid me here.

I tiptoe down these halls,
a quiet predator in the shadows,
light feet, steel-trap cunning,
and wily defiance; I shall show them
what a woman of iron mind can do

~ Eloise Faichney, 2016

(Once my student and now a dear friend, Eloise, with great
joy, I watch you fly high.)

"That's where the truth of history comes in," said Sancho.

"They could as well have passed over such matters in silence out of fairness," said Don Quixote, "for there's no need to write down actions that neither change nor alter the truth of history if they must result in disesteem for the hero. In truth, Aeneas was not so merciful as Virgil paints him, nor Ulysses so prudent as Homer describes him."

"That's so," replied Sancho, "but it is one thing to write as a poet and another as an historian: the poet can relate or sing things, not as they were, but as they ought to have been, and the historian has to write them, not as they ought to have been, but as they were, without adding or taking anything at all from the truth."

Miguel de Cervantes
Don Quixote de la Mancha

LIST OF MAIN HISTORICAL CHARACTERS
USED FICTITIOUSLY IN THIS WORK
INSPIRED BY HISTORY

Beatriz Galindo (b? – 1534)
Years ago I discovered a footnote about this fascinating woman,
known as *La Latina* (Lady of Latin), in an essay about Isabel of
Castile. A Latin expert, poet, so knowledgeable about medicine,
rhetoric and the philosophy of Aristotle, she tutored on the
subjects at the University of Salamanca. Beatriz was also a friend
and advisor to Queen Isabel, as well as being a wife and mother.
She is yet another woman forgotten by history – and a woman
who deserves notice. I hope she forgives my imagination for the
liberties I have taken with her story in these pages, but if it makes
people interested in finding out more about her, then I am happy.
Beatriz was a student of Antonio Elio de Nebrija, a Renaissance
scholar and a man known in history for writing one of the first
books of grammar for a romance language.

Francisco Ramirez (b? – 1501)
Known as "the Artilleryman" during the war of Granada. Husband
of Beatriz Galindo, Francisco Ramirez died in the taking of the
Villa of Lanjaron in Granada, Spain.

Cristóbal Colón (c. 1451 – 20 May 1506)
Christopher Columbus, as he is known in English speaking
countries, was born in the Republic of Genoa which is now part of
modern Italy. He is well known for his exploration of the
Americas.

Isabel I of Castile (1451 – 1504)
Isabel ruled Castile from 1474 to 1504. My imagined construction
of Isabel is drawn from these following works: *Isabel the Queen:
Life and Times* (Peggy K. Liss); and *Isabel of Spain: The Catholic
Queen* (Warren H. Carrol).

Ferdinand II of Aragon (1452 – 1516)
Ferdinand, Catalina's father, was one of the rulers Niccoló
Machiavelli used in *The Prince* as a benchmark for other rulers to
follow. A wily fox and able politician, he made use of whatever he
could, including members of his own family, to achieve his own
ends. This influenced my imagination in the creation of his
character. Machiavelli wrote: "...always using religion as a plea, so
as to undertake greater schemes, he devoted himself with pious
cruelty to driving out and clearing his kingdom of the Moors; nor
could there be a more admirable example, nor one more rare"
(Machiavelli 1532).

Their children
Isabel (1470 – 1498)
Prince Juan (1478 – 1497)
Juana (1479 – 1555)
María (1482 – 1517)
Catalina, later Katherine, Queen of England (1485 – 1536)

María de Salinas, kinswoman of Catherine of Aragon
(? – 1539)

Her parents
Doña Josefa Gonzales de Salinas
Don Martin de Salinas

Ahmed, son of Boabdil, King of Granada

Doña Elvia Manuel

Francisco Jiménez de Cisneros

Fray Hernando de Talavera (1428 – 1507)
confessor to the Queen

Alfonso, Prince of Portugal

Margaret of Austria

Manuel, King of Portugal

Spanish words used in this story and glossary

Alcázar: palace

Amigo: friend

Andas: litter

Cadis: judges

Chopines: platform shoes

Converto: a Jew who becomes Christian

Doña: Lady

Don: Lord

Hidalgo: Spanish noble

Habito: a loose day-gown

Hija: daughter

La Latina: The Lady of Latin

Prima hermana: first cousin

Si: yes

Toca: head covering

Mi chiquitina: little one

THE KINGDOM OF CASTILE

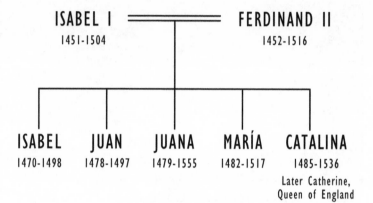

ISABEL I ════════════ FERDINAND II
1451-1504   1452-1516

ISABEL   JUAN   JUANA   MARÍA   CATALINA
1470-1498   1478-1497 1479-1555   1482-1517 1485-1536

Later Catherine,
Queen of England

THE CATALINA FAMILY TREE

FALLING POMEGRANATE SEEDS

THE DUTY OF DAUGHTERS

I

*"Follow your star and you will never fail
to find your glorious port,"* he said to me.
~ Dante Alighieri

Burgos, 1490

Doña Beatriz Galindo caught her breath and tidied her habito. She shook her head a little when she noticed ink-stained fingers and several spots of black ink on the front of her green gown. She sighed. *Too late now to check my face.* "The queen has sent for me," she told the lone guard at the door of the chambers provided for Queen Isabel's short stay at Burgos. The young hidalgo straightened his stance, then knocked once with the back of his halberd on the door, his eyes fixed on the white, bare wall across from him. The door opened and a female servant peeked out at Beatriz, gesturing to her to come in.

In spite of the hours since dawn, the queen sat in bed, her back against oversized cushions. She still wore her white night rail, a red shawl slung around her shoulders, edged with embroidery of gold thread depicting her device of arrows. A sheer, white toca covered her bent head, a thick, auburn plait falling over her shoulder.

Princess Isabel, a title she bore alone as the queen's eldest daughter, and named for both her mother and grandmother, sat on a chair beside her mother, twirling a spindle. Her golden red hair was rolled and wrapped in a cream scarf criss-crossed with black lines, a wry grin of frustration formed dimples in her cheeks before she discarded the spindle in the basket at her feet with the others. She nodded to Beatriz with a slight smile. "Good morning, Latina," she murmured, using the nickname bestowed on Beatriz by the queen. Beatriz hid her stained fingers behind her back and curtseyed her acknowledgement.

Straightening up, Beatriz gazed at the bed-hangings, unfurled behind Queen Isabel. A naked Hercules wrestled with a golden, giant lion, his club on the ground beside him. Turning to her queen, she fought back a smile and lowered her eyes, pretending little interest in Hercules, especially one depicted in his fullest virility.

Queen Isabel balanced her writing desk across her lap, scratching her quill against the parchment, writing with speed and ease. A pile of documents lay beside her. An open one, bearing the seal of the king, topped all the rest. Beatriz's stomach knotted, and not just through worry. She closed her eyes and breathed deeply. *I am free; I am always free while the king is elsewhere. Pray, it is not bad news about the queen's Holy War.* The knot in her stomach became a roaring fire. *Holy War? Jesu' – how I hate calling any war that. Pray God, just keep my beloved safe.*

She almost laughed out loud then; as one of the king's most important artillery officers, Francisco Ramirez, the man Beatriz loved and had promised to marry, did not live to be safe but lived to live. It was one of the things that made her fall in love with him. Waiting to hear the reason for her summons, she gazed around the spacious bedchamber, composing in her mind the letter she would write to him tonight:

My love, my days are long without you...

No – she couldn't write that. If she did, it would be a lie. Her days were full – most mornings she spent tutoring the girls before relishing in the long afternoons free for her own studies. She missed Francisco, but still lived a rich life without him, a richer one when he was at court.

What to write to him then? She could not tell him of her hatred of the Holy War. She could never name as holy a war stamping out any hope of another golden age, when Jews, Moors and Christians lived and worked together in peace. Francisco was a learned man, but a man who used his learning to win this war. Her learning taught her otherwise. It taught her to keep silent about what she really felt to protect the freedoms of her life. Could she tell him then of her joy of teaching the infanta Catalina and her companion María de Salinas? For six months now she had been given full responsibility for their learning. She looked at the queen. Surely the queen was happy with the infanta's progress?

As if Beatriz had spoken out her thought aloud the queen said, "I want to speak to you about my youngest daughter." She waved a hand to a nearby stool. "Please sit."

The queen put aside her quill and pushed away her paperwork. She lifted bloodshot, sore-looking eyes. A yellow crust coated her long, thick lashes.

Seated on the stool, Beatriz gazed at the queen in concern. If there was no improvement by tomorrow, she would prepare a treatment of warm milk and honey for her eyes, even at the risk of once again upsetting those fools calling themselves the queen's physicians.

"Si, my queen?" she murmured.

"Tell me, how do you find my Catalina and our little cousin María?"

Beatriz began breathing easier. Just another summons to do with the infanta's learning. "Both girls are good students, my queen," Beatriz smiled. "The infanta Catalina is a natural scholar. She relishes learning – even when the subject is difficult, but that does not surprise me. Your daughter is very intelligent, just like her royal mother. María, too, is a bright child. Slower than the infanta, but already the child reads simple books written in our native tongue, as well as some Latin. The method of having books written in Latin and Castilian placed side-by-side is working well." Beatriz straightened and lifted her head. "It was the method used to teach me when I was the same age as the infanta."

The queen exchanged a look with her listening daughter.

"I have been pleased to see how much my Catalina, my sweet chiquitina, enjoys her mornings with you." Queen Isabel brought her hands together, drumming her fingertips together for a moment. "Latina, I believe the infantas Juana and María can be given over to other tutors now that you have provided them with an excellent grounding in Latin and philosophy, but I desire you to be Catalina's main tutor, of course that includes María, her companion." Queen Isabel twisted the ring on her swollen finger.

"One day, my Catalina will be England's queen. It will be not an easy task – not in a country that has known such unrest for many, many years. I want to make certain my daughter is as prepared as I can make her, but I need your help. Can I rely on you to stay with us, and teach Catalina what she needs to know of England's history, its customs, its laws?"

"My queen, of course..." Beatriz halted her acceptance when the queen raised her hand.

"Think before you commit yourself. You are betrothed. What will happen when you are wed and, God willing, have the blessing of children? We talk of an obligation of perhaps ten years, and for you to be not only my daughter's tutor, but act also as her dueña."

Beatriz smiled at Queen Isabel. "Francisco and I are both your loyal servants. When the time comes, we will do what needs to done for our marriage and children, but I will confess to you that my real life is here, and as a teacher at the University of Salamanca. I am honoured that you wish me to continue in that role for the infanta. And to be entrusted with teaching your daughter, now and in the future... my queen, words can not describe what that means to me."

Light. So much light. Beatriz Galindo walked back to the library in light, and not just the light from the high archways of the royal alcázar. It was the light of life. Her life. Before the shadows engulfed her again, one archway opened to a garden where running water from a fountain sparkled like diamonds, light and water flashing rainbows onto the high, white stone walls. Beatriz halted by the arch, holding her habito away from her feet, and gazed out before treading into the garden. She sat on a stone bench and looked around her.

At summer's end beauty and ugliness competed for dominance. Most of the flowers were now gone to seed, even the well-tended roses drooped their heads, crimson petals and desiccated leaves of every shade of brown scattering upon an earth sucked dry and cracked by days of relentless heat. Life passed so quickly, one season dying, re-birthing into another.

Beatriz closed her eyes for a moment, raising her face to the sunlight. *Dear God, I have much to give thanks for – I will always be grateful for what I've been given.* Then she thought how complicated was this gratitude. It was a gratitude birthed from sorrow, and from loss.

A shadow fell upon her. She opened her eyes, relieved to see her dearest friend, Josefa de Salinas, smiling down at her. "You are fortunate, Beatriz, to have time to enjoy the day. I am on my way to the queen." Josefa laughed a little. "My royal cousin has summoned me to embroider the hems and collars of her new shifts. Sometimes I wish my mother had not taught me so well my skills with the needle. I may then be like you, amigo, more at liberty to spend my mornings in the garden."

The sheer, white fabric of Josefa's toca wafted in a breeze against the sides of her face. Apprehension stabbed Beatriz. Her friend's face was too pale, too thin. The deep hollows under her high cheekbones were as if strong thumbs had bruised her wan skin. A flowing black habito revealed the swell of her belly, a jewelled scallop, made of gold, gathering together the points of the toca at the breast of her gown. Beatriz did not need her knowledge of medicine or midwifery to know that Josefa's pregnancy was proving difficult. Beatriz swallowed, thinking of what she could make to help her friend. Hiding her anxiety, she smiled at Josefa. "I was thinking of my own mother."

Josefa sat beside her. "Did she not die when you were but a child?"

"Si – I was three when the black death took her. My father never forgave himself that he could not save her from suffering a terrible death. I think I have told you that my father was a famous scholar of medicine, highly regarded in all Castilla – yet all his knowledge proved useless at that time. I was just wondering how different my life would have been if my mother had lived. My father's grief was such he never married again. It no longer mattered that I was but a daughter. He consoled himself by teaching me."

Josefa laughed. "And found himself with a prodigy."

"Prodigy?" Beatriz shrugged. "I'm not certain I was ever that. Rather a child with a great passion for books and learning. I was twelve when my father's great friend Antonio de Nebrija took me under his tutorage. It changed my destiny from that of a religious order to a respected teacher of Latin at the university itself. So respected Queen Isabel sought me out when I was twenty to teach her to read and speak Latin. I have found complete fulfilment these past five years and more – not only as a teacher at Salamanca, but in my work as tutor to the queen's children." Beatriz lifted her gaze to a rose dropping its petals. *Si. Death not only destroyed the life I had then, but also planted the seeds for the life I have now. The life I was meant to live.* She refused to ponder about the dues she sometimes paid.

"You have told me the story before. But what makes you think of this now?" Josefa asked.

"I am happy today – the queen wants me to continue as tutor to her youngest child, and your daughter."

Josefa lifted her dark eyebrows, and grinned wryly. "So – I hear it first from you."

Beatriz eyed her friend. "Do you mind?"

"Does it matter if I mind, or not? Martin or I could not say no to the queen when she asked for María to grow alongside her daughter as her companion. It was a great honour for our family – and all of us saw how much the young infanta loved María. We are close kin, after all, with the queen. I must accept with good grace my daughter shares the same education as the infanta." Josefa glanced towards the archway leading back into the building. "While I would like to sit and talk with you in the sunshine, I must be away if I have any hope of finishing even one of the queen's chemises before the day grows too hot."

Josefa stood up, shook out the folds of her habito and headed towards the sunlit corridor. "No doubt I will see you soon enough," she called over her shoulder.

Beatriz watched her friend go. For a time she sat there, content to be alone with only her thoughts as company, content this sunlit garden held no dark memories for her. At last, she sighed and rose from the bench, heading towards the library. Almost at its door, she heard voices of children. She slipped into the alcove that hid her from view but also allowed her to look into the room.

Catalina and María bent their heads over a book, opened wide upon María's lap. The girls sat in a pool of light from the window behind them. It burnished their hair with gold – lighting Catalina's to a fiery red and covering María's black hair with a veil-like sheen. Even at only five, both girls took great care of precious books. *But where is Doña Teresa Manrigue? She should be here.* A tender-hearted woman, Doña Teresa carried in her pocket a seemingly endless supply of rose sugar as rewards for the children. The last time Doña Teresa left the girls alone in the library she had told Beatriz the infanta had commanded her to go. No wonder the queen desired a new dueña for her daughter.

"My turn to be Arthur!" María said, placing her finger on the page closest to Catalina. Her face a picture of concentration, María licked her top lip. "And as they rode, Arthur said, I have no sword." María's sigh was one of clear relief.

Catalina pulled the book closer to her. "No matter, said Merlin, hereby is a sword that shall be yours."

Beatriz restrained a laugh, hearing the infanta deepen her already low voice. But while one child loved learning, the same couldn't be said about the other. When Catalina pointed to the next passage there was no mistaking María's discomfort as she shook her head. "You do it. You read better."

Catalina's grin revealed missing milk teeth, giving her round face an endearing look. "I only try harder."

"You forget," María said quietly, glancing towards a hoop with an uncompleted embroidery some distance away, "Mamá doesn't care whether I read or not."

Catalina turned to María a look of determination, it was one that mirrored the queen's. Just like her mother, altering the girl's chosen course was nigh on impossible. "I do," Catalina said. "I want you to be as good as me at this. Think, when we learn about herbs from Latina and the good sisters, you can go to my mother's library to know more. Latina says knowing Latin is like having a key that will open many doors. You read now."

Beatriz grinned. Her lessons were not falling on deaf ears.

María read in a halting, uncertain voice: "So they rode till they came to a lake, which was a fair water and broad, and in the midst of the lake Arthur was aware of an arm clothed in white samite, that held a fair sword in that hand..."

"Catalina!"

Beatriz almost jumped out of her skin when the young, grating voice called. Stepping out of the alcove, she saw the infanta Juana rushing down the corridor, followed by her dueña and two female slaves. A child of ten, Juana's slight form was outlined in sun-edged shadow.

"Latina! I did not think to find you here too." Juana looked into the library. "Sister, our lady mother desires our presence in her chamber."

Catalina gazed at her older sister and then back at the book.

"Come, my sister. Latina, you come too."

The infanta Juana disappeared from view, her women picking up their skirts and rushing after her. Beatriz smiled, reminded of the goose girl she had seen only this morning, searching for herbs not grown in the royal gardens. The swish of long dresses and under-breath protestations hissed after the infanta like a gaggle of annoyed geese.

Her face pensive and full of regret, Catalina shut the book, caressing its engraved leather cover before passing it to María. The two girls got to their feet, María cradling the book in her arms. Catalina ran after her sister. Silken slippers padded against the tiled floor until fading to a whisper. Now all alone in the library, María stood on her tiptoes, returning the book to its rightful place.

Beatriz hurried back to the queen's chambers with the others.

The guard blinked in surprise, seeing her yet again, when Juana knocked and Catalina beckoned to Beatriz to follow. One by one they entered the queen's bedchamber, Juana's dueña and slaves stepping aside to wait outside the door.

The queen was still abed, still writing, appearing disturbed, even downhearted. Wondering what could have changed the queen's mood so quickly, Beatriz noticed the queen was writing a letter to the king. Looking around the room, she thought of her unwritten letter to Francisco. Should she write to him of Prince Juan, now perched on the edge of the bed, his head bent, silver-blond hair half covering his face? The prince strummed his small harp, one long, slender leg folded under the other. Or should she write of his sisters – Isabel, the eldest child of the queen, Juana, María, and small Catalina? Beatriz lowered her face to hide her smile. Perhaps her letter would turn out like her last – one where she wrote to Francisco about the Aristotle tract she was translating from the Latin to Castilian, and yet more suggestions about what he should do to protect his hearing. She had even quoted to him from her lecture about Bartholomew the Englishman to underscore her seriousness. But then too Francisco's love letters did not fit the usual pattern of a lover. So many times his letters were full of his experiments with gunpowder, even sharing different recipes he'd tried in his efforts to discover a trustworthy composition, and the success, or lack of it, he had in weakening the fortifications of the Moors. Sometimes he even asked her to seek out in the queen's library for books that would help him in his task to blow up walls that had stood for centuries. She only agreed to his proposal of marriage when he promised her their mutual quest for knowledge would never change. She had no reason to doubt him. They had been good friends since she first took up her position at court. A widower ten years older than she, with two grown sons and one married daughter, Francisco was a man who understood the passions of minds.

Beatriz returned to the present moment. Prince Juan blinked as if waking from a dream, his handsome, sensitive face that of a poet.

Humming in accompaniment to her brother's song, Infanta María, three years older than Catalina, twirled her spindle, sitting next to her adult sister, Isabel. Not one to love learning for the sake of learning like her three sisters and brother, the infanta María was a kind child who never seemed to share the melancholic natures of her more sensitive siblings. Sometimes Beatriz wondered if she was born under a kinder, happier star.

Princess Isabel reached for *Livy's Decades* on the table beside her and opened it to a page deep within the book. Her index finger pulled at her bottom lip, eyes scanning the page, turning it quickly to the next. Catalina and her small companion watched on in fascination. Beatriz smiled. She could guess the girls desired to read just as fast.

Suitably serious as the eldest child of her mother, Princess Isabel rarely wasted her time with books of courtly romance. Her mother sometimes teased her, as she also did her second daughter, Juana, by calling the princess 'my mother-in-law'. But while the queen called the infanta Juana thus because she inherited the dark bold beauty of her father's mother, Isabel gained the name because she shared her grandmother's solemn outlook on the world and desire for study and prayer. The queen held up the king's mother as yet another example for her daughters to mirror.

Small Catalina, fifteen years the younger, wanted to be just like her eldest sister, Isabel. As the companion of the infanta, María had little choice but to follow after. Both girls still preferred tales of King Arthur or El Cid, favouring the chivalry intertwined with magic and love and longing of King Arthur's court. It was a good thing the queen had a well-stocked library with a full collection of the Arthur legends, from French poems to their favourite Latin text written by an English knight. The girls were always asking Beatriz for new stories.

The queen lifted her gaze from the half-finished letter. Her worn face softened into a welcoming smile as she looked over to her youngest daughter. Letting go of the parchment, she pushed her desk aside and held out her arms. "Mi chiquitina, come! Come and embrace your mother."

Josefa, putting aside her sewing, grinned at Beatriz, placing a hand on her daughter María's shoulder. The child flung her arms around her mother, cushioning her face against her breasts. Josefa bent her head, kissing the top of María's head. She looked up at Beatriz and smiled again. "I said I'd see you soon enough." Without waiting for an answer, Josefa took her daughter's hand and led her from the royal family to the far end of the room where there were, prepared already for the night, two bed-pallets.

With not enough rooms in this beautiful but small alcázar for the queen and her court, her four daughters and their most trusted attendants slept on pallets in the large chamber near the queen's private rooms. The queen never slept alone. She shared her chambers with her daughters because King Ferdinand stayed too long away from her side. No one could doubt the queen's honour or wifely virtue while she slept with her own daughters and favoured women. Now the time approached for the court to leave Burgos to join the king at Sevilla.

A finger to her lips, gesturing to her daughter for silence, Josefa sat on a chair, picked up a border of black material, and returned to her needle. She stitched the gold, even loops of punto real, a favoured stitch of the queen. On the nearby stool was a neatly folded chemise waiting to be joined to the finished embroidery.

Firelight flickered, glinting upon the gold, silver and jewel-decorated vessels set upon a nearby table. Beatriz stepped into deeper shadows, where no candle or firelight reached, seeking not to be noticed. Her eyes rested on the royal family. The queen's blessing done, Catalina clambered onto her mother's bed and kissed her cheek. The queen wound her arms around her youngest child. She laughed softly, caressing Catalina's hair.

Prince Juan, Catalina's twelve-year-old brother, dropped his harp on the bed. His blue eyes glowing with mischief, he tickled his sister's underarm. She giggled, nestling into him. The prince stood on the threshold between pretty boy and beautiful youth. Blond down intermixed with a darker, thicker colour upon his cheeks. He tickled Catalina again.

The child giggled. "Stop it, Juan!"

Juan laughed. He flicked back the straight fringe from his eyes before reclaiming his harp and plucking a short tune. The black velvet of his doublet increased the bright blond lustre of his hair, candlelight creating an aureole around his head. Angel, his mother called him. Prince Juan well deserved his nickname. All loved him.

"Your command is mine! What song shall I play you, sister?" asked the prince.

The queen's smile embraced them both. She rested her fingers on her son's arm. He returned a gaze full of love.

"Son, not yet. I want to first speak to Catalina." She encircled her daughter with her arms, drawing her closer. "Mi chiquitina, can you remember what happened two years ago?"

Catalina looked up, bewildered. "Mamá?"

The queen sighed. Her jaw slackening, she no longer smiled. A candle gusted out, casting her face into deep shadow. Communing as if with the unseen, she tightened her hold on her daughter.

"I forget – 'tis long for a small child to remember... In truth, you were little more than an infant when the English came and I, holding you on my lap, showed you the bulls." The queen smiled slightly. "You wore your first gown of black velvet that day, one rich with jewels. The next day we promised you to their prince." She looked again at Catalina and stroked her hair. Wrapping a lock around her finger, she studied it and let it go, her face becoming strong again. "I have just received word from your father. We have promised another of our hijas to another king's son. My Isabel?"

Princess Isabel playfully peered over the book. "Mamá?"

"Come, and tell your sister your news."

Isabel strode over to the bed with all the grace and confidence of a young woman of twenty. She sat on the other side of her mother's wide bed and took Catalina's hand. "I'm to be wed."

Catalina cried out and threw herself into her sister's arms, pulling at the long chain of Isabel's heavy, gold crucifix. Princess Isabel's laugh overlaid the silence of the other occupants in the queen's chamber. Disentangling herself from her sister, she said, "Be careful, mi chiquitina."

"Married! But to whom?"

"Can't you guess?" Isabel laughed, but didn't wait for Catalina to answer. "I'm marrying Prince Alfonso of Portugal. One day he'll be Portugal's king, and I its queen."

Queen Isabel gazed at her eldest and youngest daughters with cheerless eyes. "Isabel, I hoped that service for your sister, María, many years hence. Whilst your father, before he owned to the French king's treacherous heart, wished you wed to the French prince, I wanted so much to find you a husband of suitable birth to keep you with us in Castilla. You are my first born, after all. But Alfonso remembers you too well from the time when you both were hostages together. He wants you, and only you."

Princess Isabel smiled, stretching out her hand to her mother. The queen clasped it and held it against her cheek. Catalina's wide eyes travelled from her mother to her sister. "You're leaving us?"

Isabel's eyes shone with sudden tears. "I must, mi chiquitina."

Catalina wrapped her arms around her sister. "Don't go, I beg you!"

Over her head, Isabel the mother and Isabel the daughter gazed at one another. Lines of pain scored deep in the queen's white face, rending her almost ugly. She shut her bloodshot eyes, biting her bottom lip. In the heavy silence, Beatriz could hear the drum of her own heart in her ears.

The prince swung from the bed with nimble grace. Standing between María and Juana he clasped their hands. All three of them gazed at the bed.

With a short laugh, Isabel's arms tightened around her youngest sister. "Catalina, listen. Portugal is not so far away that I cannot ever come home. In any case, I know my duty and do it willingly."

Catalina grabbed her sister's habito, as if she wouldn't let her go. Isabel frowned and shook her head, not one strand of hair daring to shift from its rightful place. "When you're older, you too will do your duty and marry your English prince. You will not fail God or your country then. I will not fail it now."

Gently Isabel extricated Catalina from her arms and dried her sister's tears. A finger under Catalina's chin, she forced her small sister to look at her.

"Child, needless weeping is not for Castilian princesses." Isabel looked at the queen with pride. "Especially hijas of our mother, the greatest queen ever known to Christendom. And what reason for tears? I am happy to wed Alfonso. I learnt to love him long ago and go to him with joy in my heart."

2

Mujer que sabe latin rara vez tiene buen fin.
Hija hilandera, hija casadera.

The woman who knows Latin seldom ends up well.
The daughter who spins is a daughter who is marriageable.

Night fell. Cold, Beatriz curled up in her narrow trundle bed, trying to get comfortable, trying to sleep. The infantas talked softly to one another in the shared chamber, the older ones engrossed in the plans to celebrate Isabel's wedding in Sevilla. At last the excited infantas settled down, their discussions dissipating to a lulling word here and there until the breathing of Juana and María became that of the sleeping. Beatriz closed her heavy eyes and began to drift towards dream, only to be startled back into wide-eyed wakefulness by Catalina's excited voice. Very young, the child's tone punctuated the growing silence. "You never spoke of him."

Covered with white furs, Princess Isabel twisted on her couch, grey shadow falling like a blanket on her slender form. Near night candles lit up her teeth and eyes.

"Alfonso? How could I? The match wasn't set in stone. Indeed, our father fought for years to dissolve the contract of my betrothal. And for good reason. I am the heir to our mother's throne after Juan, God protect him." Isabel crossed herself. "That might prove true for our father's kingdom, too. Mother wants Father to force Aragon to stop insisting on male succession." She glanced at Catalina. "Also, the King of Portugal may have agreed to settle for our sister María, once she reached marriageable age."

Catalina rolled on the narrow pallet to face her sister. "You did not want that?"

Isabel shifted like one discomforted. "You're no longer an

infant. You should know by now that what we want for ourselves matters very little. We serve, and obey."

"But, sister, your heart?" When Catalina gestured with palm upraised, it seemed to Beatriz she held to her sister the heart she spoke of.

"Heart?" Isabel's muted, grim laugh resonated in the high ceiling chamber. She glanced over to Beatriz. "Our La Latina likes to sprinkle too well her lessons with tales of romance. I beg you, don't believe them."

She lounged back, letting out a deep breath. "But you are right. For my own sake, I did not want our sister María matched to Portugal's prince. Alfonso and I became good friends during the time we were held hostage together." Isabel shrugged. "He is three years younger than me. I cared for him as I do for Juan, like I do for you all.

"But we also shared that we're both eldest children of ruling monarchs. Such children do not stay children for long." Isabel's teeth shone with an unexpected smile. "He kissed my lips when we said farewell." A dreamlike shaft of light showed her straightening her form on the couch, hands locking behind her head. When Isabel spoke again, it seemed she spoke to herself rather than her little sister. "My first kiss from a noble-born youth, not a brother or close male kin. An innocent boy's kiss, si. But even then, a kiss that promised much." Isabel turned again to her sister. "Mi chiquitina, no more questions. Time for you to sleep. Would you like for me to provide a lullaby by reciting your favourite part of *El Cid*?"

With a squeal of delight, Catalina nodded. Yawning, Beatriz rubbed her eyes. Rolling on her side, she listened to Isabel's melodious voice:

> *"Ah Cid I kiss thine hands again,*
> *but make a gift to me*
> *Bring me a Moorish mantle*
> *splendidly wrought and red."*
> *"So be it. It is granted,"*

the Cid in answer said,
"If from abroad I bring it,
well doth the matter stand...

That same night Beatriz awoke to the sound of Catalina weeping. She sighed and slipped from her bed to go to sit by the child. Catalina looked up at Beatriz. The girl took a shuddering breath, bit her bottom lip, her tears stopping. Beatriz touched the child's wet cheek, smiling at her in reassurance. Too many nights Catalina awoke like this. It was one of the reasons why María de Salinas had come to companion the young infanta. She was one who knew how best to comfort her in her night terrors. Before María, Catalina had wept until the break of dawn, or when the queen sent a priest to pray over her. Beatriz believed the child was unsettled by the long, arduous journeys from one part of her mother's huge kingdom to another. She was also a girl blessed with a deep awareness of good and evil, attuned to the world of the spirit.

Catalina sniffed and rubbed her eyes. She inhaled another shuddering breath. "Forgive me," she whispered. "I'm all right now. Teacher," she pointed, "I beg you to re-light that candle."

The oscillating saffron light of the near fire revealed the dim tower of the blown-out candle, placed near Catalina's bed. Beatriz lumbered sleepily to relight it. The candle burning bright, she returned to Catalina and sat by her side. "Why are you so afraid of the dark, child?" she asked quietly, aware of their sleeping companions.

Catalina shook her head. "Not the dark... only what it brings."

"Bad dreams come to all, my infanta." A slant of blue moonlight slipped through the window and showed Catalina lowering her gaze, as if ashamed.

"Si. But this bad dream won't leave me alone."

"Would you like to tell me about it?"

Catalina stared up at her. "An eagle sits on my chest." She brushed away fresh tears. "It pulls out my heart."

Taken aback, Beatriz rubbed the side of her face. Why would a child have such a dream? What could she say to her? She weighed up her words slowly and with care. "Believe me, nightmares don't

31

hurt us. Even in dreams we can call for God's help, and protection. He turns nightmare back into dream. When you dream this dream, pray to God to make the eagle fly away."

Catalina looked at her in bewilderment. She seemed struggling with knowledge far beyond that of a child's. "You don't understand. 'Tis when the eagle flies away I wake up weeping."

A few days later, Beatriz sat by the window, reading, near to where Queen Isabel and her four daughters twirled their spindles from their distaffs. Lifting her eyes from her book, she saw Catalina's companion stick out her tongue and Catalina's answering grin. The two five-year-olds reddened when Princess Isabel glared at them. Scowling, she gestured to them to return to their task. Beatriz closed her book, listening to the queen.

"One must first give battle before claiming victory. If you do nothing, you end with nothing. Remember well my words – those who do not recognise opportunity when it comes, find misfortune in its place. My hijas, you go to rule alongside your husbands..."

The queen placed a finished spindle in the basket beside her feet before picking up an empty one. Holding it in one hand, she sat up, the fingers of the other hand slipping under her white toca. She combed her fingers through her hair not once or twice, but three times, each time her fingers slower than the last, as if measuring out her words. "Si, you will rule too, but never let them know that. Men believe they possess the upper hand. The wise woman never lets her menfolk know otherwise."

Twisting her spindle back and forth, Princess Isabel stroked back a few loose strands of fine red/gold hair escaping from her silver hair net, seemingly far-away in her own deep thoughts. Shimmering with rainbows, tiny pearls glistened like tear drops throughout the weave of silver. On her stool, Juana swivelled from watching her older sister, her deep blue eyes now turned to the queen.

"Mother... may I ask who has the greater power – you or our lord father?"

The queen's face spoke her surprise with the lift of her thin eyebrows. Taking in her daughter's seriousness, she smiled. "Your question gives me pleasure, my Juana. You should think about such matters. As for the answer – your father and I work in partnership and I share my rule with him. He is my king, and my beloved lord."

Twirling her spindle with confidence, María piped in, her usual reticence seemingly all forgotten. "I don't understand, Mother. I hear the priests say husbands are always the heads of their wives. But you and Father –" the infanta shifted upon the stool, clearly ill at ease, "'tis not like that at all."

The queen dropped her spindle onto her lap, now swinging her approval to her third daughter. "My Joy," she said, using María's nickname. Queen Isabel used it so often her siblings had taken to using it, too. "You're right to remember well the teachings of the church. But God places us in a peculiar position – a position where we serve Him by offering up ourselves. That is the duty of our royal blood."

"But will not our husbands be our heads, Mother?" Infanta María darted a look at Beatriz. "Yesterday, Latina discussed with us the words of Aristotle." The young infanta's face frowned in concentration. "Juana – do you remember?"

"'Men's courage is shown in commanding and women's in obeying,'" Juana answered.

Thoughtfully, the queen picked up the spindle again, her long fingers pulling at the woollen thread from the distaff, keeping the thread taut and even. She glanced aside at Juana. "'And the male is naturally more fit to command than the female, excepting where there is a miscarriage of nature.'" The queen laughed with grimness. "I have heard it all before, and too many times. Aristotle also said, 'The male is by nature superior and the female inferior; one rules and the other is ruled.' I confess something to you, my hijas. I think often of the words of our ancestor, Alfonso the Wise. He said, 'Had I been present at the creation, I would have given some useful hints for the better ordering of the universe.'" Her spindle stopped twirling and she yanked at the thread. "This world is a hard one for women, but we make the best of our lot. Since time began, men and women suffer and learn... women most of all."

The queen straightened. "Learn from me here, my hijas. Let your husbands think they are the head, let them be the head when times allow, but always be ready to do what God tells you is right. Listen to your hearts and souls, as well as to your minds." She drummed the spindle against the black velvet of her habito, pulled taut over her thigh. "You four are hijas of two proud royal houses. Your marriages will work towards giving our land stronger ties and power throughout Christendom, all for the glory of God. Think too what it means for your brother if we place his sisters in positions to help him as king of two kingdoms.

"My hijas, work towards forging strong friendships and alliances with people who will best aid and shield you in the future when you no longer have my protection. Whatever befalls you, be watchful. Keep your people close. Never forget to reward those who deserve it, those close to you, and those you want closer. Punish those who betray you and never, ever show yourself weak.

"Hijas, remember this, too – keep your hearts and minds chaste and your bodies from ill and wanton company. Your grandmother raised me in honesty and with much care for my purity, and I have done the same for you girls. 'Tis not just your bodies I speak about here. I tell you in truth, we gain nothing if we lose our souls. Rulers, too, must remember this." The queen grinned, a smile embracing all her daughters in its warmth. "We are the blood of the Trastámara. Strong, God-fearing women make up the fabric of our royal house, women you can be proud of – think you of your ancestress, Saint Isabel. My four girls will be worthy of them, for already you make me proud. Enough said." She glanced at Catalina. "Child, do you wish to begin us in Latin conversation?"

Dropping her spindle upon her lap, Catalina sat straighter, her hands holding the sides of her square stool. She nodded, her eyes alert, shining, eager.

The queen laughed, a gentle laugh she saved for private

moments with her children. "Mi chiquitina, your poor mother became a student far later than you. Pray, give me at least a few minutes before you outpace me. Indeed, if all you girls could remember who is queen here?"

Seeing the queen's proud gaze, Beatriz joined in with her daughters' laughter before re-opening her book and resuming her reading.

B

If you can't bite, don't show your teeth.
~ Castilian proverb

"Could we not go and see my brother?" Catalina asked. Beatriz sighed. Their imminent departure had disturbed today's lesson, again and again. All morning, servants came and went, emptying the library of the queen's most precious books. Bad weather slammed the door shut on any hope of being allowed outside this morning. The girls had struggled for the last hour to complete their reading in the midst of what seemed the confusion of an overturned beehive. No wonder Catalina wished to escape from the hectic bustle of a court making ready to move once again.

Putting down her quill, Beatriz gestured her defeat. Without any more discussion, Catalina pulled María in the direction of a far more secret door, hidden underneath a huge wall tapestry at the side of the room's fireplace, with Beatriz following close behind. The secret door opened to a secret passage going from one wing of royal apartments to the other – not only to ease the way for the king to come to his wife, but also to aid a safe and quick escape for the royal family. For years now the prince had possessed his own establishment, practising the art of ruling within the security of his mother's court. While the king was with the army, the prince occupied his father's apartments.

One guttering torch, set high in a blackened sconce, lit dimly the short passageway to the spiral staircase at the end of the corridor. First to bound over the last, shortened step upon the staircase, designed to trip and announce an unknowing assassin, Catalina pushed open the hidden door to the prince's bedchamber.

A sudden burst of light from a nearby window illuminated Princes Juan and Ahmed playing chess together. Ahmed, the nine-year-old son of Boabdil, Moor king of Granada, had been held as a hostage for his father's freedom and good behaviour since the age of two. Lovingly called Infantico by Queen Isabel, he was treated like a member of the royal family and raised as a Christian, and a loyal Castillan.

Catalina called out her greeting and the two princes turned. Ahmed's dark, huge eyes flashed in welcome, his smile stretching across his plump face. Only his thickly lashed, dark brown eyes showed his Moorish ancestry, for his skin was as pale as all of Queen Isabel's family. Blond-haired like Prince Juan, the boys could have been mistaken for brothers. Prince Juan frowned. "Sister, pray tell me that you asked permission of our mother to visit me?" The prince coughed.

Catalina coloured, biting her bottom lip. Her brother sighed. Rising from his stool, he paced over to his chamber's door and opened it. He stuck his head into the next room. "Miguel," he called. "Tell the queen the infanta Catalina is here with me." Shutting the door he turned back to his sister. "Thank God, I hadn't sent Miguel on another errand, and he was alone. He is one of the few who knows of the secret way between these chambers and our mother's. Anyone else would have wondered how the three of you slipped by the guard."

Ahmed chuckled. "'Twas the way I used today, too."

Prince Juan returned to the stool and grinned. "With my royal mother's permission – something my small sister often forgets to seek in her eagerness to visit me." Crossing long leg over long leg, his tapered fingers tugged at the sag of his red hose. Juan lifted his gaze to his sister. "Or have you come for another reason?"

Beatriz curtseyed. "I beg your forgiveness, my prince. It was my place, not your sister's, to ask the queen's permission. I'm afraid all the disruptions today caused me to forget."

Catalina glanced around the room and almost skipped towards an unused stool. Sitting on it, she placed her hands before her, fingertips touching fingertips, studying her brother. She smiled her most enchanting smile. "We could not study, could we Latina? Even in the library we were made to feel in the way. Is it then wrong to want to see my brother?"

Prince Juan laughed. "Moving court does not trouble me. My men refuse to let such trivial matters concern me." He studied the unfinished chess game. "All I need to do is sit and play with Ahmed until I'm wanted again."

Ahmed pushed forward one of his pieces and picked up one of the prince's pawns. "I'm winning this game."

Prince Juan screwed up his face and rolled his eyes. "Not for the first time. My father is right. I dream too much."

Catalina bounded off her stool. "Can I play against Ahmed next?"

Rising from the chess table, Prince Juan gazed towards his harp. He coughed again – and took a deep breath, as if fighting it. The prince was unwell so often Beatriz kept a well-stocked supply of soothing mixtures of horehound, honey and lemon for his coughs. But hating his times of weakness, Prince Juan worked hard at hiding any sign of illness from everyone, especially his parents.

The prince wiped his mouth. "Take over the game, mi chiquitina. I have a tune in my head I cannot silence." He dipped his head to Prince Ahmed. "Do you mind? Catalina will give you a better game than me, especially today."

Prince Ahmed gestured to the empty seat across from him. "Come, mi chiquitina. Let's see if you can gain victory."

Watching Catalina consider her move, Beatriz put her hands in the deep pockets of her gown and drew them out again in disappointment. Staring down at empty hands, she sighed. Usually, she had small books in her pockets to read at times like these. Now she prepared for boredom. María too shifted from foot to foot, but then Prince Juan turned and spoke. "María. My vihuela is still unpacked. Take it up, cousin, and sit by me. I need your help with my song."

Happiness lighting up her face, María grabbed the vihuela next to Juan. She gazed at him with joy, with worship, as if unable to believe he trusted her with one of his most loved musical instruments, let alone believe he asked her aid to make music. The prince had played vihuela for years and María only for the last nine months since companioning Catalina.

Knowing the gentle prince would not expect her to ask permission in his private rooms, Beatriz settled on a stool, words of Aristotle coming to mind:

> ... *shall we rather suppose that music tends to be productive of virtue, having a power, as the gymnastic exercises have to form the body in a certain way, to influence the manners so as to accustom its professors to rejoice rightly? Or shall we say, that it is of any service in the conduct of life, and an assistant to prudence? for this also is a third property which has been attributed to it.*

Beatriz turned to the window, and began planning her next lesson for the girls.

Later that day Prince Ahmed plopped down next to Beatriz on the stone seat built as part of the protruding oriel window. The boy gazed down at the steep, rocky cliff-face that defended one side of the queen's alcázar just as surely as did her soldiers, maybe more so, as it was difficult to imagine any – friend or foe – surmounting the sheer, inhospitable cliffs. Turning to her, Ahmed commanded. "Tell me of my mother."

Her mind distracted by wondering how long it would take the royal court to reach their next palace, Beatriz laughed, shut the book she was reading and placed it on her lap. "Again, my prince?"

"Pray, one more time," Ahmed flashed a wide smile of perfect white teeth. "Until I ask the next time."

Beatriz settled against the cushions, preparing to tell the oft-told story. "She was a daughter of a famous general who spent his fortune in defence of your father's kingdom. In gratitude, your father, my prince, showered a constant stream of titles upon him: Alcaide of Loja, Lord of Xagra, Mayor of the Alhambra and

Sheriff of the Kingdom of Granada. With such a renowned father, it is not then not too surprising your mother became the wife of the king." She smiled a little, knowing she had reached Ahmed's favourite part. "I saw her once with you... Your mother held you in her arms before surrendering you for your father's freedom. The veil on her face did not hide her unforgettable eyes. How piteous they looked when she passed you, her infant son, to the queen's chamberlain."

Ahmed yanked the sleeve of his white shirt. Edged with lace and bordered with embroidery, every stitch of it came from the queen's own hands. "Would she remember me, do you think?"

Beatriz stared at him. She hooded her eyes, compassion flooding her heart. "A good mother never forgets the child she bore into the world. My prince, never doubt that your mother is a good mother. She did not need to come and hand you over at the queen's court. Only when Queen Isabel promised she would care for you like her own children did she let you go. One day, you'll know from your mother's own lips how little she forgot you."

Furious, Ahmed bounded up from the cushions and stood over her. "Why doesn't she write and tell me that now? My father writes to me but my mother, never."

Beatriz bent towards him. "My prince, your father always writes a message from your mother."

Sitting again beside her, Ahmed's lower lip trembled. "A few words – that the king, my father, includes for her."

Gathering her thoughts, Beatriz gazed at the book on her lap before eyeing Ahmed again. "Your mother would write if she was able. Do not fall into the mistake of believing what you see at Queen Isabel's court is the same elsewhere. Dear prince, not all women know how to write."

Ahmed's thick brows puckered in confusion. "Time after time you've told me my mother is intelligent. And my grandmother too. I can easily read, why not them?"

"Many know how to read without knowing how to write. 'Tis a far harder skill to learn, my prince. Do not think harshly of your

mother when countless men have also not learnt to wield a pen."
Beatriz opened the book. "Do you know what I have here?"

Ahmed peered at the cover page. "*Garden of Noble Maidens*," he
read without hesitation.

Beatriz grinned. "Well done, my prince, and from the Latin too.
I would not expect you to know the story behind this book, but the
queen received the first copy as a gift for her seventeenth birthday.
By then, she had lost her younger brother and it seemed more
likely that our queen might succeed her brother, the king. An
Augustinian friar wrote this book for her, to guide her, so he said.
It speaks of all the attributes expected of a maiden – chastity,
modesty, watching her tongue and humility. The friar also writes
that women descend from Eve, the original sinner. He wrote this
book as a reminder to Queen Isabel, a reminder of women's
inferiority. My prince, our queen is perceived by many men as the
best of the worst, a woman who must also strive to be an example
to other women. And so she has done – from the time she first
became queen. So many women at court – and I count myself
amongst their number – reap the benefit of being ruled by one of
our sex.

"Many men of your father's faith also do not question women's
inferiority. One day, Prince Ahmed, you might fully understand
why your mother never writes."

41

4

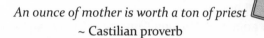

An ounce of mother is worth a ton of priest
~ Castilian proverb

The huge andas shook, shuddered, and jerked. Pitched almost off her seat, Beatriz bit her tongue, swallowing back the metallic wash of blood. Outside, the oxen master yelled and cracked his whip. Pity filled her heart for the poor beasts pulling the heavy andas along this ill-made road that jarred her very bones, the scream of protesting oxen cutting into her as if she was whipped, too. But she already felt whipped. The queen's court at Sevilla would include the presence of the king. Listening to the loud voice of Josefa's husband commanding the queen's escort today, she squirmed again, unable to find any comfort from the hard seats or the beautiful brocaded cushions, made mostly for display.

Queen Isabel sat across from her, little disturbed by the constant jar and rock of the journey, hand overtop the other in her lap. Josefa de Salinas and the infanta Catalina dozed close on her left and right. Just like Beatriz, little María, seated next to Catalina, shifted her position yet again, unable to find the same escape.

Heads close together, Queen Isabel and her eldest daughter murmured with Doña Beatriz Bobadilla, one of the queen's dearest friends, speaking too softly for Beatriz to make out any more than a few disconnected words. Juana twisted beside them, her heart-shaped face dark and scowling. She peeked through the thick curtains, allowing in a sliver of piercing light. Juana's eyes glowed catlike. Her jaw jutted out and another furrow appeared between her dark brows. When her mouth twisted like her body, Beatriz dropped her gaze and clasped her hands tight together. She well knew the signs. Very soon Juana's hot-blooded temper would break, unable to withstand the long hours of both heat and confinement.

Strong wind slapped the untied leather on the outer walls of the andas, while the shell breathed in and out as if alive, buckling and expanding with every hot gust of wind. The air stifled rather than offered any relief. Juana leaned across her sister. "Please, Mother, can we not open them further?"

The queen turned to Juana with a frown. Her eyes stern, she shook her head. "There is a time and place to show ourselves, but not while we dress to avoid the heat of the day. And hija, do not interrupt while I am speaking to others."

Tears of frustration fired Juana's eyes. She slumped back in her seat, wringing her hands. Her eyes raked the back of the andas. The strong wind pulled at the unsecured opening, revealing a momentary glance of the outside world. The hot sun already seared the earth and the very air itself, assaulting the winding road and the long cavalcade before them in a dazzle of blinding light. Juana's voice almost whined when she spoke again. "Mother, please, I beg you, I cannot bear to be thus enclosed. Please, when we next stop, can I not ride a mule?"

Jutting out her own chin, Queen Isabel stared at her daughter. Seemingly defeated, Juana cowered in her seat.

"Learn to bear, hija, learn to bear." The queen clamped her lips shut as if biting back harsher words.

Juana grabbed her mother's arm, in one last desperate attempt. "But Mother –"

Queen Isabel shook her off. "Must I always repeat myself with you? Don't be foolish, girl! I have already told you that when we near Sevilla all of us will make ready to change into one of our new gowns for Isabel's wedding celebrations and ride together into the city." The queen's face softened. "My Juana, can you not be patient until then?"

In answer, Juana shifted in frustration and swung out a leg that connected with María's knee. The child yelped, her gaze crossing swords with Juana. But Juana already seethed with repressed fury. María dropped her eyes, wisely choosing a hasty retreat, and made herself smaller against the wall of the andas.

Offering her little cousin a glance of sympathy, the queen turned a face to Juana as hard and unyielding as their wooden seats. Paling, Juana muttered a quick, under-breath apology to María.

Queen Isabel drew a cushion behind her and settled back against the thick padding of the andas. She inhaled and let out a deep breath. "Shall I tell a story to pass the time?"

Excepting for those still dozing, everyone seemed to sit straighter, the groans of creaking timber, the snap and whip of untied leather, the continual crazed rocking of the andas, the early afternoon heat that caused them to drip with sweat, all forgotten. Juana and Isabel turned to their mother, identical eyes wide, delighted and full of yearning.

"Oh, Mother, please," murmured Isabel.

Catalina stirred in her seat, sleepy and annoyed, half-opening her eyes. "Are we stopping again?"

"The queen is going to tell us a story," her small companion answered. All the girls wide-awake now, the sisters riveted their gaze on their mother, reminding Beatriz of the long-necked swans swimming last summer in the river near the royal residence.

The queen laughed, teasing humour returned a vivid beauty to her eyes. "Has it been that long, my hijas?" Her mouth thinned into a straight line. "Organising your sister's wedding has taken much of my time." She straightened her shoulders. "But you must realise an event like this takes days and days of careful preparation to ensure all is done properly, and as it should be. Your father and I both want Isabel's day to be glorious. We've engaged the services of the finest musicians in the land and commanded the making of many fine jewelled gowns for our beautiful girls to wear." She smiled for Isabel alone. "This is the wedding of our first born. We will show the Portuguese how much we treasure you."

Isabel kissed the queen's hand. "As I treasure you, Mother."

Juana leaned across Isabel. When Juana's older sister frowned in response, Beatriz found herself thinking, not for the first time, how much Princess Isabel resembled her mother. Not only in appearance but in spirit.

"What of the story?" whined Juana. "Please don't forget the story."

The queen considered Juana, her face becoming more lined and full of worry. "And what story shall it be? A true one or a fable? Perchance a story from the good bible?"

"A true one." Juana glanced aside at Isabel. "Our sister is leaving us. Mother, could you not tell us again the story about how you rescued Isabel when she was a child?"

Princess Isabel beamed, and Catalina stirred in excitement. "Mother, yes, that one! Please!" the child said.

The queen patted Juana's hand. "Good. You make my heart happy that you ask for this story, my Juana. It shows you've put aside your jealousy of your sister." She glanced at her eldest daughter. "Very soon, Isabel will be counting on you to take her place."

Imparting a gentle smile to her sister, Isabel nodded. "Juana will do this well. Father will see my sister better when I am no longer here. She only needs this chance to come into her own and show him how truly able she is."

Queen Isabel pursed her lips, the lines of age deepening around them. Her eyes fixed on the tapestry that backed the wall of the andras before her. As if caught up in the scene showing Saint Michael fighting the dragon, she seemed oblivious to her waiting daughters. At last, she gave a short laugh. "Your father may not be so observant, but I know well the abilities of my hijas." She reached across Isabel and clasped Juana's hand. "My passionate, beautiful Juana, in a family of great hearts, you truly have the greatest heart of all. I know it has been hard for you to grow up in Isabel's shadow. I do not wish to ever speak against your father, but he has had little time to know you as I do. He lives a hard and dangerous life as a soldier. That must remain his focus while we fight our Holy War.

"With Isabel gone, he will see you more clearly and look more to you with approval. Try to keep your emotions under control, my Juana. Nothing annoys your father more than to see his hijas forgetful of who they are. Never forget you're a royal daughter twice over."

Intertwining her hands tight in her lap, Juana blinked away tears. She grimaced in pain – or perchance for other causes. She spoke in a barely heard whisper. "My mother, I pray every day for my lord father to look more kindly upon me."

The queen's eyes darkened. Before she shut them, for several heartbeats, Beatriz saw a door opening to deep wells of pain and grief.

"I know you do, child." She sighed. "Isabel's marriage gives our hearts reason for joy. As for your father, he is only harsh because he wants what is best for our kingdoms, and the best for all our children. Let's begin this story."

Queen Isabel smiled at Catalina. "Isabel was then little older than our chiquitina," the queen laughed grimly. "If you think today is hot, my children, it compares little to the heat we endured then. None escaped it. It scorched the land in the hottest summer in living memory. In the middle of that awful summer, word came to me that Isabel was imprisoned at Segovia –"

Princess Isabel laughed. "Not right, Mother?"

The queen glanced at Isabel with a merry glint. "Pray, mine own young Mother-in-Law, are all my girls interrupting me today?" Beatriz turned away a smile, hearing the queen use her often used nickname for her eldest daughter.

Her laughter ringing out like bells, Isabel lounged against the andas and waved her hand. "My esteemed and most prudent queen, forgive me. Pray, lady mother, go on."

Her gaze again on Saint Michael and his uplifted sword, Queen Isabel's eyes darkened as if with memories. "Even at six, my Isabel acted older than her years – much like chiquitina." She shrugged. "Isabel was yet my only living child. For seven years, before the birth of Juan, she wore the mantle of my successor. She needed to grow up fast. Your father and I made certain of that. Your sister did not panic at the sound of near battle. Despite her young years, her quick thinking ensured she and her attendants escaped to the inner tower of the alcázar, fleeing from the clutches of men who soon captured Don Pedro de Bobadilla. He was left in charge of Segovia whilst my dear amiga and her husband Cabrera spent time at my court." The queen smiled aside at Doña Beatriz Bobadilla.

"'Twas one of the few times I ever saw you weep, hearing of the imprisonment of your good father."

Glancing aside at Queen Isabel, Doña Beatriz shrugged. "My queen, I foolishly allowed myself to become distressed. You soon had the situation in hand."

The queen nodded and returned to her story. "The messenger told us Isabel and her people were in safe-keeping. But for how long? It was only a matter of time before these disgruntled rebels realised that they could gain a greater hostage for their bargaining if they turned their attention to Isabel.

"Thank the good God, I was then a young and hardy woman, used to spending days in the saddle. Without wasting any more precious time, I mounted my best horse, leaving orders for Cabrera and Doña Beatriz to follow with a troop of cavalry. Only two companions did I take, two men I judged could aid me best – the Count of Benavente, a man well-proven in battle and wisdom, and Cardinal Mendoza, whose advice had rarely led me astray. We left Tordesillas as the sun reached its zenith and rode and rode. The only time we stopped was to give ourselves a chance to speak of the best course of action once we arrived at Segovia.

"At night we journeyed without torch-bearers, but a full moon helped us find our way through mountain passes. Refusing to give way to sleep, we rode until the break of dawn and well into the next morning.

"My heart lifted at the first sight of the Roman aqueducts, and then I saw the alcázar, shadowing its beauty high over the city. I spurred my horse to greater speed, leaving both the count and the cardinal in the wake of my dust. The poor cardinal," Queen Isabel gave a short laugh. "I yelled at him, 'Dig your heels in! Use your whip, make the horse gallop!' A ghost of a man by this time, the cardinal struggled to keep himself upon his mount. But this mission was far too urgent to stop or give him any pity. That could wait. The sun attained its zenith again by the time I reached the city gates. I held my head high, drawing to myself every iota of my being when I said to the rebels: 'Tell those cavaliers and citizens that I am Queen of Castilla, and this city is mine.' Without showing fear, I rode through the gates. None dared shut me out. None dared doubt I came to take back what rightly belonged to me. Si, what was mine. I spurred my poor, exhausted horse one more time, galloping straight to the tower where my Isabel took refuge.

"As good fortune had it, a large number of loyal citizens had added their numbers to her bodyguard. They opened the gates with joy. When I took Isabel into my arms, I praised God for keeping her safe and vowed out loud, whenever possible, Isabel and all my children, yet unborn, would stay protected by my side. But our tears of relief needed to wait for another time. Events in this rebellious city had not come to an end.

"Outside, the people bayed for blood, howling their hatred and demands. Fearing the fury of the mob, the good cardinal and Count Benavente wished for me to bar myself safe within the tower.

"But they spoke to a queen hearing well the voice of her unhappy people. My heart told me they wouldn't hurt me, that their hatred wasn't for me. I showed no fear standing at the tower window, my little Isabel holding my hand." The queen's eyes met her daughter's. "How proud I felt of my girl. Without showing any trepidation, I asked my people what they wanted. Voices called as one: 'Remove Cabrera!'" At the name of Doña Beatriz Bobadilla's husband, Queen Isabel smiled reassuringly at her friend. "I told the crowd I'd give the city into the keeping of a servant, loyal to me, but who would also honour them. I wanted no further dealings with those involved in leading the insurrection, only those faithful to my rule.

"'Long live the queen!' echoed between the towers, and I knew victory was mine. The rebel leaders escaped with their lives and peace was restored without further bloodshed.

"For a time, I relieved Cabrera from his post and stayed in Segovia for two months, attending to the complaints of the city. Most of the problems stemmed from a long list of misunderstandings." Queen Isabel shrugged. "Perchance a little over-eagerness to be firm with the city on the part of my loyal Cabrera –"

Men shouted in sudden warning. Whips cracked, oxen bellowed in pain. The andas pitched forward and then violently to the left. The queen grabbed onto the stiff tapestry behind her, sewn securely into the wall. Her head whipping around, she looked at her daughters, as they fell hard against one another, crying out in pain and fear.

Flung one way and then another, Beatriz snatched at the stiff tapestry, grasping for a handhold. Loud cracks, snapping leather, bellowing oxen muffled the incoherent cries of her companions.

The andas jerked again, jarring to one side. Josefa, seeing her daughter perched perilously on her seat, reached out to little María. One more time the andas tottered, tilting over to one side. Josefa lost her balance and toppled between the facing seats. Her body thudded loudly on the floor, her cut-off cry smiting all to a terrible stillness. Josefa remained there, unmoving, silent. "Mamá! Mamá!" her daughter cried, her eyes entreating the queen for help.

A babble of voices rose to a crescendo outside. The andas now steady, Beatriz, with caution, followed the queen, moving from her place on the upward slope. Crouching over Josefa, they gently rolled her over to her back. She lifted her eyes to meet the queen's eyes. Queen Isabel waved Josefa's daughter back without even glancing her way. She gently shook Josefa's shoulder. "Cousin?"

Fanning out her hands either side of Josefa's belly. Beatriz let out a breath of relief. "I felt a kick. The babe lives!" she said.

Josefa moaned. Beatriz gazed at her friend's white face and now opened eyes, and her heart skipped a beat. Her pupils enlarged and skin as white as pure alabaster, Josefa looked terrified, and in great pain.

Beatriz helped the queen seat the dazed Josefa between them. Outside, men's voices boomed, shouting over one another until the sound became a cacophony of confusion. Horses squealed and snorted, their hooves thundering around the andas like a violent storm.

One side of the andas opened up with a loud slap of leather. Beatriz blinked her eyes at the sudden rush of light. Josefa's husband appeared, the strong angles of one side of his face all harsh shadows, the other bathed in light. After an anxious glance at his drooping wife, he vanished from sight. Beatriz heard him take charge. "Heave! Heave! Heave! Come on, men, work together. Get your backs into it, keep it steady. Right that wheel on its axle! You – over there. Check the ropes of the oxen. Remember, the queen is inside!"

With another violent jerk and shake, the andas became level again. Emitting a soft whimper, Josefa's head fell against the queen's shoulder. Queen Isabel bit her bottom lip and glanced aside at Beatriz. "How far to Sevilla, my friend?"

Trying to hide her growing fear and alarm, Beatriz lowered her head. "Hours away, my queen."

"Shall I call a physician?" asked Queen Isabel.

Placing her palm on Josefa's chest, Beatriz concentrated on counting the beats of her friend's heart. She rubbed her face. *Mother of God, help me. Josefa's heart beats too fast.* She gazed at the four infantas. Even Juana stayed still and quiet. It seemed a door had opened to a part of life none of them wanted to see. Even Isabel, a woman full-grown and old enough to be mother of both Catalina and María, kept her eyes fixed upon her lap.

Beatriz turned to Queen Isabel, keeping her voice down. "My queen, you know I speak the truth when I humbly say I am as learned as them." She smiled grimly. "Remember, the two physicians accompanying us today were both once my students at Salamanca." She put her hands upon Josefa's belly. "I can care for her. I do not think her labour has started, but she's hurt. I cannot easily judge how badly this might be while we remain cramped up here. The sooner we reach Sevilla the better."

"I can care for her." The enormity of her words echoed in her ears. She looked at the child María wiping away her tears. Comforted, the small girl gazed at her as if she seized onto her words with hope. The child believed in her. Beatriz found herself praying that the child would still believe in her in the coming days.

5

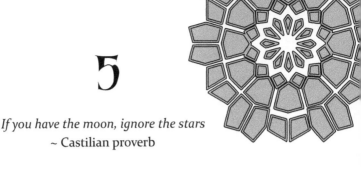

If you have the moon, ignore the stars
~ Castilian proverb

Beatriz cursed the hours it took them to reach Sevilla, more aware than ever of every rattle, every sway, every bump in that teeth-chattering andas. Those terrible, drawn-out hours seemed as slow as a dreadful winter changing into spring. The infanta María whispered in her mother's ear. Nodding in reply, Queen Isabel popped her head out of one of the openings. She uttered a brisk command, and the cavalcade came to a stop.

"Children, not much longer now. Go and stretch your legs for a few minutes."

The crest of a high hill overlooked the outskirts of Sevilla. The infanta Catalina and her small companion wandered a little distance away, gazing at the winding track leading to the city. The panorama of unyielding, sun-scorched landscape, hills and valleys went on forever. Catalina twirled around as if in dance, her arms outstretched as if claiming freedom. Her older sister hurried over to her. "Stop it, Catalina," said Isabel. "You're showing the men you do not know how to behave."

An agonised scream cut through the andras. Beatriz spun around to Josefa like a spinning-top.

"Mamá!" María yelled. Her skirts bunched up in her hands, exposing naked legs, the child ran back toward the andras.

Beatriz gazed down on Josefa. Lines fanned out like fine webs around her tightly closed eyes. Other lines deepened from nose to outer lips. She looked grey, older than her years and almost unrecognisable. Opening her eyes, Josefa snatched at Beatriz's hand in desperation and screamed again. Beatriz's fear rose, real, solid, and impregnable.

Josefa moaned, more softly this time. She turned to Queen Isabel, voicing a few words of a strained apology before a louder cry strangled her words. Pain darkened her unfocused eyes to almost black. Shifting side-to-side, her agony was plain and horrible to see.

Rubbing Josefa's belly, Beatriz whispered to the queen, "I fear her travail has begun." Little María clambered inside the andas. Beatriz glanced her way, unable to speak one word of reassurance to the child.

Queen Isabel took something out of her pocket and placed a small, golden rectangular box into Josefa's limp hand. She closed her hand over it. "Hold this to you, cousin. 'Tis my fragment from the robe of the Virgin I carry always. I had it with me for all my childbirths. The good Mother of God will keep you safe."

Josefa didn't seem to hear, or see. She gave another moan and shifted again. "Pray, forgive my weakness." Removing her hand from the queen's, Josefa stared at the tiny gold reliquary with distaste. "The fall hurt my back. 'Tis not my babe, 'tis not that!" Her eyelids fluttered closed. "'Tis not that..."

Beatriz rubbed at her wet eyes.

Josefa came to childbed before her time, giving birth to a dead boy the very same night they reached Sevilla. For days Beatriz and the queen's physicians feared her lost too, a knowledge sweeping Beatriz to the brink of a deep, bottomless void. For Josefa's little daughter it was more than the brink. For three days María haunted the doors outside her mother's chambers, knowing her mother fought a battle for life. Within, her father refused to budge from his wife's side. Forgotten by her parents, shut out from their lives, María barely registered when, sooner or later, Beatriz led her back to the royal chambers.

On the third day the chamber's heavy door swung open. Fray Hernando de Talavera, the queen's elderly Hieronymite confessor, came through its narrow opening. The dark brown scapula covering the priest's white habit served only to make the harsh angles of his fleshless face more severe and deepened his dark, cavernous eyes. Beatriz strode over to him, María closely following.

Like so many times in the past, the priest gazed kindly at María, but this time a kindness overlaid with pity. Despite his unhidden disapproval of her, Beatriz held Fray Hernando in great regard. Like her, he was a respected professor of the university at Salamanca. He always spoke to children just as he would speak to adults – and always what he believed the truth.

María ran to him, clutching at Fray Hernando's scapula and then Beatriz's habito before falling to her knees. Her efforts to question them became lost and muffled in tears. Beatriz raised María up, keeping her arm wound around her.

"My mamá..." she sobbed.

With a helpless gesture, Beatriz turned to the priest. Fray Hernando paid her no mind, his eyes were only for the child. Never before had Beatriz seen him so gentle.

"Come here, child," he said, taking María from Beatriz. Bending down, his aged bones cracked as he gripped María's thin, frail shoulders. "The crisis is coming, child. Perchance in the next hour we'll know... Pray, child, as we all are. María, if death does take your mother..." His grip tightened on her shoulders. "Little one, she goes to God's care. Go with your teacher, child, and wait for us to send word to you." The priest shuffled away in the direction of the chapel.

Beatriz clasped María's hand and led her to the library. María stopped her. Her eyes were wide, her mouth opening and shutting.

"What is it, child?" Beatriz asked.

"I don't want Mamá with God. I want her here, with me."

Tired, miserable, Beatriz hugged María. "I know. I want that, too, as do all the people who love her. I promise you, we never give up while there's life. My heart tells me that God will hear our prayers and let paradise wait for your mother a while longer."

María wept. It took all of Beatriz's control not to weep, too.

53

Early morning of the next day, María stood again outside her mother's door. One hour passed and then another until Beatriz sent a hesitating Doña Teresa Manrigue to approach her.

"María, come with me," she coaxed, her voice sugar sweet, just like the rose-sugars she kept in her pocket. "Our queen does not want you here, little one. Becoming so upset does not help your mother. You're upsetting the infanta too. She refuses to do her lessons unless you are with her. Look, your teacher is waiting to take you back to her."

Doña Teresa took the child's arm, but she shook her head and refused to budge, rooting herself to the ground. María stared at the door of her mother's chamber. Doña Teresa pleaded with her, bribing to give María her own bag of rose-sugar if she returned with Beatriz to the library. Tut-tutting and muttering her frustration, Doña Teresa scurried down the corridor. She came back with a tall and broad manservant. Without a word, he picked the child up as if she weighed nothing at all.

"The infanta commands your presence," he said. María sobbed her helplessness as he carried her back to the royal apartments, with Beatriz close behind. Letting the child down outside the library, he strode away to other concerns.

María entered the large library like a sleepwalker. Catalina gave a cry, bounded up from the table and ran to embrace her friend. For the remainder of that day, María sat next to Catalina. Catalina held her friend's hand as if that alone would prevent María from being pulled down into the depths of terrible currents of grief and despair. Carefully choosing a book to read to the girls, Beatriz once more attempted the motions of everyday life. It was impossible.

The dark tide drew back the morning of the next day. A few words of hope travelled down to them that the queen's physicians believed the battle won and María's mother's life saved at last. Unable to say no to María, Beatriz took her to her mother's chamber. As if the child conjured him out of thin air and unvoiced yearning, her father flung open the door. Almost a stranger to them, he stood against the light, hollowed cheeks, face unshaven, curded from his usual tan to an unhealthy paleness, dark rings under red-rimmed eyes. María ran into his outstretched arms.

"Mamá, Mamá," the child said through her tears, as if she could speak no other words. He hugged his small daughter tighter to him, before gesturing to Beatriz to approach them. "Come. Come and see her."

Whiter than the white chemise she wore, Josefa outstretched her arms to her daughter. María became an arrow shooting to its target.

"My María." Stroking María's hair, Josefa said her daughter's name like a caress.

Sobs racking her, María nestled her face into her mother's breast, tightening her grip on her shoulders. Her father gently pulled María from her mother. "Careful. She's still not well."

Josefa gazed at him, her dark eyes wells of grief and loss, wells with depths that Beatriz could only imagine. "I am better today." Chalk-white, Josefa's hand curled in a tight fist upon the bedclothes.

Martin squared his chin, his usually generous mouth a hard gash in his wan face. He clasped the limp hand at her side. "Si. Better today." He shut his eyes, the skin around them wrinkling into fine lines. Tears beaded his thick, long eyelashes and fell down his bristly skin. María edged closer to her mother's side, her frightened eyes going from one parent to the other. Believed blithe by many, these days changed María's father forever.

Josefa's hand tightened on her husband's. "I am here, and I will bear you more children."

Her husband opened anguished, tortured eyes. Raising his chin, he tightened his mouth, and shook his head. "This is not the first time I've sat by you, wondering if you'd die. No more. I've spoken to the queen this morning. When you are better, you will go home to our other children and no longer stay here at court."

María let out a cry. Her mother's arm wound around her daughter, pulling her closer. "Hush, I go nowhere."

Martin grasped his wife's shoulder. "Josefa, what of our other three? Don't they also need their mother?"

Turning her head, Josefa wiped her wet face with the puffed sleeve of her chemise, staring at the white pillow next to her. "My mother cares well for them, you know that. 'Tis far better that they stay safe at home." Her distressed eyes veered back to her husband. She took a deep breath. "I wish María had remained there too. I have told you, she who goes with wolves learns to howl."

Beatriz stared at Josefa. Did she mean the royal family? She knew Josefa loved the queen, her cousin. Catalina? Catalina a wolf? Never. The king, though... he was a wolf like none other.

Martin shrugged, and then spoke out loud the very thoughts pounding in Beatriz's mind. "Those prowling too near our wily king may turn wolf." He smiled at his wife. "'Tis your good sense that has always guided me best about him. But the queen, your cousin, keeps our daughter safe with her children. There's no danger for our child."

Josefa acted as if she didn't hear him. "I tell you again, husband, I like it not she and the infanta remain so close. We but lose another child."

He stroked a falling tear from her cheek, rubbing it between index finger and thumb as if he caught something precious. His grim face softened. "My love, were you not also close to your cousin, the queen, from childhood? You, Latina and Beatriz de Bobadilla are trusted as none other." Martin reclaimed his wife's hand. Shaking it gently, he brought her eyes back to him. "Beloved, we cannot change the fact the little infanta befriended our María so the child asked her mother for her as a companion. Our family serves the royal family with their lives. But our noble queen is your good amiga too. She has listened to me and agrees you must go home."

"Martin, I –"

"No more arguments, sweetheart. This is the third child lost to us while journeying with the court, and every time the physicians battle for your life. They tell me you will die if something like this happens again. Josefa, enough is enough!"

Josefa's far-too-wan face pinched more around eyes and mouth.

56

"You want me gone from you? Our youngest child left alone at court?"

Martin nuzzled into her neck, his cries tearing out of him.

Beatriz led María away to the nearby embrasure. How she feared for the child. The last few days had seen the threads of María's childhood snap, one by one. Soon, it may be too late to prevent the snapping of the final threads.

Josefa wrapped her arms around her husband. "Beloved, don't. I cannot bear it."

Martin gazed at her with bloodshot eyes. "And I cannot bear to lose you. I beg you, please listen and go home. Please, Josefa."

In answer, Josefa moaned softly, as if fighting a different type of pain to what she experienced in the andas. She shifted her head one way and then the other on the pillow, before wiping her face and kissing Martin.

"I'll bear you more children. Going from court won't change that, or the fact that childbirth is always a woman's war."

Their black hair intermingling on the pillow, Martin rested his head next to hers. He brought her hand to his mouth, kissing its inner palm. "You speak of war, beloved. Hear me... given the opportunity, leaders worth their salt map out their battle engagements. In my own soldiering, what aids me to victory is the study of war and my own experience. For my own safety and that of my men, I remember well the lessons taught to me by both history and life."

He kissed her cheek. "I learned this here. Three times you've journeyed far with the queen while with child, only for you and the unborn babe to suffer for it. Three sons have been lost to us, in almost as many years. When you stayed at home, you did not lose our babes. Thanks to the care of your good mother, you bore our children safely there, and every child lives and thrives.

"Coming to attend the queen has worn you out, and put your life in unnecessary danger. Not once, or twice but three times now have I seen the priest make ready with the last sacrament. You hold my heart, Josefa. Take you from me, and I am little more than dead too. Beloved, I beg you, please go."

Josefa held his face between her hands. "I want to stay at court." She took a deep breath. "What if you need me? I would never forgive myself if you're hurt soldiering with the king, and I discover it too late... far from you at home..."

Martin drew her closer to him. He kissed her, first a rain of kisses along her brow and then her cheeks, before taking his mouth to hers. Still holding María's hand, Beatriz blushed, stepped away and stared at her feet for a moment. Martin traced down from Josefa's temple to the corner of her kissed red mouth. Her lips opened to the gleam of white teeth.

"Believe me, love. I could not forgive myself if I caused your death by giving you a child when you are too unwell to bear it. I love you, body and soul, Josefa. The doctors tell me it will be long before we can bed together again. Having you here, close to me, is too much temptation. You must go, beloved!"

Josefa wept and wept. Beatriz stood in the shadows, forgotten, with their daughter, swirling in her private ocean of desolation.

6

Walk until the blood appears on the cheek,
but not the sweat on the brow
~ Castilian proverb

Dear Francisco,

Soon I will be very lonely at court. Not only have you been gone for months, but the queen's cousin and my good friend Josefa returns to her home in Vitoria. Poor Josefa is unhappy about leaving, but her fragile health has forced the queen to command it. The queen well knows what it is to lack the strength of body to bring forth a living child. In the early years of her reign, she lost baby after baby due to waging battle for her crown.

At the moment, Josefa waits for the queen's physicians to give permission for her departure. I – and the queen, too – visit her every day. I take her daughter, my little student María. The poor child cannot hide from me how she dreads the day when her mother leaves. Whilst five is very young to lose a beloved mother, we can only thank God the loss is not permanent.

We are in the midst of celebrations for Princess Isabel's wedding...

"Come home with me," Josefa pleaded.

Alarmed, Catalina looked aside at María. She shook her head so fast it could have been a spinning top.

The queen laughed. "Look at María. And my Catalina, too. We'd need horses to drag these two apart, just like when our girls first met over a year ago. I remember well that day. The storm that drove us to your home to take up the hospitality of my aunt, your good mother. Come the morning of the next day, few could separate Catalina from María." Queen Isabel studied the two girls. "Do you wish me to make the command?"

Josefa frowned and lifted her gaze from her sewing, dropping her embroidery onto her lap. Her skin remained as white as the sheets of her bed, but the aging shadows around eyes and mouth lessened with every new day. Her natural vitality slowly returned the youthfulness of a woman who, like Beatriz, had seen no more than twenty-five summers.

Josefa considered her daughter and then Catalina, shrugging her slight shoulders. "I kiss your hands in gratitude, my queen, but I think not. Our two remind me of two girls I once knew – two cousins, one older, the other younger – who called themselves sisters. Every time life separated them, the younger one's heart broke. God willing, I would rather not give our girls reason for the same grief."

Queen Isabel picked up Josefa's still hand. "Si – love binds us to those we love. I would want it no other way." She lifted her chin. "I make this vow to you, I will be as a mother to María. Even without kinship, our long, loving friendship means I could do no other."

Josefa gave a wry smile. "I am grateful, Isabel. I cannot lie to you, my prima hermana, I'd prefer María to grow up with my other children. But like the sun rises in the morning and sets at night, María already knows her place is to serve your hija. My heart tells me this is what God wants. And why should my daughter not love your daughter? All my life I have loved her mother." Tears welled in Josefa's eyes. She spoke in a voice both trembling and plaintive. "Who will care for you, Isabel, as I do when you cannot sleep, and work throughout the night? None attend to your needs as well as I." She glanced over at Beatriz. "Latina forgets the whole world when she loses herself in her study. I always make certain you at least have a drink by your side during the long hours to matins, or ensuring there is enough candlelight for you to work by."

Queen Isabel shook Josefa's clenched hand. The smile she bestowed upon Josefa was one Beatriz had never witnessed from her before – young and tender, speaking of a lifetime of loving memories. "Don't cry. Don't dare think you've failed me. You have not, my Josefa. You have exhausted yourself in my service and suffered because of it.

"Now it is time for me to take care of you. I will look forward to your letters. Si, María and I will write to you. Let you revel in your hija's improving hand and sharpening wit. My Catalina will make certain of that.

"Next summer I will journey through Andalucia. I give you notice today I will visit you at Vitoria and see you as I pray to see you – healthy and more than ready for argument once again."

Brushing away tears, Josefa laughed. She gazed up at the queen as if she was the only person in the world. Her mouth trembled. "How I shall miss that. These years spent in your service have meant much to me. How I wish I could stay. My greatest regret is my body proved too weak to both serve you and give my husband more living sons. My body betrayed me." Josefa wiped her face with the sleeve of her chemise. "My Latin will grow rusty while I care for my children and my apricot trees."

Queen Isabel bent to kiss her cousin's pale cheek. She framed Josefa's face with her long, gout-swollen fingers. Their gazes met again.

"Your apricots and horses will make you strong and well again," the queen laughed. "Not forgetting your older children. They have been too long without you." She rested her hands on Josefa's shoulders. "I'll send you books. Many books – books for my good aunt to enjoy too. As long as I know you remain safe and well at Vitoria with your orchards, riding your horses, and improving your Latin, my heart stays light." She kissed her cousin again. "Let's us enjoy these final days together while you regain your strength, and remain content our separation will only be through distance and not yet death."

Alone, Beatriz leaned against the garden's high wall in the royal alcázar at Sevilla. Her black cloak and sheer toca lying at her feet, she held her arms tight across her chest, trying to control her breathing. A shaft of sunlight struck and hurt her eyes. She rubbed them, her fingers coming away with her tears. She crossed her arms over her swollen, painful breasts, swallowing the blood in her mouth from when she had bit her tongue. The tears started again – she let them fall, unchecked.

Gathering an assortment of herbs growing in abundance in this private royal garden, she had not expected to be disturbed, disturbed by the loud snapping of dry twigs that had announced the arrival of the king.

Don't think of it. Forget it. She yanked up the neck of her gown, covering and hiding from view the bruises left by his fingers on her breasts. She rubbed her neck and tried to swallow, her throat hurt. She didn't need a mirror to tell her she would need to find a dress with a high collar to hide what the king had done to her.

She tried to repair her dishevelment, and began to walk slowly towards her rooms. Beatriz cocked her head, stepping into a part of the garden awash with green light. She felt unreal, as if she had fallen in another world of nightmare. Without thinking, she crossed herself, resetting on her head the toca. She wished it could make her disappear.

Beatriz stepped into the garden's deeper shadows and saw María coming through the gate. The child looked at her with surprise. "Latina," she blurted out.

"Have you come to enjoy the sun's warmth, too?" Beatriz said quickly. As if in denial of her words, she shivered, averted her face and swallowed, her hand going to her throat again. It hurt. Really hurt. This time she feared the king had meant to strangle her.

María, disturbed and frightened, stepped towards her. "Mamá – is all well with her?"

"Your mother?" Beatriz narrowed her eyes against the bright

light streaming on her face. She untied and retied the loose ends of her girdle, as if letting loose the beads of a rosary in prayer. "When I saw her this morning she gave me no cause for concern. Has something happened since then?"

María looked even more bewildered. She gazed down at the toes of her black leather slippers, peeping out from beneath her skirts, and then back at Beatriz. "Something is wrong, my teacher..."

María glanced at the path leading to the royal chambers. The doorway was open in the high stonewall. A climbing rose spread its certain claim over the grey stone. Butterflies flittered a graceful dance around the yellow roses creeping above the door. Only the royal family ever used that door, for its path led straight across a courtyard to the chambers of the king and queen. Go too far and guards barred the way with pike and sword.

María turned and faced her. "Why is the door open, Latina? The queen commands it locked."

Beatriz shifted uneasily. "Why should I know, María? You ask questions for no good reason." Her words broke and snapped, like the very twigs under their feet. She gazed at the sky. Not one cloud – so beautifully blue, it seemed to mock her.

María blinked. Distressed, her eyes filled with tears, she repeated, "Something's wrong..."

Beatriz bowed her head, straightening the folds of her gown, refusing to meet María's eyes. She shrugged. "Si, something's wrong, but 'tis not for a young child's ears. Go from here, María. Go and enjoy these days too soon ended, when childhood gives you freedom denied to us who are no longer children."

Her eyes shining with tears, María gave Beatriz a deep reverence. Her head pounding, Beatriz felt like she had lost her footing. Again the abyss opened up before her. She raised her hand to her aching temple. *I should not have taken it out on her. Next lesson, I'll beg her forgiveness.*

Before she left the garden for her own chambers, Beatriz shut the door, watching María head in the direction of the library. The wind brought to her ears the gay long notes of the hunting horn threaded with the muted rumble of galloping horses leaving the grounds of the alcázar. In the distance, she saw the billowing dust of the party accompanying the king on his morning hunt. Soon, the sounds of men and horse became but a whisper of rumour upon wind.

Despite the warmth of the day, Beatriz gathered her cloak around her body, and tossed her hood over her head. She cloaked herself in another sense than the physical. Following the path that would take her back to her rooms, her eyes no longer saw the world around her, but looked blindly around, overcome by despair and defeat. Beatriz stumbled. Wanting to vomit, she sat on a nearby stone bench and bowed her head. *I am trapped. Trapped, with no way to escape.*

Catalina and María stared at her when they came to the schoolroom for their morning lesson the next day. "You're wearing a nun's habit," stated the infanta.

Beatriz glanced down at her shabby grey gown of the Franciscan order. The girls had been little more than babies when she had stopped wearing it every day. "I am still a lay member of my order in Salamanca. I almost took my final vows, but realised my problem with obedience is one I never want to solve." The girls looked disconcerted. "I am allowed to wear the habit if I wish. I'm a member of the third order of Franciscans." Catalina and María continued to gaze at her in bewilderment. Beatriz took a deep breath. "I'm wearing it today because I needed a reminder of humility. Yesterday I was unnecessarily harsh to María. I hope you can forgive me, child?"

María beamed. "Si. But you don't need to wear your habit, Latina."

Beatriz eyed the child almost skipping and dancing with Catalina to the table where their books were waiting. The coarse fabric of the habit chafed her skin, as if reminding her of her lie.

She swallowed, touching the wimple of her habit. She had pulled its cords a little too tightly this morning, but at least it covered her bruised neck and chest. She prayed to God the habit would give the king reason to think again before coming her way. He respected the church. Surely if he remembered how close she had been to taking her vows he would leave her alone.

Sweet heart,

I miss you sorely. I do not often say that, do I, love? But my dear friend is gone. Last week, Josefa left with her husband for Vitoria. The queen's physicians deemed her well enough for travel, but, love, how bitter sweet that day was.

Her daughter María is bereft. Court life never disturbed the child overlong with Josefa also here. Josefa offered a buffer, a semblance of normality for the child. I pray to God I can do the same. The queen promised her cousin she will be a second mother to the little one. As yet, María can not hide she aches for her own.

Once a year, before the onset of Lent, María will go home with her father to spend Easter with Josefa. No doubt the passing of time will teach the child to adapt with ease from one place to another without Josefa's help.

Si, María's home is no longer with her family. Catalina is the child's true home, her place of belonging. As I, too, belong – to you. Today I find myself yearning to be your wife. Is that strange for me to say? I – who always tell you, 'There is no hurry. Let's be patient, and marry when you can leave the king's army.' Farewelling my friend leaves me melancholy... These last days, only teaching gives me any joy...

7

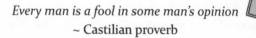

Every man is a fool in some man's opinion
~ Castilian proverb

Beatriz saw him again and again during the weeks leading up to Princess Isabel's wedding. He stood alone in shadows, away from sunlight, away from the hum and bustle of court, his eyes full of dreams. *Just like a mystic,* she thought. A mystic burning bright with the fire of a zealot.

Noticing Beatriz's curious eyes on him again, Catalina whispered. "'Tis the Italian, Cristóbal Colón. Father calls him the Jew." Beatriz looked aside at Catalina and lifted an eyebrow. Catalina answered with an embarrassed shrug. King Ferdinand made no effort to hide his dislike of Jews.

With so many Jews in powerful positions in his wife's court, Beatriz knew Catalina often felt confused about the different standpoints taken by her parents. Beatriz hoped to guide the girl – hoped to help open her eyes so she appreciated people for their hearts and souls, rather than view the world through unnecessary prejudice. God knew she received enough of that herself as a woman scholar navigating a world mapped out by men. "He wants my parents to pay for ships and men. The king, my lord father, says the man is a charlatan and wastes my mother's precious time with some foolhardy plan to discover a sea way to India and the land of the grand khan."

María gazed blankly at Catalina.

"Do you know what grand khan means?" Beatriz asked.

Frowning, María gave it quick thought and offered an answer. "King of kings?"

Beatriz smiled. The children were listening to her lessons.

"Si," Catalina said. "Mother told me that the khan sent word to the pope for men of God to come to him. None have because the journey is too full of danger. Cristóbal Colón believes he can discover a way to make it not so."

"I think the king is right. Seafaring ships disappear over the ends of the world," María said earnestly.

Catalina laughed. "That's only a fable. Don't you remember Latina telling us otherwise?" she reminded her friend, with another glance in Cristóbal Colón's direction. "Geraldini and Santángel both have my lady mother's ear. My mother likes the Italian. She believes God has sent him to her. He will get his ships."

Catalina pulled María back into movement. One more time, Beatriz gazed over her shoulder. Seemingly a true Italian – even if a Jew – with heavy, hooded eyes, large, hooked nose, sensual lips, and strong chin, the man reminded her of a bust found in their present alcázar, a bust of a long ago Roman Caesar. Cristóbal Colón took no notice of two small girls and their woman tutor padding softly in the long, narrow corridor, away from the shadows and into the light of a new day. Even Catalina, a daughter of the royal house, aroused none of his attention.

Behind the infanta Juana, a frowning Doña Teresa Manrigue gestured to them to quicken their pace. Beatriz ceased wondering about this stranger, forced to face the moment at hand. With her trailing skirts slung over an arm, she rushed with the small girls to join the queen and her other children to attend yet another festivity celebrating Isabel's proxy marriage to the Prince of Portugal. Two more of the queen's women followed a few steps behind.

Beatriz hurried faster than usual, but for far different reasons. If she didn't hurry, concentrating on walking in her long gown with grace, she might succumb to her desire to run in the opposite direction. She had no wish to watch another bullfight.

Beatriz hated bulls. She had always hated them. An immense, overpowering primeval fear made it so, a fear surging up within her whenever the inescapable smell of a bull came near. Seeing them, smelling them, even from a safe distance, swamped her in a violent tide of terror. Her heart beating hard and furious against her chest, Beatriz felt sick and dizzy. It took the clasp of and Catalina's hands to stop her from dashing away from the entrance of the arena. Already, the heady, ripe smell of beast walled her in its imprisonment.

Looking down at their white, pinched faces, it seemed the girls also shared her fear. And not only the girls. The queen also hated bullfights. Time after time she sat there with a white, drained face, empty of expression. Her head set against the high back of her chair, she kept her eyes fixed, watching the bull rage and fight for its life against the matador.

Just days ago María had experienced her first bullfight. The child wept – and the queen had noticed. Later, when Beatriz accompanied Catalina and María to the queen's private chambers, Queen Isabel took María aside, crouching down to speak to her in the embrasure of her huge window.

"I detest bullfights." She lifted María's chin, making the child look straight into her eyes. "Can I trust you with my secret of how I pretend otherwise?"

María nodded and attempted a smile.

Queen Isabel rested her hand on María's shoulder. "You are your mother's good hija, si?"

María nodded again and the queen laughed. Cocking her head to one side, she peered out the window before turning back to María. "I must appear brave before my people, small cousin, but – I tell you in truth – only the stupid and those lacking any foresight do not fear. Little cousin, you too descended from kings, please believe the truth of my words. When we pretend bravery the pretence often becomes real. Very real. If we face fear we often find we turn a lion into a cat. A cat is easily dealt with, si?" Queen Isabel smiled when María nodded. "My small kin-child, promise me you'll pretend to be brave until mantled by true bravery."

Remembering now María making that promise, Beatriz steadied her gaze upon the queen's thickened fingers, drumming on the arm of her seat. The jewels in her rings winked in the sunlight. Overheated in her gown, Beatriz attempted to push down the fear and horror swirling in her stomach, making her feel ill again.

Loud laughter erupted from the king's stall. His vulpine face full of eagerness for the kill, King Ferdinand leaned forward in his chair and joked with the grandees standing near him. Beatriz lowered her head, praying he would not notice her. The king always took great delight in the battle of life and death waged before their eyes. A vivid, magnetic and pragmatic man amongst men, he seemed to live for such moments.

Beatriz hooded her eyes against witnessing the men's enjoyment, but she lifted her head when she heard the excited laughter of Prince Ahmed and Prince Juan. Watching Prince Juan copy his father depressed her. A poet and scholar, Juan was a youth who never revelled in bloodshed. His behaviour today disturbed her. Why, she asked herself, must he assume the mask that belonged to men like his father? Could he not show the public the sensitive, gentle boy he really was?

Still and silent, the queen and her daughters sat with rod-straight backs against their chairs. Placed behind Catalina, Beatriz kept her hands locked together in her lap and steadied her breathing. She thought of the morning song of birds, new books she wanted to read, tomorrow's lessons – anything and everything rather than to return her eyes to a bleeding animal full of justified fury, no longer seduced by the matador's dance, but fighting for its life. Hearing the king laugh again, Beatriz recalled the words of Aristotle: *Man, when perfected, is the best of animals, but when separated from law and justice, he is the worst of all.*

The bull gave a tortured bellow. Beatriz looked down to see the matador pull his short spear out of the bull's back. She hated bulls? Watching the animal's pain-glazed eyes roll back in its distress it was no longer hate she felt but great pity.

Side-stepping with a dancer's grace, the matador again speared the bull deep into its shoulder. The open wound gushed an outpouring of blood, a red rivulet against the bull's black skin. The crowd roared its approval and so did the king. In answer, the matador flourished a half-turn to the royal stand. A foolish, costly mistake. The bull lowered its head and charged.

Beatriz closed her eyes. She heard Catalina gasp and Juana

scream, a scream penetrating the silence in the royal stands.

Below them the bull gored the matador to death. Sickened, faint, Beatriz swallowed back vomit. Hot urine splashed down her thighs. Her heart in her throat, the matador's terrible screams cut through her. Twisting, she looked behind her, seeking an easy way of escape through the queen's crowd of women. She just wanted to grab Catalina and María, and run away from this living nightmare, but obedience to the queen forbade it.

Holding long spears, twelve men or more rushed into the arena. From a safe distance, they aimed and threw their spears. The bull, focused on its revenge, stayed oblivious to the arching spears until too late. One last furious bellow sounded below. The beast buckled, collapsing on the dying matador.

Catalina turned and looked at Beatriz with terrified eyes. The child had grabbed the back of her seat, holding it so tight her knuckles became white. Hysterical, Juana sobbed and sobbed. Beside her, a very pale Isabel took her arm, and shook. She whispered, "Quieten yourself, I beg you. Father watches."

Juana hiccupped, her tears stopping, as if knifed at their very source. Ducking her head, Beatriz looked aside at the king. Black fury darkened his already dark skin to a frightening guise. Reminding Beatriz of the bull just minutes before its death, his gaze snapped upon the queen's as if a bolt of lightning. Without warning he stood, his anger making him seem tall. His men followed suit. The king turned his back on his daughters and the queen, striding fast from the stands. Queen Isabel sighed, stirring in her seat, her face stern and pale. "Let's follow."

Stiff brocade gowns rustled in a chorus, skirts swept the ground. With their women helping to hold up their trailing gowns, the queen and infantas carefully manoeuvred through the stands. High and low, the multitude watched the royal family's every move as they left the arena.

After entering her chambers, the queen commanded the majority of her attendants to stay in the outer chamber. Only those closest to the royal family were admitted to her private bedchamber.

Turning on her heel, the queen faced her second daughter with worry and frustration.

Juana fell to her knees. In a hoarse voice, she pleaded, "Mamá, I beg you, forgive me."

Wordlessly, the queen shook her head. Her eyes huge, Juana visibly shuddered. Isabel rested a hand on her sister's shoulder and stood protectively beside her. Swallowing hard, Isabel's gaze veered to her mother. Her eyes pleaded, begged.

Looking at her two daughters, the queen's shoulders slumped, her face softening. "Hija, be warned. Your lord father will surely take you to task about your behaviour today."

Juana's mouth trembled. Tears ran down her cheeks. "I didn't mean to do it," she said.

Shaking her head again, the queen sighed. "I hate the blood of the bullfights too, Juana, but they belong to our land just as surely as we do. Even Catalina did not cry out like you, and you are five years the older. You must never show fear, not now, not ever, my daughter. Showing fear renders you powerless." Queen Isabel swallowed. "You gave your lord father and I much reason for shame today, my Juana."

Juana crumpled against her sister. Isabel, putting her arm around her, looked at her mother and spoke. "Mamá, can you not please talk to Father and crave his forgiveness for my sister. It was a terrible thing that happened today. Surely he can understand the reason for my sister's great distress."

Queen Isabel's eyes narrowed. Lifting her chin, she gazed at Juana, but spoke as if she wasn't there. "Your sister shamed us. Shamed our family in front of the whole court and our people." Rubbing the side of her face, she took a deep breath. "Si, I will speak to him, but if he calls for Juana to come to him, she must go."

"Oh, please, no." Juana sobbed. Anguished, she gazed beseechingly at her mother.

Her arm still around her ten-year-old sister, Isabel tried again. "Mother, we celebrate my coming wedding..." Isabel's eyes filled with tears. "I cannot be happy if my sister is punished. Pray, Mamá, could you not tell Father that?"

Queen Isabel ran her thumb's knuckle across her forehead and between her eyebrows, her teeth worrying at her upper lip. Forgotten, the trail of her gown dragged on the floor as she paced to the window. Flinging open the shutters she leaned on the stone windowsill. The harsh sunlight fell on her face, aging her.

"Dear God, dear God, give me strength," she muttered, turning back to her daughters. "What if I ask your father to let me punish you instead, Juana?"

Juana dropped to her knees again. She knotted her hands before her, looking up like a reprieved criminal. "Oh, thank you, Mamá." She grabbed her mother's dress, kissing its dusty hem.

Her eyes narrowing with sudden pain, the queen pursed her lips. "My hija, I cannot promise this will suffice with your father." She reached down, then drew back her hand to clench it for a moment. With a deep breath, she touched Juana's bent head. "Child, get up now. I will do my best."

Juana's great fear did not surprise Beatriz. When the King of Aragon deemed his children guilty of wrongdoing, he punished them sorely. If he witnessed it, that alone ensured his quick anger and chastisement. But for Juana, the king always reserved a crueller punishment. Many times in childhood he whipped her bare buttocks with a rope and ordered her locked alone in a chamber, often for a day and night. She saw no one but a silent servant who brought her food. Sometimes a whole week passed before Juana was allowed to resume her place with her sisters. Beatriz heard Juana often crying in the night when her father was at court. The king seemed to possess little love for Juana. He gave more kindness and love to his bastards – even to hunting dogs he sometimes kicked in passing – than to his second eldest daughter. He suffered the infanta's presence with barely hidden contempt.

Many of the court paid Juana little attention because of this. None desired or wished to bring the king's disfavour upon themselves. Each time he resumed his place by his wife's side, the king eroded Juana's confidence, making her fear him more with every new and greater punishment.

Time after time he dismantled the queen's careful care of their most sensitive daughter. The king made the intelligent Juana feel stupid, worthless, defenceless – a shame to the royal houses of Aragon and Castilla.

When he returned to the battle-front or vanished to his kingdom of Aragon or to the distraction of a new mistress – Beatriz thanking God for it, even knowing it caused the queen great pain – it took weeks of the queen's tender nurturing to stop Juana from jumping at shadows, biting her nails to the quick, screaming in the black of night. Beatriz pitied the girl. The infanta craved her father's love, his approval, but all he gave her was pain.

Despite the closeness of Princess Isabel's wedding, this time was no different. The king refused to allow the queen to buffer Juana from his anger. First whipping Juana, he then locked her in her chamber for two days. When the infanta returned to her sisters' side, she was a frightened waif who recoiled at her father's every glance.

8

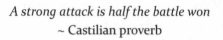

A strong attack is half the battle won
~ Castilian proverb

Two weeks before Isabel's marriage, Beatriz brought Catalina and María to watch another tournament and noticed the queen fixing her attention on a tall man standing amongst the group of men gathered behind the king. The queen beckoned to Catalina. Approaching her mother, she dipped a curtsey, her eyes alight with curiosity.

Queen Isabel took her daughter's arm. "There's an English lord you should meet." The queen turned again to her husband and his companions, catching the gaze of the more plainly garbed man with the king's grandees. She gestured to him. "Pray, come, my good Lord Darcy."

The Englishman, squinting against the bright sunlight, walked towards Queen Isabel. His hood slipped back. To her surprise, Beatriz saw a handsome youth rather than a mature man. His sky blue eyes shone brightly, perchance brighter because the sun had tanned his skin to a dark golden honey. Streaked almost white by the sun, his blunt mane of silver-blonde hair, cut far shorter than the long French style favoured by the grandees, framed an oval face. He bowed low. "Your Highness, gracious and noble queen, you greatly honour me by your notice."

Queen Isabel proffered her be-ringed hand for his kiss, a slight smile teasing at her lips. She held out her free hand to Catalina. "My good lord, pray indulge me in the pleasure of introducing my hija, one day your future queen, if it so pleases God, many long years hence." The queen smiled broadly. "My youngest and beloved hija, the infanta, Doña Catalina and, with great pride, also known here as the Princess of Wales."

The young lord bowed. His bright eyes blinking against the glaring sun, he bowed once again to Catalina. "The queen honours me by this greatly desired introduction. Elizabeth, by the grace of God, Queen of England, consort of our gracious King Henry VII, spoke of you to me, as also did Arthur, our well-beloved Prince of Wales. We look with pleasure to the day when you come to our fair land, Your Highness."

Catalina blushed. "Thank you, my lord." She licked her dry lips, then spoke to the English lord in slow but perfect Latin. "I am eager to see England."

Lifting an eyebrow, the queen gave a short, gruff laugh of pride. She glanced at her husband. "That day will come soon enough. But I think Lord Darcy can see for himself the reason England must wait. Perchance he could write now the truth of it to King Henry, our good brother. My small hija needs time to grow to maturity. What better place to do this than by her mother's side?"

The English lord dipped his head. "I cannot argue against your wisdom, noble queen. Perchance I can beg a boon and talk to the princess. I am told I am a good teller of tales. I am certain she would enjoy hearing about the English court, and Prince Arthur."

Queen Isabel smiled. "Lord Darcy, come you to my chambers tomorrow. I want to know everything of England." Her eyes lost their light as she gazed down at her small daughter.

Before noon the next day, Queen Isabel summoned Beatriz to bring the infanta and her companion María to her chambers to meet again with Lord Darcy. Greeting her mother and the English Lord, Catalina sat on a large cushion by her mother's side. María quickly sat on the floor next to her. The infanta's eyes glowed with interest as the young man began to speak of England and its royal family. Darcy spoke long about Prince Arthur. The small infanta bent forward when he mentioned how the heir to the English throne loved his lessons and playing his harp. He told Catalina of the prince's new puppy, a recent gift from his mother. Beatriz could see the English royal family come alive for Catalina. The bright, blond, blue-eyed Arthur teaching his little dog tricks, reading books, playing with his little sister, Margaret, learning music from his own mother and sometimes King Henry himself. Darcy also told them his queen hoped for another child to add to her nursery soon.

"Her last letter told me the same," Queen Isabel said, sewing at the altar cloth she worked on for the Church of the Holy Sepulchre. "Very soon her children will out-number mine. She is a good mother, I hear." She smiled down at Catalina. "Already she acts as mother to my daughter, troubled she will find English water unfit to drink." Queen Isabel laughed. "There's no need for her concern. One day, your queen will discover that her son's bride is no weakling."

Time passed and the stories of the royal family changed its direction to other members of the English court. "I believe you knew Lord Rivers, my lord, a man I was proud to own as kin?" the queen asked, handing to Doña Beatriz Bobadilla the still unfinished altar cloth before taking up her spindle. Amused, Beatriz noticed Doña Beatriz folding the altar cloth into a perfect square. Bending down to María, the older woman whispered, "María, show me your hands." The child held out her hands, while Beatriz turned back to listen to Darcy's reply.

"Yea, Your Majesty, I knew him." Lord Darcy crossed himself. "May his soul be at rest with God. It was because of his tales about this most glorious Holy War that I decided to earn my spurs here when the time came. My father was not pleased to let me go, but I am near to nineteen." He lifted his chin. "Old enough to act the man's part."

"Both sides, child," Beatriz heard Doña Beatriz murmur nearby. María looked bewildered, turning her hands backwards and forth. She paled when Doña Beatriz placed the altar cloth into her hands. "Put it back in the queen's sewing chest."

María's face lit up. Straightening her shoulders, she almost skipped by the time she reached the open, nearby chest. Turning with empty hands, she gazed towards Doña Beatriz, and then, at a loss of what to do next, to her tutor. Beatriz smiled, beckoning María to come to her side.

Queen Isabel frowned and put aside her spindle, and began to twist her rings on her swollen fingers with difficulty. *Dandelion tea. When I return to my rooms I will brew dandelion tea and make certain the queen drinks it tonight.* "Rivers was a brave and handsome man, despite losing his front teeth fighting for us."

"My husband and I liked him well." Her eyes became thoughtful. "He lost his teeth fighting in the manner of your countrymen. While I did not witness the engagement, the king told me of it. Rivers dismounted from his steed at the head of his three hundred men and, armed with sword and axe, amazed all with his battle frenzy. He scaled the walls of Loja as if he wished to take the conquest single-handedly. But a stone hit him in the face and shattered his teeth, and knocked him unconscious. His injuries kept him abed for some time.

"The king and I visited him once he began to recover. I told him of my sadness that such a handsome man could be left with such inconvenient an injury. My lord husband has lost teeth in battle, so he also commiserated with him. Rivers replied, ''Tis little to lose a few teeth in the service of He, who has given me all. Who reared this fabric has only opened a window, in order to discern the more readily what passes within my soul.'"

Women's laughter rippled through the chamber like the chiming of bells, and Lord Darcy grinned. "Rivers was a good commander. He fought for King Henry at Bosworth, the battle that vanquished that evil York tyrant-usurper, and child-killer.

"Queen Elizabeth had no desire to see her uncle to leave their court, but 'tis hard for men to be younger sons, as I am, and be always in the shadow of the older. Poor Rivers was shadowed by four brothers. For certes, he died doing what he wanted and shining none but his own light."

Queen Isabel took hold of her spindle and twirled it. She sighed. "I wish he had remained with us. He was an amusing man, proud of his race and his relationship with my family, as well as your noble queen. Rivers was forefront at our pageants and festivals. His magnificence feasted our eyes. I miss him greatly. Perchance, he might be now still living if he had stayed here. Even if he had lost his life here, dying fighting a crusade is a far more glorious death than dying as a mercenary against the too often faithless and Godless French."

The queen's eyes hardened when she mentioned the French. Leaning back in her chair, she screwed up her lips as if tasting something unappetising that she wished to spit out.

Lord Darcy sipped from his goblet, and then placed it back on the table. "I agree, Your Grace. I can only applaud your great dedication and sacrifice to this holy enterprise."

Queen Isabel smiled at him. "My lord, I am queen for God's purpose, and what better one than this?"

"May I have permission to speak, Your Grace?" Doña Beatriz Bobadilla stepped from the embrasure to the queen's side.

Queen Isabel turned to her, and then back to the English Lord. "Of course. Lord Darcy, Doña Beatriz Bobadilla is like a beloved sister to me, and has been so since we were children. She has aided me many times in my life." She clasped Doña Beatriz's closest hand. "Once she even took an assassin's dagger meant for me. Praise the good lord, the dagger simply glanced off her padded gown and gave enough time for my soldiers to seize the would-be murderer." Queen Isabel laughed with grimness. "Men might wear armour, but Doña Beatriz proved that day we women sometimes embroider our gowns so densely they may serve the same purpose. I will never forget, but for the grace of God, I could have lost one of my dearest amigas that day. I trust her with my life, and the lives of my children. Pray speak, Beatriz."

Beatriz Bobadilla dropped a curtsey. "Beloved queen, I thank you." Her face grave, she turned to Lord Darcy. "I desire for you to know more about Queen Isabel, so you can tell my words to your king and queen. Our beloved and illustrious queen is achieving what no other Castilian monarch has done before, ridding Castilla of the blight of the Moors. You are right to mention her sacrifice, for Her Highness works tirelessly and sacrifices much to gain this victory."

Darcy bowed once to Doña Beatriz and then swept a deeper one to Queen Isabel. "Good queen, you but need to talk to the soldiers to know the great love and esteem they possess for you. Your men call you a saint and gladly lay down their lives in your service. Madam, I am honoured to count myself one of your knights."

Smiling with all her charm, Queen Isabel outstretched her hand. "It has been a very pleasing visit, my lord. I look forward to watching you in our tournaments and speaking again with you at the nightly revels. These weeks are joyful times for myself and my family. I am most glad you are here to share them. Until we meet again, God go with you and keep you safe from harm."

Darcy bowed and backed towards the door. One last bow and the room again became the queen's chamber, empty of men.

Queen Isabel sniffed and lay a hand on Catalina's shoulder. "Hija, listen now to your mother... I see you like Lord Darcy, he seems a good man. But, child, the English vice is treachery, more so than our countrymen's. They keep their kings looking over their shoulders and worrying every shadow hides an assassin or traitors of their own blood plotting their overthrow. Trust is a gift that must be earned. Catalina, do not trust any of them until given sure proof of their mettle..."

Her heart sad, Beatriz stared at the small infanta. *Assassins. Traitors. Treachery.* The five-year-old looked wide-eyed, anxious and uncertain. Since Catalina was three years old, the child had learnt lessons of queenship whether she wanted them or not.

Merry music swelled and throbbed in the huge, candlelit chamber where another night of festivities hailed Isabel's approaching wedding. The king's return to court brought many of his closest men from the most recent battlefield. One man was Beatriz's betrothed, Francisco.

Standing next to him, she gazed over to the half cycle of courtiers. "Our first meeting in months, and we are surrounded by the court," she said.

Francisco smiled wryly at her. "While you keep delaying our marriage, sweetheart, it is probably best we meet not alone. I might be tempted to persuade you otherwise."

"Do I need to crave your forgiveness, Francisco?"

He laughed. "Now I am with you, perhaps. But I'm not a youth. I am willing to be patient for what I want. Just as long as I have your promise you will not make me wait too much longer to call you my wife."

Beatriz eyed him. "Did you not tell me you desired no marriage until your skills are no longer so needed by the Queen?"

"I'm beginning to think that day will never come. I only wait now for you to say it is time."

She reached for his hand. "Soon, I promise we'll call the banns soon. Just be patient a while longer, please."

Francisco enclosed her hand in both of his. "I am a man of my word. I promised to give you all the time you need. As long as I have your promise to be my wife, I'm content."

Beatriz smiled at him. Francisco had asked her to marry him not long after the king had first assaulted her. Still coming to grips with that, his declaration of love and proposal of marriage had left her sobbing in his arms, the arms of her good friend. She confessed to him her lack of virginity, telling him of her rape, but not of her rapist. She feared what would happen if he knew. She had expected her confession would douse cold water on his desire, but discovered anew Francisco was a man of compassion, and still determined to offer her his love. Eventually, it seemed right to agree to be his wife.

A flash of bright colour caught Beatriz's eye. Close to the wall, near the door, the infanta Catalina and her companion María giggled together, imitating the dance moves of their elders. Both girls wore what looked like their best gowns.

Still holding Francisco's hand, Beatriz pushed her way through the seemingly endless crowd, ducking her head when she noticed the king, hand-in-hand with the queen, measuring out another dancing step, suddenly swing his eyes towards her. She shivered. He seemed an unhooded, hungry falcon catching sight of its prey. How she despised the man. She glanced at Francisco. She could never tell him her rapist was the king. In the work he did on the battlefield, he needed his wits about him. Giving him cause to hate the king could place him in greater danger. At least she was safe from the king's unwanted attentions while Francisco was at court.

Beatriz reached the girls. "Infanta! María! What do you do here? Doña Teresa will be beside herself if she discovers you not in your chambers."

Appearing suddenly guilt-stricken, the little girls stepped closer to one another.

Amused, Francisco, winked and grinned at her. Beatriz couldn't stop herself grinning back. "Forgive me, Francisco, I must take these two back to their chambers before the queen discovers their disobedience."

Francisco nodded, adoration shining from his dark brown eyes. "I look forward to continuing our conversation and the pleasure of your company on your return."

Beatriz smiled at him, her dear friend, the man who wanted her as his wife, and turned her attention back to the two small girls. "No argument from either of you. Come now."

Taking their hands she hurried to the door that would take them back to the royal chambers. "Night is no time for two small girls to take it into their minds to leave the safety of their bedchamber. I should by rights tell the queen," she scolded.

She almost laughed when she saw Catalina and María share a smile. She shook her head. They knew her far too well; she would never tell on them. Tomorrow, translating Aristotle or some other dead philosopher would seem far more important to her than their small transgressions.

Catalina stopped her at the door. Some distance away but in view, the king, queen and Princess Isabel sat on the dais. Cardinal

Mendoza, a man both respected and feared throughout the queen's kingdom and beyond, occupied the chair beside the princess. A duke sat next to the cardinal, and next to the duke another noble, the Portuguese lord, an elderly cousin of Alfonso and his proxy at the coming wedding, two bishops, and finally Ahmed. The only child at the table and white-faced with exhaustion, he looked uncomfortable and unhappy

"Why is Ahmed there?" Catalina whispered to Beatriz.

She shrugged. "He is the first born son of the Moor king. The queen believed it right that he should be here, for the Portuguese to see him."

Garbed in regal gowns, twenty women danced with cavaliers before the king and queen. Applause and murmurs of appreciation rippled around the chamber as the dance ended. Again the music rose and fell, the women returned alone to the floor, with girdles tied around their waists. The royals on the dais clapped, and Princess Isabel bent towards her mother and whispered. Queen Isabel smiled and nodded. Glittering with jewels and in a golden gown almost exactly like the queen's, the princess stepped out to the floor with a lady from Portugal. Servants handed them girdles, and they joined the jubilant dance.

The women left the floor and the musicians struck up a solemn tune. This time the king and queen, hand-in-hand, stepped from the dais to dance a measure both grave and graceful. Jewels emblazed their royal garb, glittering and flashing with every movement in the light of countless candles and high torches.

"I love it when they dance." Catalina drooped, her face pale and miserable. Breaking free of Beatriz and María, she stepped towards the dim corridor. "I want to leave. I want to go back to my chamber."

"Why?" María asked, gazing back at the slow dance of the king and queen and around the chamber blazing with candlelight. Music throbbed and soared, and then plummeted to speak to all hearts.

"I hate it..."

Bewildered, María looked at Catalina, and then up at Beatriz.

"Hate?"

"What do you hate, child?" Beatriz asked the infanta.

Catalina knotted her hands together. "My sister is leaving."

Gazing back at Princess Isabel now talking animatedly to Cardinal Mendoza, Beatriz tried to think of words of comfort. Nothing came to mind.

Beatriz stood a short distance behind Catalina on the royal dais near the high altar. In the cathedral of Sevilla, a thousand and more lit-candles, reflected by mirror, gold and silver, mimicked the brightness of day. The smell of incense was heady and sickly sweet, making her head spin and ache, adding to her depression. Called back to battle, Francisco had left that very morning. Beatriz hoped it would not be long before the king followed after, or that it was true that the king had found himself a new leman. She had never been that. She was but the bitch he kicked in passing.

Below, her hand atop the king's, Princess Isabel walked down the aisle of the cathedral to Alfonso's proxy. Isabel, pale and petite like her three sisters, was so beautiful she could have been a figure painted in an illuminated book. Beatriz had never known her other than as an adult, but today, on her wedding day, the stillness of Isabel's face made her appear utterly young, and vulnerable. *Thank God she possesses her mother's strong mettle. The girl will need it.*

With her head held high and eyes fixed straight ahead, Isabel displayed every iota of her usual pride as she paced towards the taking of her vows. The measured steps of Isabel and her father seemed a strange dance timed to the slow chanting of monks.

Isabel's slender form gave her the illusion of height, an illusion aided by high chopines. With every step she took, gold-patterned heels peeped out from under her gold-cloth gown. Each short, determined, cautious step bespoke constraints, constraints her position placed upon her. Even if she wanted to run away, her chopines forbade it as surely as if she wore fetters, fetters no one saw, but securely locked upon all the daughters of the queen. Beatriz sighed. Fetters placed too well on all women. But for the daughters of the queen the fetters were merciless.

Isabel stepped closer to Alfonso's proxy, and closer to her heart's desire. This marriage was one she never dared to voice and hope for. Taking her place next to the prince's proxy, Isabel, her face solemn, knelt for the cardinal's blessing.

The Princess Isabel now utterly and indissolubly joined to Alfonso in marriage, the weeks of celebrations arrived at an end. Another week passed and the queen and king and their two courts accompanied their eldest daughter to the border of Portugal and Castilla. Following closely behind Catalina and the rest of the royal family, Beatriz rode her mule to crest the last hill of their journey. Spread out far and wide on the green, lush valley below shimmered the colourful pageant of the richly dressed courtiers of Portugal. Mounted on horses, the king and prince were far more richly dressed than the superbly garbed men and women of their court.

Prince Alfonso leaned forward, eyes scanning the approaching company. The wind blew his long blond hair around his tanned face. He smiled – a smile of joy blazing out across the distance. The seventeen-year-old prince forgot royal protocol. With a loud cry he heeled his horse into a gallop, heading towards the mantle-covered, slender girl riding down the hill.

Reaching level ground, Isabel halted her mount. She bent low, patted the mule's neck and murmured soft words, all the time watching her prince ride to her. Coming close, he vaulted from his horse and ran the short distance separating them. A gentle wind lifted Isabel's thin veil and brushed its caress against her pale cheeks. The gossamer veil could not hide her smile. From the way her shoulders shook, Beatriz suspected she laughed, or perhaps wept – tears of happiness. She had hoped for this day for so long.

Now at her side Prince Alfonso held out his hand to Isabel, with palm upraised. Beatriz grinned at Catalina, trying to lift the child's spirits. Not too difficult to discern the desire of the prince – he wanted Isabel's hand in his.

Caught up in the moment, Beatriz heeled her mount closer to the royal family, wanting not to miss a moment. Isabel clasped Alfonso's hand, her eyes glittering with unshed tears. Beatriz had never seen her so elated. Isabel leaned towards Alfonso, whispering something to him, her face hidden from all but the prince by the falling mantle hood. Seized by a sudden gust of strong wind, Isabel's hood fell back as she lifted her head. Silken red tresses, aflame in the sunlight, escaped her veil to intertwine with his golden hair. The prince laughed, kissing the inner wrist of Isabel's thin hand. It seemed to Beatriz that an illuminated page came to life.

Sharing their joy, smiles of two courts encircled the young couple. Despite years of reservations about this match, especially from the still disgruntled King Ferdinand, their union symbolised and strengthened the new peace between Castilla, Aragon and Portugal.

Queen Isabel and King Ferdinand gazed at one another. The king shrugged and, in the full view of everyone, he exchanged a rare, tender smile with his wife. They bowed in their saddles to King João, King Ferdinand lifting his black velvet bonnet to him. Returning the courtesy, King João's countenance spoke to all of his great pride and delight. There could be no doubt of his love for his treasured and only legitimate son.

Taking the bridle of Isabel's mule, the prince led his bride across the border. King João and his Portuguese subjects followed close after them. Cries of jubilation and the beat of many drums and trumpeting of horns marked the crossing from one country to another.

Princess Isabel turned in her saddle, gazed at her parents and waved. Almost in unison, they dipped their heads to her and raised their bonnets. A final wave and then Isabel faced Portugal. She did not turn again.

In Portugal, Isabel wedded once more the heir of its throne, but this time without proxy. For months Beatriz heard news of Isabel's happiness with Alfonso. The queen reassured those closest to her, and so herself, that Isabel dwelt in peace and joy with her husband. Deciding upon this marriage had been the right and only decision for her eldest daughter.

Isabel's wedding signalled the new era of concord between Castilla, Aragon and Portugal. Queen Isabel trusted her oldest daughter to do everything necessary to assure peace remained in that quarter, because a far more important war demanded her attention – a war moving closer to victory.

Her daughter's departure aged the queen. For twenty years she had doted on her eldest daughter. In recent times, Isabel was one of the few to whom the queen opened up her true and secret heart. With the king now returned to the battle-front, Catalina seemed the only daughter able to raise her mother's smile.

g

War at the outset is like a beautiful maid
With whom every one wishes to flirt.
At the end it is like a despised hag
Bringing tears and sadness to whomever she meets.

~ Samuel Ibn Nagrela

From a distance, flower puffs of white and myriad vibrant colours seemed to embroider the brown, summer-seared hill. Closer still, Beatriz picked out the magnificent silk and brocade tents of the king and his grandees, surrounded by simpler soldier tents. Banners fluttered in the air everywhere. The tent city competed in colour and beauty with the looming Moorish city of high, reddish stone towers.

It was not simply the rich hues of the royal camp bespeaking the glory many found in the queen's Holy War. Gazing at men in battle gear, hoping to find Francisco at the camp, Beatriz remembered María recounting her father's conversation with her mother Josefa on their last visit home: "Castilla belongs only to those of the true faith. Soon our land will be cleansed of those heathen unbelievers."

"Mamá was sitting by the fire, sewing a new shirt for Father. Flames reflected in her eyes, and she looked at my father with fear. I could see my father's eagerness to share the thrill of battle did not enthral her. When she returned to sewing, her needle flew in and out of my father's shirt in unspoken anxiety.

"She hates this war, Teacher. But she is a soldier's wife. Her duty binds her to silence just as Father's duty means for him to go back to war.

"My mamá does not like women who farewell their men with whining and beating their breasts for what none can change. She told us she will not be like Andromache, the wife of Hector of Troy, and plead with our father not to fight. She always bids my father, 'Godspeed' when he rides away from our home.

"As soon as we see him no more, Mother goes to her chamber. I believe she weeps there."

Beatriz stopped the pull of memory. Up ahead, Queen Isabel, mounted on a chestnut mule covered by trappings of crimson edged with gold embroidery, gently rocked within her stately saddle-chair. Catalina's proud gaze was all on her mother.

A beat of drums, a swelling of trumpet notes and a roar of thousands rose to the heavens at the queen's approach. Many soldiers broke rank, rushing towards her, kneeling, uncaring of the dirt, along the road bringing her to them. Beatriz caught the answering cries of dismay from the defended citadel of the Moors in the wind.

His dark eyes alight with grim merriment, and garbed in a crimson doublet with breeches of yellow satin, the king rode his favourite black stallion towards his wife. A group of proud grandees closely shadowed the king. The men galloped their mounts as if invincible.

Queen Isabel tossed aside her deep scarlet mantle, freeing one arm to rein in her mule. Her agitated movements opened up her black velvet brial to its skirt of scarlet brocade underneath. Her three daughters wore gowns similar to the queen, even down to wide black hats with thick gold thread worked around top and edge.

The queen straightened her shoulders. Beatriz noticed pain flickering across her face. Travelling about Castilla caused the queen immense discomfort, swelling her legs to almost twice their normal size. Days of journey forced her to stay abed for as many days. She became sicker and sicker with every new year.

Coming within speaking distance and pulling hard at the reins of his horse, the king saluted her. King Ferdinand's huge black beast pranced beside the queen's mule as if eager to return to battle. "Did I not vow to you I'd pick out the seeds of this pomegranate? One by one, I have done so until there remains only one seed left."

Angry shouting came from the walls of the fortress. On the battlement flashed the glint of armour and scimitar. Clusters of men waved lances, threatening to throw them on the queen's soldiers below. Tossing his brocade mantle over his shoulder and displaying his sword with its eagle-winged hilt, the king grinned. His missing front tooth caused a slight whistle when he spoke. "Hear the Moors, wife! They rent their clothes and tear out their hair at seeing you come hither. They know time runs out for them. By sword or gunpowder, be assured, lady wife, conquest will soon be thine."

Studying the citadel of their enemy, she offered a smile half-shadowed by her sunhat. Her bow almost touched her mule's neck. She gazed back at the king. "Yours and mine together, husband, as it has been for every day since we first joined hands and our two kingdoms."

The nearby stallions disturbed Beatriz's nervous mule. Calming her mount before it decided to break away, she wondered yet again about the king and queen. She long knew the queen's devotion to her husband surpassed his shallower affections. Almost every year she bought off another mistress whilst publicly and affectionately caring for the resulting bastards. It seemed to Beatriz the king loved his wife as the queen, and all the power her queenship brought him, rather than the ailing, fast-aging woman too often following him with doting, increasingly anguished eyes. Suddenly ill, Beatriz trembled, hunching under her cloak. *Dear God, please make the king leave me alone. Make him forget me, please.*

Removing his bonnet, the king dipped his head and smiled. "My queen and lady wife, there is a loyal subject you must congratulate."

Catalina reined in her mule, restless like Beatriz's, and watched her parents. She beckoned María de Salinas to come closer. The bells on the harness of Queen Isabel's mount rang a discordant sound as her eyes searched the men at her husband's back. She gestured, calling out: "My good Marques of Cadiz and Count of Cabra. Pray ride to me, my lords."

Two men heeled their horses toward the queen. Followed by his banner bearer, one man edged his coal-black horse away from the other, stopping the huge beast before it chanced to overtake the king's.

Forced again to attend to her fidgety mule, Beatriz recognised the banner of the Count of Cabra. Set upon a sanguine field was a crowned Moor, a gold chain around his neck, with twenty-two banners placed around a shield. The queen had told her the tale behind it. Seven years ago, the count had taken into custody the King of Granada after the defeat of his army, which saw the death of many and the taking of twenty-two banners of their enemies. Thus, the king and queen gave to the Cabra family the title of Don and awarded the gift of this banner. That same victory had seen Prince Ahmed handed over as an infant hostage for the release and good conduct of his father.

Before the count rode the Duke of Cadiz, a hot-tempered man who yet possessed a great heart, with the one-eyed ambition that came from proving himself worthy of the titles he inherited despite being his father's bastard. With no other son to inherit, his father had wed his mother when the duke was a youth and already a demonstrated victor of famous battles. Coming from the enemy side in the early and uncertain years of Queen Isabel's reign, now he was Godfather and sponsor to Prince Juan himself, having long proven his loyalty to the queen and her cause.

He squinted against the bright sunlight. Yanking his costly helmet off, his hood slipped back with the shake of his head revealing a mature face, older than the king's or the queen's, but a face so comely it drew Beatriz's attention and made it difficult for her to look away. Long days in the sun had tanned his skin to brown leather. His dark, deep-set eyes glittered like jet. Firm cleft chin, sensual mouth, long, red hair streaked by silver curled around his face. The magnificent lord bowed low in his saddle to the queen. The duke lifted eyes that widened before hooding against the glaring noon sun. A hand shading his face, he bowed once more. "Gracious and most noble queen, pray forgive me for staying on my horse."

Riding closer, Queen Isabel proffered her hand for his kiss. "My good duke." She exchanged an amused look with her husband.

The Count of Cabra, a dark-haired man with a network of lines mapping a story of humour and careful diplomacy on his face, approached to give the queen homage.

The queen gazed at her two leaders. "Now, my congratulations must be to either of you, or maybe both, as has proven the case for many years in the past. Tell me, which is it now? Cadiz or Cabra?"

With a gruff, deep laugh, the count came closer. "The duke this time, Your Highness!"

The duke smiled. "A small thing, my queen."

Horse hooves shuffled and shifted in the dirt. A protesting neigh pierced the air, as the king half-wheeled his horse to face the queen. "A small thing, Rodrigo? I do not think it a small thing when you saved so many from a grim fate. When bad weather caused soldiers to lose themselves in the mountain passes, the duke here lit beacons around his tent to guide the stragglers back to the campsite. Without that action, I would hate to think how many good men we would have lost on our journey here."

"I was but in the right place at the right time," the duke shrugged. "Any man with common sense would have done the same."

The queen patted her restive mule. "You have a gift to be always there at the right time and the right place, my lord duke. I count myself fortunate to have you in my service. Your good sense and great prowess has brought great glory and victory to our Holy War."

The duke bowed. "My queen, I am proud and honoured to serve you."

"And I am proud and honoured to number such men as yourself and the good count as my leaders." Queen Isabel grinned. "Now this tent my husband mentioned, 'tis the same magnificent tent I have seen on other occasions? If my eyes do not mistake me, I see it yonder?"

Beatriz followed the direction of the queen's pointing finger. The duke's pavilion travelled with him to every new battlefield.

Decorated in Moorish taste, with inner compartments divided by walls of painted silk and curtains, the tent's splendour left the tents of all the other nobility pale and lacklustre beside it. It dominated the city of tents as if an alcázar itself, even daring to compete with the tent of the king.

The duke bowed in the saddle. "Gracious queen, allow me the pleasure of surrendering it to you."

Her objective achieved, Queen Isabel's eyes glinted with humour. "I thank you, my lord duke. You are as generous as always."

Before settling her court into the camp of her army, Queen Isabel kept her eyes on the king and his men as they returned to the battlefield. She became so still, her face acquiring a strange look – as if her apparent calmness hid a thousand thoughts, a thousand heartaches. For the rest of the day, not even her daughters dared speak to her.

IO

Habits are first cobwebs, then cables
~ Castilian proverb

Sweet Francisco,

I thank you for your letter explaining your absence from the camp. How like you to not send another to search for gunpowder supplies – and how wise are you to not trust this task to another. Your work is dangerous enough without you chancing your life on ingredients of inferior quality.

Here at the camp we grow more impatient day-by-day for the king's summons telling us that Granada is at last conquered. While the days are slow, their pattern remain the same: Matins, morning meditation, state business. The queen often attends to this abed – her strength diminishes daily and is not what I desire to see...

"Who will care for you as I do when you cannot sleep and work throughout the night?" Josefa had asked the queen before leaving her service. The queen's sleepless, too often pain-fraught, nights distressed Beatriz, her children and all those loving her, and for good cause. Most days Queen Isabel ruled her kingdom with no more than four hours sleep, sometimes less. But an arduous day ruling rarely caused her to neglect her other roles. By late afternoon, when the worst of the heat had passed, she allowed time to attend to her duties as wife and mother. She wove fine linen to make her husband's shirts, setting her daughters and her women also to this task. While they wove and sewed, she instructed her daughters on the word of God and lessons in statecraft. Listening to her lessons on ruling, Beatriz's pity grew for the queen's daughters. *Thank God I am a teacher and not born into royalty. Life is hard enough without that.*

Catalina listened to her mother with great devotion. Day-by-day she learnt from her an example of patience and hard work, an example that never wavered despite her mother's increasing ill-health. Every evening night fell to the ringing of bells that called to Angelus when the queen chanted the much-loved prayer, "The Angel of the Lord declared to Mary: And she conceived of the Holy Spirit."

Her three young daughters responded in unison with the next part of the prayer, leading in the other women. Beatriz saw Catalina drinking in her mother's closing words: "Behold the handmaid of the lord: Be it done unto me according to Thy word. Hail Mary..."

These daily rituals of the church seemed to serve yet another purpose. The queen stamped upon herself and her daughters the conviction that, through their royal birth, they were God's handmaidens, committed to serve God through the ruling of Earthly kingdoms. That God placed them thus allowed them no other choice.

June brought with it not only the hottest days of an unrelenting summer, but also their long-awaited summons. The queen and her court re-joined the king at Gozco, camping closer but still at a safe distance from the battlefield. There, the court watched victory ripen like the pomegranate itself in summer, and see it fall – fall, luscious and red, bursting with its jewelled seeds ready to eat, seeds of death and life, into Queen Isabel's waiting palm.

While soldiers readied the queen's encampment again, Beatriz looked over at the near hill, blinking against a noon sun, inhaling and exhaling air so hot it seemed to scorch her lungs. On the apex of the hill, King Ferdinand's splendid tent commanded the highest view, overlooking the combined armies of Aragon and Castilla and the red walls of their ancient enemies.

Beatriz turned her head, rooted to where she stood, hearing the loud flap of canvas. Strong winds billowed out the huge banners of Santiago, Castilla, and Aragon into confusion. Set before them, shards of cutting sunlight broke against the ornate, silver standard of a fourth banner. The holy banner of the crusader's cross flapped and whipped uncontrolled against the banners of the two kingdoms. All the banners seemed engaging in battle for supremacy when Hernando de Talavera, the queen's confessor, emerged from the king's tent into the strong wind. Windblown, his body bowed before the wind, his face ageless in its austerity, his long, white robes joined the flap and billow of the banners.

Another dawn broke, awaking Beatriz to the hand-bells of priests, calling the faithful to prayer, intertwined with the call of prayer in the citadel of the Moors, a song like a cry echoing down to the queen's encampment. Every day the call competed with the Christian bells. Christian and Moor mirrored one another in their worship of God.

Each morning, the earth trembled as horses passed their tent, signalling the start of a new day for the queen's cavalry in the field. Battle-drums and war-cries became a normal part of Beatriz's life. The screams of the wounded and dying from nearby tents pierced her dreams, awaking her, bathed in sweat.

One night she opened her eyes, shaking with the remnants of nightmare, fighting to regain the solid ground of reality. Outside, men laughed, fought and sang drunkenly. A chorus of countless cats screeched, as if twirled around and around by their tails. "Santa María, what's that?" she asked in fright.

Their night candle doused some time while she slept, the tent's inky blackness left her dislocated and confused, and still enmeshed in the web of her foreboding dream. She started, hearing the exasperated voice of one of the queen's ladies. "It's the bagpipes, Beatriz. Those English devils run amok again. Every night they feast and drink, making so much noise I cannot sleep."

Hearing the unholy scream of bagpipes begin again, Beatriz remembered her nightmare, and remembered the terror that had birthed it.

Only the day before bright sunlight had slanted upon Queen Isabel's stout form, glittering the gold in her gown with every movement. From the safety of the highest house in the village of Las Zubias, eyes burning with zeal, the queen stood at the un-shuttered window of a chamber on the upper storey, watching the brave and noble Cádiz routing the Moors to savage defeat on the plains of Granada. Close to his royal mother, his three young sisters and little María, Prince Juan pointed out the king coming to the duke's aid.

María's father, Martin de Salinas, recovering from a head blow and forbidden the field this day by both physician and the queen's command, kept his royal kinswoman company. Overlooking the battle as if a bullfight, he explained the battle manoeuvres, and their strange dance between life and death.

Steel clashed and sparked against steel, man clashed and sparred against man, sword-to-sword, dagger-to-dagger. The wind carried the screech of metal, often followed by the shriek of death. Red dust billowed and swirled, spreading through the air a thick, undulating curtain, veiling warrior and horse from one another, causing a state of confusion, disaster and more violent death.

Galloping horses drummed a rhythm to the sway of war. Their manes whipped by speed and wind, some steeds crashed to the earth, their bellies torn apart by spear poles fixed into the ground.

Death whined for prey in the high-pitched wind. Again and again, clouds of black arrows soared, arching into the sky, marking many with death, and maiming just as many.

Not wanting to watch, Beatriz gazed around for water. Her lips and mouth dry, a poem drummed continually in her head – a poem of a great leader, a leader once both Vizier and Nagid of Granada, a man who dared challenge the glory of war. Years ago her father, proud to trace his lineage to him, had read his poems to her from a precious volume handed down the generations from eldest son to eldest son. Now one of its poems came back to haunt her:

> *The horses lunged back and forth like vipers darting out of their nest.*
>
> *The hurled spears were like bolts of lightning, filling the air with light.*
>
> *Arrows pelted us like raindrops, as if our shields were sieves.*
>
> *Their strung bows were like serpents, each serpent spewing forth a stinging bee.*
>
> *Their swords above their heads were like glowing torches, which darken as they fall.*
>
> *Still, my gallant men scorned their lives, preferring death.*
>
> *These young lions welcomed each raw wound upon their heads as though it were a garland.*
>
> *To die – they believed – was to keep the faith;*
>
> *To live – they thought – was forbidden.*

Garland on a battlefield? Beatriz saw none here. A man screamed foreign words that meant nothing to her, but she understood his terror, his agony, his desire for life. Martin de Salinas pointed to men garbed in English colours. "They call for Saint George!"

"Mother! See the English archers find their target!" Prince Juan spoke in awe.

The crackle of gunfire, followed by tell-tale wisps of blue smoke, intermingled with the scream of man and horse. Even from this safe distance, Beatriz just desired to cower, seeing one man smote by an arrow straight into his eye.

Tall like his countrymen, an English soldier hacked down a

terrified Moor with his battle-axe. From their vantage point, the Moor looked to Beatriz just a boy, no more than fourteen. The axe left him broken and bleeding upon the earth. His assailant swung his axe again, down on the boy's neck, before rushing further into the heat of battle. A wing of Castilian cavalry swept over the slender body, trampling it under-hoof. When the tide of horses swept by, it left nothing of the Moor but a sack of bones, gore and blood.

"Ahmed," Beatriz whispered. It could have been Ahmed trampled to a bloody death. She swallowed back bile. For his own safety the prince remained some distance away until his father finally admitted defeat.

"Oftentimes they're slow to engage, my queen," De Salinas said, "but in full battle the English show their true worth. Your Grace, good soldiers to have on our side."

Thoughtfully, De Salinas fingered his chin before dropping his hand back to his side. The tips of his long fingers possessed calluses from his vihuela. Beatriz found herself staring at them. *Why did men make music as easily as taking up a sword?*

De Salinas cocked his head, looking aside at Prince Juan. "My prince, did you know the English believe themselves the most perfect race placed upon the good Earth? The English think themselves better than not only the Moors, but also our men. Indeed, they proclaimed their lord commander better than any grandee. My soldiers little desire their fellowship."

The prince chortled, his laughter ringing strange to Beatriz's ears. He leaned out the window, watching his father engage in combat. "Do they, cousin?" The smile masking his lower face failed in its journey to his humourless blue eyes. He suddenly seemed so much older than his years. "As long as they fight for us with courage, I won't tell them any different."

"Civil war in their barbarous country," De Salinas continued, "have given these men a taste for blood and battle. The English wield both sword and battle-axe with great might, refusing to give ground even when defeat stares them in the face. They're good, staunch comrades in arms, as long as they remember to try not to outdo our men in their wish to keep all the glory to themselves."

Beatriz's stomach churned, its hollowness leaving her both dizzy and ready to vomit. Racked by the awful torture of watching men and boys kill one another, she wiped her sweaty hands on her gown, her mouth simmering to desiccation with each quickened breath. She stepped farther away from the royal family. *Please God, pray let this soon be over.*

Swallowing back bile, Beatriz opened her eyes again to the battle. She no longer had a sense of foe or friend or Englishmen. All she saw was a mass of humanity coming together, and then coming away lessened. Men and beasts littered the field – the dead alongside the wounded and the dying.

Countless ravens gathered in the battlefield, fluttering in short, considered flight, picking at unclaimed bodies where men no longer fought. Drawn back and gone, the tide of war took its deluge of blood to soak elsewhere. The harsh, uncaring, grating caws of raven interwove with the screams of men and beast.

Raven eyes – jet-jewelled and cold – burst into Beatriz's mind and took hold of her scattered wits. No matter how hard she tried to banish them away, the vision lingered, becoming more substantial with every breath she took.

Her breathing quickening again, she took another step away from the royal family, trying to banish her vision. Its cruel form haunted her without mercy. The ravens became as if tailed demons – black like ebony, glistening with a greenish slime, their eyes now red, burning embers withering her soul. They seemed to stand all around, taunting, stalking her as if in a game of cat and mouse.

Beatriz crossed herself and prayed. She looked towards the window – a window revealing not only the bright summer's day and hazy blue hills, but the black emptiness of bloody, violent death.

She turned away from the increasing carnage, her hands no longer palm-to-palm in prayer, but knotted together across her chest – gripped tight enough to hurt. She could no longer thread together the reason, the need, the purpose for this battlefield.

Beatriz owned the queen an intelligent woman, but her utter

concentration on this battle only confused her. The queen's dislike of the dance of death between bull and man was known to all those close to her. It was yet another reason to love the woman ruling Castilla with such an iron grip. *Why, then, bring children here to watch this?* This battle seemed as senseless as the bullfights where men tormented dumb animals to their deaths.

She remembered the years she spent as a child in the convent, when she took mice away from the kitchen cats despite the disapproval of the nuns. She had yearned to ask them: "Why kill just for the sake of killing?"

She was of the blood of El Cid and a long line of warriors. Her ancestor Samuel Ibn Nagrela traced his descent from the house of the warrior King David, the same house that saw the birth of the Lord Jesús. Fed a feast in childhood of crusade stories, hundreds of years of battles won and lost, she had realised early in her life that war was no game.

On this battlefield rode the flower of Christian chivalry. Men left the camp enthused with a strange kind of joy. Even when they returned bloodied and broken beyond all hope of saving, their eyes still shone until death darkened them forever. Beatriz's heart throbbed to the words of her ancestor:

> *These young lions welcomed each raw wound*
> *upon their heads as though it were a garland.*

Bewildered, Beatriz shook her head, wondering if men lived just for this one moment, the one moment when, god-like, they dealt out death. She did not understand this war – nor the death of men, Christian or Moor. *Holy war? A war the good God wanted? God wanted men to hate and kill one another?* She could not believe it.

Men believed to die here opened heaven's gates, and took one straight to paradise. There were no angels singing, only the cries of savage death and the cawing of crows. Shutting her eyes, Beatriz seemed to hear the evil cackle of demons. Their cackle became louder every moment she stayed in this chamber.

Carried by the uncaring wind, the screams of men and beast

assailed her, tearing her heart into shreds. In the midst of a wide-awake nightmare, she looked again out the window. Demons swam all around her, red eyes spewing tongues of fire and flame, fangs pointed and dripping blood. They wanted prey. They wanted her. Unable to block out the sounds of war, unable to stop watching out the shutter-less window, she trembled, fighting an urge to scream: *The window! Shutter it! Please! I beg someone! Shutter it! Don't let the children watch this one moment longer. Oh please, someone! Close the shutters!*

Queen Isabel stood at the window as if transfixed. Even Juana and María seemed surprisingly undisturbed, locked upon the crest and fall of battle, the crest and fall of life and death.

Catalina took María de Salinas's arm. "Come." Beatriz saw the child's white, sick face. She knew it a mirror of hers. "Come and play with me."

Uncaring for their rich velvets, the two girls sat on the dusty floor. Motes rose, spun, glittering like flicks of gold in a slanting sunbeam.

Upon her square palm, Catalina offered to María silver-gilded knuckles. Earlier this morning, unaware that her mother would take her where no child should ever go, she had scooped them from the chest in her chamber to put in the pocket of her gown. The two girls had been innocent then. How could they be innocent now? Beatriz winced seeing Catalina's trembling smile.

"You call first," the child said. Tears ran down Catalina's pale cheeks. She met María's eyes, and Beatriz seized on the one light in a far too dark afternoon. From the first moment the two girls had become friends, they shared a kinship beyond flesh.

Catalina tossed the knuckles up in the air and, like the motes just before, the silver knuckles winked and glittered in sunlight. The girls became children again, while Beatriz tried to shutter out visions of Hell.

II

*The world and its desires pass away,
but the man who does the will of God lives forever.*
John 2:16-17

Dear love,

I continue to wait eagerly for your return. Did you not tell me, love, that you witnessed the king knighting his son in sight of the beleaguered city of the Moors two years ago? Yesterday, Prince Juan had his first taste of battle – a carefully dealt out taste. The prince's life is far too precious for his parents to tempt fate overmuch.

The queen's daughters would prefer not to spend their days at camp, but victory over the Moors is so important the entire royal house must witness it. They are guarded well – perchance, too well. The lives of the girls are more confined here than when we live in the great comfort of a royal alcázar. We are crowded together in a tent, although the infantas take turns to sleep with their mother in the magnificent tent loaned to her by the Duke of Cadiz...

A peculiar red-tinged orange light flickered against Beatriz's closed eyelids. Drawn out of the eddy sucking her into sleep and dreams, she opened one eye and then the other. Her eyes stung, watered, blinked. The orange glow wavered, illuminating the tent. The light grew stronger until – moment-by-moment – it eclipsed the amber light of the tent's lone candle.

Surfacing from her drowsy haze of confusion, Beatriz coughed – signalling a sleepy chorus of coughs from the infantas and their attendants. Beatriz's throat and lungs started to hurt. She wheezed, and the reason hit her like cold water. She bolted up in bed, her heart racing. Fear opened in place of her stomach. She breathed smoke – not the smoky air of a camp numbering hundreds of tents, but increased a thousand-fold, and more. A woman screamed. Drums and trumpets sounded the alarm. Voices shouted. More screams cut through the air, closer this time, cries of women intermingled with squeals of terrified horses.

Outside the tent men yelled and swore. Heavy feet crunched upon earth, stumbled, ran. The queen, her deep voice heightened by rare panic, screeched, "...leave me! See to the prince and my daughters. Make certain they're safe."

Fearing the camp attacked, Beatriz shook her two charges awake. At almost the same moment soldiers, some dressed only in heeled hose and shirt, rushed into the tent. One carried a torch and pointed to Catalina and her sister María. This night saw Juana sleep in her mother's tent. Without any concern for decorum, ignoring the girls' startled cries, the men bundled the two infantas and small María in blankets from their beds and carried them into the night. The other occupants of the tent had only the fire's light to help them to safety. Drawing a blanket around her shoulders to cover her shift, Beatriz hurried after the men, coughing every step of the way.

She gazed over her shoulder. The other women emerged and ran from the tent. Turning slightly, she saw the queen's pavilion. Glowing bright like a blazing funeral pyre, its red and orange flames lit the night sky.

The wind gathered strength. Embers flared out, catching the top of the infantas' tent. Flame-tongues licked until the blaze took hold. Metal gleamed then turned into molten rivulets. The pavilion she had just left became buckling walls of flames. The fire ate and ate, its sparks spreading to yet another tent, gorging upon the silk and metal.

Making her way to Catalina and María, Beatriz shivered, iced both by terror and cold night. Her naked toes curled in pain against the hard, stony earth. She limped in agony by the time she reached her royal charge. Nestled under the queen's arm, engrossed in watching the night spectacle, Catalina reached to clasp Beatriz's hand in hers. Little María ran to her, taking her other hand.

On the other side of their mother, the infanta María stood beside her older sister, Juana, who held Prince Juan's hand. All of them were robed in blankets. Even King Ferdinand seemed to have had a close escape. Marching back and forth, directing soldiers fighting the fire, he wore just his white shirt and hose and held his sword, buckler and cuirass, as if ready to do battle. He scanned the efforts of his men, the fire flames flickering in his dark eyes.

Hearing a cry of warning, Beatriz glanced over her shoulder. The fire gorged everything in its path, enveloping the nearby sleeping booths made from tree branches, rough and ready protection from the elements for many soldiers. Compassion tugged at Beatriz's heart. They would be left without sleeping places this night. They would not be the only ones.

The fire continued to feast. The night air filled with the crackle and snap of a ravenous beast. Unsatisfied, greedy for destruction, the beast grew in size, becoming grotesque, a monster on a rampage. A hoard of soldiers formed bucket lines and struggled to quench its advance.

"Men, let not the Moors benefit from this night's work and discover us with our guard down! Cavalry!" the king yelled. "Mount your horses! Ring the camp and protect the queen!"

Answering his command, a battle-horn swelled its long call into the night. The thunder of a thousand or more horses stormed around them, the queen's cavalry rushing into the black of night. Gathered together and safe, as if on an island of calm, chaos and darkness lapping at its shores, Queen Isabel and her children stood close to one another. The gusty wind radiated a wall of heat in their direction. They had made their escape just in time. Good fortune had robbed the blazing pyres before their eyes of the dead.

A dismal dawn broke over the camp the next day. Low grey clouds intermingled with mist and lingering smoke. Exhausted soldiers salvaged through the smouldering ruins, carefully sifting the remains of the queen's tent for any signs of evil intent or for anything worth saving. The exquisite pavilion of the Marques of Cadiz destroyed, Queen Isabel, her three unwed daughters and their closest attendants shared a large tent undamaged by the fire, wearing upon their backs clothes given to them by those still with possessions after the dreadful night.

Garbed in borrowed gowns too big for them, Catalina and María stood with Beatriz on the edge of the destroyed camp, watching the soldiers at work. Over-tired from a sleepless night, long moments passed before anyone spoke. Catalina stepped onto the scorched encampment. She dug into the ground with her slippered toe, examining the little pile of earth as if wishing to make sense of it.

"Jesu'. The very earth itself is black and seared." Catalina lifted her head. "You spoke to my mother? Do they know how it happened?"

Beatriz joined Catalina, studying the scorched earth too. Sunlight broke through the heavy cloud and glinted off some object half-buried in the soil. Cleaning it with her foot, Beatriz picked up a small mass of shapeless metal. "Whatever this was once, none now can tell." She sighed and dropped it back on the ground. "So much destroyed in a single night – our clothes chests and furs the least of it." She pushed back a strand of hair blowing in her eyes. "How did it happen? My infanta, last night, the queen prayed alone for the safety of the king and the prince. When the pavilion filled with smoke, Queen Isabel wasted no time taking flight with your sister."

Catalina took Beatriz's arm. "Was it treachery?"

Beatriz tried to smile her reassurance, but a nasty taste was in her mouth. When she looked at Catalina she shivered. God knew she would always protect the queen with her life, even if it risked her soul. "Treachery is always a possibility," she sighed, not wanting to think about it. "But the queen believes the fire was an accident."

"Can you be certain?" Catalina asked.

Beatriz shrugged. "The queen commanded a taper be taken from near her couch and placed elsewhere. It appears the attendant placed it too near the hangings and forgot the strong wind last night. Thank God only our possessions were destroyed. It could have been far, far worse. Our good queen came too close to death here."

While the queen and her court escaped a fiery death, the wheel of fortune turned elsewhere, giving with one hand, taking with the other. One month after the fire, when the sun was high in the sky, a horseman rode into the camp, his horse – rolling-eyed and frothing blood – ridden to the ground. Rumour of his grim news spread around the camp as fast as the blaze that destroyed the queen's camp, but 'twas not until the next morning that their grieving queen told her attendants the story come from Portugal.

A week before, Prince Alfonso hurried home to his wife at nightfall, galloping his untried, half-broken stallion, a recent gift of King Ferdinand, on the uneven ground of the Tagus riverbed. It was to be the good prince's last twilight before night fell on his mortal life forever.

The queen told her women a swooping owl had spooked the prince's horse. The animal wheeled from the rough track into rougher terrain, an unseen hole snapping the horse's leg. Alfonso was tossed from his mount, then the animal crashed down on him.

Alfonso's Castilian groom took him to a fisherman's hovel before going for help. By the time the king's physician came to the prince's aid it was too late to move him. Alfonso lay for two days close to death. The King of Portugal, the Queen of Portugal, his mother and his wife remained by his side. Both women held on to him as if that alone held him to life, but he never regained consciousness.

Death came for him on the second night.

Queen Isabel and most of her inner court now resided in a new and more comfortable dwelling, a small Moor alcázar taken in conquest, half a day's journey from the battlefield. The queen waited there while her soldiers built for her a half city and half camp, naming it Santa Fe: Holy Faith. Santa Fe would offer her better protection and comfort than the king's camp. Beatriz spent much of her time in the queen's chamber, teaching Catalina and María their lessons. With Queen Isabel unwell, full of unrest and worry about her eldest daughter, Beatriz knew Catalina's presence helped to lighten her mother's mood. Often she wondered if the queen really noticed them at all, especially the day when the message arrived from Portugal.

Reading it the queen gasped. "My Isabel has locked herself in a dark chamber. She has not slept or eaten since Alfonso's death. She weeps and weeps and refuses to wear anything but sackcloth." She read a little more. "Sweet Jesu', she's cut off all her hair! Her women fear for her. They think she may try to take her own life. Queen Leonor fears the same. She writes that they have taken Isabel's dagger from her. My daughter must return. I shall write so now!"

Thus, the King of Portugal sent Isabel home.

Beatriz abandoned any hope of teaching the girls when outriders brought them news that Isabel's cavalcade was but a day away. The next morning she took them to the balcony overlooking the winding road ribboning its way to the alcázar. Grateful for the balcony's stone bench, Beatriz read a book as Catalina chewed at her thumbnail, looking down at hills and valleys, spreading out to become the blue mist of distance.

The sun passed its pinnacle while María strummed her vihuela. At times, Beatriz scrutinised Catalina. The child stayed at her post as if she could not move. Her book unexpectedly boring, time trudged slowly onward like a spark igniting a damp log.

At last Beatriz heard a fanfare of trumpets. Catalina let out a cry. Half sobbing, half laughing, she picked up her skirts, running from her chamber. María put down her vihuela and raced after her. Beatriz followed until, breathless, she reached a large gathering of courtiers come hither to welcome the queen's eldest daughter.

The andas halted before the steep, narrow stairs and the king helped his daughter out. A ghost-woman emerged from the andas, shrouded in black veils billowing in the gusting wind, overtop a widow's white headdress. Sheer black gossamer veils did little to conceal Isabel's haggard, ill face.

Her women kneeling behind her, Isabel curtseyed. The king raised her up, kissing her cheek in welcome. He took her up the steps for her mother's greeting. Isabel pulled back her veil as a sign of respect. With exhausted grace and lowered eyes, she dropped to her knees and kissed the king and queen's be-ringed hands. Queen Isabel bent to speak to her daughter. Despite her closeness, Beatriz could not hear Isabel's reply, only softly mumbled words.

The king and queen gazed at each other before they assisted their daughter to her feet. Isabel kept her head bowed as her mother kissed her. She did not look at either parent, she did not look at anything. The long trail of her gown dragging behind her, she stumbled up the steps like one blind.

Catalina shifted from one foot to the other. Unwilling to wait one more moment, forgetting protocol, she rushed down those last few steps to her sister. Blanching, Queen Isabel swung an alarmed glance to the king, reaching for her youngest child. Too late. Catalina flung herself at Isabel, wrapping her arms around her sister's body. Her older sister took a backward step and stood like stone, her arms stiff at her sides.

"Isabel!" Catalina cried, hugging her again, this time tighter, almost pushing her sister back another step. Isabel stared ahead, far too lost within her own grief to be conscious of the grief she herself caused, unaware that her youngest sister's mouth trembled, or that Catalina's tears welled, running down flushed cheeks. Grim, his eyes hard, the king separated Catalina from his older daughter.

The princess returned to them a stranger. Over the coming days she wafted through the court, her drawn, sorrowful face hooded by a mantle, garbed in mourning from head to toe, speaking little, and only when spoken to.

There were moments when she resumed some semblance of her former self, but a misspoken word or deed soon caused Isabel to disappear like a genie into its lamp. The light extinguished from her eyes, she withdrew into the shadows of her deep hood. Ever protective, the queen kept her eldest daughter close and even insisted the girl sleep with her at night.

Two weeks after Isabel arrived home, Beatriz and her two small charges slipped passed the queen's attendants. Either gossiping over their sewing or playing chess, the women paid them no mind. Catalina pushed open the heavy oak door to her mother's bed-chamber and froze. Isabel knelt at her mother's side, head cradled upon folded arms on the queen's lap, sobbing and sobbing. Never before in Beatriz's life had she witnessed such grief, not from man, woman, or child. Isabel's sobs tore out of her and cut deep like a dagger.

Free from layers of head-dressings, Isabel's naked head showed no longer the silken, glorious red-gold hair once envied by so many at court, but a skullcap of reddish bristles pressed against the breast of the queen's black velvet robes.

Beatriz strangled back a cry. Jagged, ugly, half-healed scabs scored Isabel's scalp. The rumour then was true. The princess had slashed her head with such frenzy she drew blood. Some of the wounds looked already scars. No wonder her women feared for her. No wonder there were mutterings about her sanity.

Beatriz saw in her mind Prince Alfonso standing eagerly at Isabel's gold stirrup, his blue eyes looking at her, lit with love. She remembered Isabel bending to speak to him, her tresses curtaining them in a shimmering veil. A gust of wind had intertwined his hair with hers, and their two right hands clasped, as the young woman and man took an unspoken troth, in love and faith before all, and an unspoken vow to share a life together. Only eight months passed before she returned a broken-hearted widow.

María and Catalina gazed at one another, their faces pictures of bewilderment. *Still so young.* Beatriz sighed. She tried hard to shield the girls from the harsher realities of life. Now Isabel's grief was as if a dark, heavy cloud covered the sun. About to shut the door, Beatriz paused. Isabel spoke, her voice hoarse, drowning in tears. "Mother, oh, my mother, please, I beg you, please let me go! Please let me take the veil. There's nothing left for me here. Nothing!"

Through the narrow crack, Beatriz saw the queen close her eyes. She grimaced in pain and stroked her daughter's shorn head. Grief and unhappiness etched deeper the lines on the queen's face and dragged down her mouth. She held Isabel's face between her hands. "Dear one, you ask for the impossible. I wish I could say otherwise, but I cannot. You are next in line to my throne after Juan and perchance your father's throne, too."

Anger lit fire and life to Isabel's eyes. "I never wanted any other crown other than that of Alfonso's consort. Father never wanted me to marry him. Time after time he delayed our match, or suggested Alfonso wed María instead, even knowing Alfonso and I already loved one another! Mother, you never told me Father attempted to bribe the pope to dissolve our betrothal. Alfonso's father spoke of it to me."

The queen blanched. "Your father believed he was doing right. I too was not in favour of this match, but I knew you'd set your heart to it." Queen Isabel lifted her daughter's chin, forcing her to meet her eyes. "Fortune did not look kindly on it. It was not meant to be for you to remain long Alfonso's wife. It must be as it was before."

Isabel jerked her face away, as if burnt by her mother's touch. "I have three sisters. You don't need me. Let Juana take my place. She's old enough. More, Mother, she hungers for it!"

The queen rubbed her temple. "Isabel, 'tis not as simple as that. Your life is given by God for the good of Castilla and Aragon. It is your duty to serve, just as it is mine. Nothing changes this. Not even Alfonso's death."

Clasping the sides of her shorn head with her hands, Isabel collapsed onto her mother's lap, and the floodgates opened to even rawer grief. The queen, appearing torn apart herself, rocked her daughter, attempting to console her.

Catalina grabbed Beatriz's hand. She pulled her from the door and closed it, shutting away the darkness within. "No more!" The small infanta stamped her slippered foot. "No more, I say! Let's go somewhere else. Let's go now!"

Dragged along by Catalina, out of her mother's ante-chamber and into the corridor, Beatriz's stride quickened to keep up with her. She looked at Catalina – not knowing what to do. She felt swept into Catalina's whirlpool of unhappiness.

Catalina no longer seemed to see the long corridor before them, and not just because of her short-sightedness. Without warning, she dropped Beatriz's hand, picked up the skirts of her black velvet *habito*, and ran.

Gathering up her own skirts, Beatriz sped after her, catching up when she reached the library. Catalina leaned her face against the wall, her hands on either side of her. As if fighting for air her breaths rasped fast and uncontrolled. Beatriz gripped her shoulder. "Child..." She swallowed. "I am here. I am here." *Oh dear God – what else can I say?*

Catalina's hot tears dripped onto her hands. Beatriz's eyes blurred with tears too. She remembered writing in her yet unfinished letter to Francisco: Queen Isabel's daughters wept with good cause. Yes – they wept for good cause, and left those who loved them feeling helpless.

A few days afterward Beatriz saw Isabel smile at last at her youngest sister. True, a faltering smile, but a faltering smile was better than none. By the end of the month, Isabel had resumed the long habit of older sister caring for the younger members of the family. Isabel never realised how many times it was her younger siblings doing the true caring.

Prince Juan spent all his free time at his sister's side, often playing his vihuela for her ears alone. Almost every day her three sisters requested Isabel's company while they sewed or embroidered together. When the princess took her needlework, either outdoors or indoors, to sit with her sisters, María, Juana and Catalina gently drew from her stories about her time in Portugal. The stories she told often diverted Beatriz from the book she brought to read. So many times Isabel seemed to speak of her months away from her mother's court as if of a story of distant legend in which she played no part. She rarely spoke of the young prince she had given her heart to. Those memories she locked away with her ability to reclaim joy.

"This story is for our chiquitina," Princess Isabel said one warm, blue-skied morning. Lifting her eyes from her almost completed eagle of Saint Juan, she resettled against the cushions on a large rug flung out to cover the grass. With Juana summoned to her mother's this day, to talk over her betrothal to Philip the Fair, the remaining infantas, accompanied by their more favoured attendants, took their leisure by doing needlework.

Beatriz dropped her book to her lap. Now returned to sewing, Isabel's needle flew through the fabric without one mistake. Under the princess's deft and experienced hands, the bold lines of the eagle took animated shape, wings spread wide, sharp beak opened as if about to swoop down on its prey. The warmth of the day made her drowsy and Beatriz drifted as if in a dream.

"There was a hidalgo at the king's court, an adventurer called Hatchet-face. His true name was Pedro Vaz da Cunha, the victor, so he boasted, of countless battles. He must have come close to losing his life in one, for it left him with one eye and his face badly scarred, thus earning him his nickname.

"When I first met him, Hatchet-face had with him a page, a pretty youth of some seventeen years who answered to the name of Perkin Warbeck. Pedro claimed to his friends that the page was in fact an English prince. Dressed in rich brocade and silk, the page truly gathered to himself the presence of one. More bewildering and strange, some foreign men at court behaved unto him as if indeed in the presence of royalty."

"A page treated like royalty? How can that be?" Perplexed, the infanta María reached into the shared sewing basket for a card of scarlet thread.

Isabel gave a small smile. "'Tis strange, my sister. But not as strange as the rest of this tale. Hatchet-face and his page accompanied the king from Lisbon to Evora and finally to the king's favourite hunting grounds at Setubal. Hatchet-face also had with him Edward Brampton, a man I once met with our mother when you were but an infant, Catalina. He came as part of the English party negotiating for your hand in marriage to Prince Arthur. Brampton's name and adoptive country well hid his tangled history. Whilst sponsored to the true faith by Edward IV, the man was a lowly born Portuguese Jew and, I believe, a bastard. I spoke to Brampton one day..." Princess Isabel's lips tightened, her eyes slanting sideways from her sewing. A frown deepened lines between her fine brows. She gazed at the nearby budding white roses, her pale face strangely composed.

Isabel turned glazed eyes back to her sisters. Beatriz thought of still, deep waters that hid so much. Uneasy, she shifted on the rug. *Is Isabel keeping a secret from her sisters? Why do I feel a threat of some kind?*

Isabel started sewing again. "I thought Brampton treated his page strangely – sometimes like a son, sometimes with deference, but also like a man burdened by a responsibility he no longer desired or wanted. At those times, his eyes simmered with resentment. Once I asked him why the page distressed him so." Isabel laughed briefly, noticing Catalina widened eyes of surprise. "I am a grown woman, Catalina..." Isabel took in a deep breath, "... and a woman then happily wedded. I can speak to men if I wish, and knowing Brampton in the past gave me the liberty to address him directly." Seeing Catalina's confusion, Isabel leaned towards her. "Believe me, my sister, there are times when women must question men, otherwise we risk knowing nothing at all.""

"And Brampton? What did he say, my lady princess?" asked little María.

Her face no longer clouded, Isabel smiled. "Nothing that day. But another time we were out hunting and I found my horse alongside his. He told me then his tale. I have repeated it to the queen since coming home." Coming to the end of her thread, Isabel gazed at her sisters. "Mother said it was ludicrous – spun from moonbeams and an addled brain of a mad man." With a flicker of annoyance, she pushed back a few strands of hair. Since her hair started to grow again, it often escaped from beneath her head veils, tickling the hollows of her cheeks.

"Brampton's story was that the last York king put his nephew Richard into his care, making him vow to take him to Flanders if he lost the battle with Henry Tudor. When King Richard was no more, Brampton said he could do no other than keep his promise to his dead sire. Thus, Brampton claimed the page with Hatchet-face was the White Rose himself and the rightful King of all England."

The full implication of her words spun around them a net of silence. Beatriz saw Catalina narrow her eyes. The child looked over to the same bush of white roses that had captured Isabel's attention just moments before. The flowers trembled in a sudden gust of wind, and petals swirled in the air, drifting to the ground. She turned back to her older sister. "There were two sons of King Edward. What of the older one, the one named for his father? Wouldn't he be the rightful heir? How did Brampton explain that?"

"Mi chiquitina, you're learnt well from Latina. I did think to ask this question of Brampton. He said it was believed someone poisoned the older boy. Believing he protected the boys by placing them in the Tower, King Richard took the news of his nephew's death to heart. The suspicion of poison just made it worse.

"King Richard hid the younger boy in the home of a man he trusted and made Brampton vow that if all went wrong for him, he would take his nephew to Flanders and to his aunt, the Duchess Margaret. This Brampton did, but with Flanders so close to England the duchess feared discovery by Tudor spies. She, in turn, entrusted Brampton on another mission, to take the boy to Portugal, and she placed him in the care of Hatchet-face. Proven loyal in the past to those who paid him well, this man's protection would cause those wanting to capture the youth to think twice before treading on dangerous ground."

"You don't think the story is true?" Catalina asked, her sewing forgotten on her lap.

Isabel shrugged and rethreaded her needle. "Like I said, Catalina, our lady mother says no. But when mystery surrounds the death of princes, there will always be fables following soon after. I doubt we'll ever sift the truth from this story, but what's important for us to know is that the king who sits on England's throne made it his by sword and conquest, and he's the rightful king in our parents' minds. Henry Tudor is not likely to welcome back one claiming to be the son of the York king, especially when he now has sons of his own." She sighed. "As for this youth. He disappeared from the Portugal court not long after I first saw him. Mother now tells me he reappeared in Burgundy and declared himself Richard IV of England. If this young man is who he claims to be, I think he would be far wiser to forget all about England's crown. It would be shrewder of him to make a new life elsewhere and just disappear, especially from those hoping to use him." Her fingers paused, and Isabel gazed into nothingness. "If those of royal blood are fortunate to escape their fetters, let them stay that way."

Later that same day, Beatriz made sense of Isabel's sudden unease. Ushered from the room where the queen's attendants sat and sewed together, once again Catalina pushed open the door of her mother's bedroom to hear the faint voice of Isabel.

"Will you tell Catalina about what you ask of the English king?"

Beatriz peeped through the crack created by the open door. At the other side of the room the queen and her eldest daughter, heads bent over their sewing, sat close together, facing the shutter-less window.

"No. I want her to be a child a while longer."

Isabel turned her head. In fright, Catalina almost shut the door, but not enough to prevent them from hearing further.

"Do you really think it necessary, Mother? All speak of Warwick as if he is an innocent, even weak-minded. No one, surely, would seek to place a crown on one such as he?"

"The weak and innocent are used and shaped to the purposes of the strong, my hija. I do not like asking for his death, but your father convinces me of its need. Warwick is now a young man of seventeen and is looked on by many as a strong claimant to the English crown. I will not allow my youngest child to leave me until I know this particular problem has been dealt with. Our chiquitina will go to England in safety – as safe as I can ensure – or not all.

"We have been long in secret talks with Henry VII about this matter, but the English king refuses to do what we ask, even when we point out Warwick alive only places in danger Henry's own sons. While I understand the queen cares not to forget her close kinship with the youth, she must understand I simply cannot send Catalina to England while he lives. Henry and his gentle queen must own the difficult responsibility in wearing a crown and the painful decisions that accompany it."

Softly closing the door, Catalina almost dragged Beatriz away. Feeling like life repeated itself, she allowed Catalina to lead her, this time to the safety of the infanta's bedchamber. Once there, Catalina collapsed on the clothes chest at the end of the bed and looked at her. "Warwick? That's the son of Richard III's older brother, the one Edward IV executed for treason. He is in the Tower of London, isn't he?" she asked.

Many of Beatriz's lessons included long study of the court and nobility the infanta would one day rule. She eyed Catalina and shrugged. "Like your sister said, most believe him simple-minded and no threat to anyone."

"But Mother thinks he threatens me?" Catalina chewed at her thumb. "My mother said she asked the English king for his death.

You heard her say this too?"

Beatriz nodded. The horror she saw on Catalina's white face made her blink and glance away from her. She tightened her lips and inhaled her deep breath. "She does it for your safety, Catalina." She dared look at the child again. Her horror hadn't lessened, rather she trembled and held herself, as if stricken with fever.

"Someone to die? To die for me, Latina? I did not ask it. I do not want it!" Catalina burst into tears and flung herself on the bed.

Beatriz stood by her. Lying on her back, staring at the ceiling, Catalina no longer cried, but heaved in deep breaths as if struggling for air.

'Let her be a child a while longer,' Queen Isabel had said. *A child a while longer?* Looking down at Catalina's pale, still face, Beatriz wondered if the queen wished for the impossible.

12

'Allah has grievously visited my sins upon my head. For your sake, my people, I have now made this treaty, to protect you from the sword, your little ones from famine, your wives and daughters from outrage, and to secure you in the enjoyment of your properties, your liberties, your laws, and your religion under a sovereign of happier destinies than the ill-starred Boabdil.'

Granada fell at last, cannon crumbled its final walls of defence before winter brought its own desolation and famine. Ravens circled the skies. Flocking and fluttering on the broken city's walls, the ravens seemed an edge of black lace on the fabric of reddish stone.

Knowing many hated the defeat, and fearful of his people's unrest, Boabdil set the second day of January as the date for the final surrender. Waiting for that time to come, Queen Isabel and her court no longer dwelled in the alcázar found for her after the fire, but at the newly readied Santa Fe.

Messengers went to and fro, exchanging a flurry of letters between the two courts, royal protocol the main matter of concern. Boabdil's mother refused to allow her son to humble himself to the king and queen, insisting the ceremony not include the king of the Moors kissing the hands of the victors.

Suspecting that Boabdil's mother might yet disrupt the smooth transition from one ruler to another, King Ferdinand and Queen Isabel chose to gentle the way of the vanquished. Word was sent to the Moorish king to come forth on horseback on the morning he was to give them the city keys. An offer of homage was all that King Ferdinand and Queen Isabel desired and expected from him, homage they agreed to decline on the day.

The promise that Boabdil would be treated with all due respect to his rank at last satisfied his mother. The final terms of surrender now agreed, Boabdil swore his loyalty to the Castilian crown and freed the city's captive Christians. The queen summoned those caring for Ahmed to bring him to the Santa Fe.

The last night before the city's hand-over, Beatriz stood with Francisco, watching together as the sun set behind the mountains, both of them relieved of duties for a time. The royal family wanted to spend this night with Ahmed, saying farewell to a boy brought up like a beloved son and a brother. There was no certainty any at court would ever see him again.

Grieving too about Ahmed's approaching departure, Beatriz studied the sun-kissed mountains and then the hill of La Sabica. *How the walls of the Alhambra ringed it in a fit marriage.* The setting sun turned the walls a deeper red, giving it glorious luminosity. The Alhambra meant crimson alcázar – crimson, the colour of blood. The colour of fire and war.

Surrounded by the jubilant expectancy of the camp, Beatriz listened to the cold, cutting wind, tinged with death, defeat, and despair, bringing down to Santa Fe the lament of the Moors.

"Why so downcast, love?" Francisco asked, putting his arm around her. "Believe me, there's no reason for pity. The terms given to the Moors are generous. After a war lasting so many years, the victorious do not usually allow the defeated leave to keep so much."

"But, Francisco, how can you say this when their city no longer belongs to them?"

Francisco frowned. "The queen has been more than fair to the Moors. She promises to allow those who wish to stay to keep their religion and laws, governed by cadis of their own faith, men overseen by governors trusted by the queen and king. For three years they will be exempt from tribute, and those wishing to return to Africa have free passage to do so."

"And the secret promises my small infanta heard her mother speak of?"

Glancing around in alarm, Francisco took her arm. "What secret promises?"

"The queen assures Boabdil and his descendants of lands that will replace this city not only for a short time, but for all time. The king and queen will also pay him thirty thousand *castelanos* of gold on the day he leaves the city."

A grim smile tightened her lover's mouth. "Thirty thousand castelanos... more like thirty pieces of silver. 'Tis the final betrayal of a weak king. His signing of the treaty broke the heart and spirit of the city. Many Moors would rather die than see this day finally come. Many believe they have lost so much they might as well lose all. You remember the recent rebellion, when one of their prophets provided the spark for the city's populace to burst into flames? That man declared the king and other Moor leaders cowards and no longer true Moslems. Thousands and thousands, women as well as men, armed themselves, paraded in the streets and shouted for the fight to continue. One leader said, 'We are men. We have hearts, not to shed tender tears, but drops of blood. Let's die defending our liberty.'" Gazing up at the city, Francisco gripped his sword's hilt as if thinking of battle.

Disturbed by his action, Beatriz gnawed her bottom lip. "I thank the good God those words fell on deaf ears."

Francisco continued. "For a day and a night the king dared not emerge from the Alhambra until the prophet, perchance murdered by the king's own men, disappeared. The King of the Moors knows there's nothing more to be done but admit defeat. He is a beaten man, full of despair and guilt. He blames all his misfortunes on coming to the throne in rebellion against his father."

The setting sun spilled a crown of gold over Francisco's black hair and made his face difficult to see. Some distance away, soldiers lit night torches, cutting around the camp a trail of light to follow as dark fell. Very soon, the red fading from its walls, the city's stones would be silvered by starlight.

Her eyes on the guttering torches, Beatriz combed her fingers through her untidy hair, remembering the tale of how men built the Alhambra by torchlight. Now, when the Moors owned their beautiful city this one last night, the light of the torches seemed to throb out a silent dirge to her that the city's very beginning predicted its end. Perchance 'twas true of everything. Life was an unending circle of birth and death, beginnings and ends. Her own mortality opening before her like a black hole, she swung her gaze back to Francisco.

As if catching her mood, he gripped her shoulders. Kissing her, his fingers dug into her flesh. Usually so gentle, she knew he didn't mean to hurt her, but was forgetful due to his unspoken fear. Tomorrow Francisco would be gone again – once again risking his life as one of the few who understood gunpowder and its myriad uses in battle. Si – war ended here. Tomorrow the Moors would yield up all their artillery, their city gates, towers and fortresses to the king and queen. But there were still battles to be fought and won before peace could truly be claimed.

The hours sped by to the city's handover. In the dark of night, leaving their king behind, Boabdil's family stole out of the city, going a way determined in great secrecy when the last treaties were signed. They said his mother rode in haughty silence, while the sobbing of his wife and concubines invaded the dreams of those fortunate enough to find any sleep that night. Boabdil's household went to a hamlet overlooking the city, and there they stayed in wait for their vanquished king.

Dawn broke to the boom of signal guns from the Alhambra. The snow peaks of Sierra Nevada glowed blood-red, as if nature took upon itself the duty to spread out the Moors' banner of defeat. Under countless standards, the Christian multitude gathered, garbed in their finest. The queen even convinced Princess Isabel to put aside the colour of mourning. From Santa Fe, led by the king and queen and their two courts, an army trekked across the Vega to halt at the village of Armilla, half a league from the city.

There was already one there who was important in these

happenings despite his tender years, the childhood companion of the royal children, Ahmed.

King Ferdinand went on ahead to meet the Moor king. The queen later relayed the day's happenings to her attendants who didn't see for themselves.

Before the advance of the queen and king, their armies and cavalry, old Cardinal Mendoza, accompanied by Don Gutierrez de Cardenas, entered the city via a road outside the walls. A horn swelled its long note in signal.

Accompanied by fifty of his companions, Boabdil rode forth from the Tower of the Seven Floors. Once outside the city's walls, he swung from his horse and approached the cardinal on foot. Mendoza dismounted to meet with him. For a few minutes they spoke so none could overhear. Then Boabdil lifted up his voice: "Go, senor, and take possession in the name of the powerful sovereigns to whom God has been pleased to deliver them in reward of their great merits and in punishment of the sins of the Moors."

Boabdil took a gold ring from his finger and gave it to Don Inigo Lopez de Mendoza, Count of Tendilla and kinsman to the cardinal, the new governor of the city. "With this ring Granada has been governed. Take it, govern with it, and may you be more fortunate than I."

Boabdil rode on to King Ferdinand – who now approached the city. He offered to dismount and kiss the king's hand, but, as promised, King Ferdinand prevented him from doing so. The Moor king leaned across and kissed the king's arm, while at the same time delivering to him the keys of the city.

"These keys are the last relics of the Arabian empire in Spain. To you, oh king, we give our trophies, our kingdom, and our person. Such is the will of God. Receive them with the clemency you have promised, and which we look for at your hands."

At the village of Armilla, Boabdil rode in on the wind that brought also to their ears the music from the city, the music of Christian victory.

"My father comes," said Ahmed in a small voice. Holding their hands, he stood between the infantas María and Catalina. Wondering how Ahmed recognised his father, Beatriz noticed the Italian, Cristóbal Colón, watching them closely as he stood with a small gathering of the queen's inner court.

Queen Isabel waited for the Moor king to make his way to her. Seeing him about to kneel and offer her homage, she put out her hand and stopped him. "There's no need for that."

The queen turned, beckoning to Prince Ahmed. When he reached her side, she rested a reassuring hand on his shoulder. Her eyes shut for a heartbeat, and her mouth trembled. "Kneel, infantico mine no longer, kneel for my blessing." The prince's eyes were huge when he fell to his knees. "God bless you, Ahmed, and keep you safe from all harm." Queen Isabel raised him up. "You've been a good son to me, a beloved son, and a beloved brother to my children. I and my family will never forget you. Go with my love." She turned from him without saying one more word. Mounting her horse, Queen Isabel jerked savagely on its reins. The animal half reared in protest, the queen wheeling it towards the Alhambra. Beatriz saw her slowly ride and a gust of wind gathered strength and began to whine. It seemed she heard the wings of time rush by.

Boabdil embraced his son. Ahmed gazed at the royal children one last time before, accompanied by a few companions of King Ferdinand, he rode off with his father. The king's men witnessed the Moor king re-joining his family on the bridge just outside the hamlet.

That same night, the grandees recounted their last sight of Boabdil. The Moor king stopped at the bridge and looked back at the royal banners unfurling from the highest towers of the Alhambra. The great silver cross of the crusade rose on the Torre de la Vela, the pennon of the Apostle of Saint James flapping beside it. Despite the distance, all could hear, rising to the heavens, a shout of "Santiago! Santiago!" A Christian multitude sang *Te Deum Laudamus*. Then there was a roar for King Ferdinand and Queen Isabel. Boabdil wept.

His mother looked at him in contempt and snarled at him, "You do well to weep like a woman for what you failed to defend like a man." Thus, Boabdil and his family departed for their life of exile. Never did Beatriz or the royal family see Ahmed again.

While the main war was now over, here and there many Moors still refused to admit defeat and chose to battle on. For years rebellions broke out in the mountains where the last insurgents fought to their deaths and the deaths of others. Sometimes insurgents came to the city itself.

Life at the Alhambra often caused Beatriz to forget this. Si. The Alhambra. A place of perfect beauty – and a homecoming like none other. The place where Catalina's childhood ended, swiftly, violently, like an eagle swooping down on its prey.

I3

Beatriz loosened the reins in her hand, reaching down to pat the neck of her patient horse. *Such a pretty chestnut mare. How I love to ride.* On a horse, she felt free, all the constrictions of her life falling away. Next to two horses, one white and the other black, Prince Juan waited for his sister, his hooded peregrine upon his wrist. As was often his wont when riding forth with his sisters, Juan robed himself in simple, though still costly, garb. He sought anonymity rather than proclaim to all and sundry his rank. Watching and waiting a short distance away, the prince's companions, six noble born youths, sat on their own horses.

Hunting dogs lolled and scratched, brave and silly ones darted and gambolled in game between the horses' legs, gaining curses from the young men each time they unsettled their mounts. The companions talked amongst themselves, remaining at the ready to ride at Prince Juan's spoken command.

Behind Juan there was a sudden flurry of movement, flash of sleek colour, toss of chestnut head and canter of hooves. A stable boy rushed out with yet another saddled horse. Despite its leather hood, the falcon flapped its wings in fright and screamed. The stable boy reached the prince and fell to his knees, holding out the reins as if offering a gift of gold.

Murmuring his thanks, Prince Juan took the reins from the boy before stroking and calming his bird. The prince shared a smile with Diego, the horse-master. Catalina hurried to his side, with María de Salinas a few steps behind her. "What did I tell you, good

Diego? I ask my sister to ride with me and again she brings her shadow."

Dipping her head to Juan's words, his sister beamed at him, tying the ribbon of her wide straw hat more tightly beneath her chin. "Shame, brother, you steal our mother's own nickname for our cousin!" She glanced at Beatriz. "Latina told María to come. She would have been lonely otherwise."

Glad of her hat's deep shade, Beatriz grinned at Prince Juan. At fourteen he already dwelled in another world to the one her two charges knew at seven. But then he was the queen's only son and heir to two kingdoms. Only within the inner circle of family and a trusted few did Juan show the boy he still was.

Seeing María falter and struggle for composure, Beatriz beckoned to her. She leaned from the horse and whispered close to the child's ear: "Rest easy. He is only teasing because he loves you."

María beamed and shuffled a little dance – knowing the truth of this.

The prince gave his falcon and his horse's reins to his waiting page. From one wrist to the other, slate-grey feathers ruffling in protest and flecking with shimmering rainbows, talons seeking a perch, the hooded falcon screamed its long and piercing *kek*.

Prince Juan mounted effortlessly. Mane bristling, the horse arched its neck and wheeled in a half-circle, ready at the lightest touch of a heel to burst into a gallop. The prince pulled the reins, bringing his stallion under control. Prince Juan's black hose already showed a shapely, well-muscled leg from hard hours of dedicating himself to physical activities. Despite times of ill-health, his shoulders became broader and less boy-like day-by-day.

The horse-master stood with thumbs hooked into his wide belt, chewing mint loudly, watching the prince contain his spirited beast. Diego nodded and smiled with pride. As if as an afterthought, he gave a brief bow, spitting out mint leaves to the ground as he turned to help Catalina onto her horse.

Astride and settled, she gathered the reins in her tiny hands and straightened her back. Eager for her turn, María took the reins of the spare horse from the stable boy. Beatriz suppressed a smile, noticing the stable boy still gazing at the prince with unhidden adoration.

Snorting, the horse nosed María's hip, pushing her back a step. The child looked into the mare's liquid brown eyes, as if gauging its character, giggling when it nosed and pushed her yet another step. Warm brown eyes with long, thick eyelashes wooed little María closer. She patted its nose and rubbed the side of a hand between her gentle eyes, murmuring words of pleasure.

With a friendly nicker, the horse pranced and pricked her ears. María laughed again and stroked her neck. Closing her eyes, she fanned her fingers, stroking backward and forward on the mare's neck. Her feet jigged in excitement, her hand on the mare's neck, waiting for the horse-master to finish with Catalina and come to her. Beatriz shortened her reins, bettering her hold, also impatient and eager to begin their outing.

Diego expertly re-adjusted the saddle straps for Catalina's shorter leg. Her feet, booted in soft leather, bore down in the gold, ornamented stirrups.

"You ride today Isa, my infanta. She's more demanding than your usual mount, but you're ready to meet the challenge. Now, let me see how you sit on her." Diego, one of the best horse-masters in Queen Isabel's kingdom, circled the horse, making certain Catalina held her reins not too tight or too loose. Bow-legged from a lifetime on horseback, he stepped back, his dark eyes going from horse to infanta. With a short laugh he relaxed, giving a gap-toothed smile before dipping his head to her. "Brave infanta – our noble queen will delight when I tell her what a good horsewoman she has in you. Take Isa around the yard, my infanta. See how she feels, while you let her get used to the feel of you in the saddle. Remember, don't let Isa act outside her place. You're her mistress, not the other way around."

Diego lightly smacked Isa's rump. The horse arched its neck and flicked its mane, edging forward and then a little backwards, its hoofs crunching into the stony earth. Laughing, Catalina leaned over and whispered in its ear. With a jubilant neigh and a shake of its head, the horse shifted and shuffled, cavorting almost on one spot.

The olive skin around his dark eyes crinkling, Diego laughed. As if remembering Catalina's rank, he dipped his head, but then became master again. "Stop her playing, infanta. I'll get Doña María onto her mare." Keeping an eye on Catalina, Diego stepped over to María.

Beaming, Catalina firmed her seat and pulled back tight reins. With a loud "Yah!" she dug in her heels, the horse answering the command with a sudden gallop.

Diego watched as Catalina concentrated, using all her strength to gain full control of Isa. She seemed so tiny on a horse standing at least fifteen hands. Beatriz released her breath when Isa tossed her mane, let out a joyous neigh, and settled into a steady trot, finally giving herself over to the fearless girl on her back. Diego turned, grinning up at Beatriz.

Away from their riding lessons, Catalina and María giggled at Diego's green teeth. Whatever the season, he always chewed leaves of mint growing near the stables. He told the girls it kept him in good health. But the girls never laughed about what Diego taught them. He knew the name of every horse in the stable as if it was his beloved child. No matter what its temper, any horse, in the first hour or so of meeting Diego, became gentle, wanting to eat out of his hand. Whenever he rode, it was to see a centaur come to life. Beatriz doubted there was a horse alive that could or would throw him.

Queen Isabel employed the best teachers for her five offspring. Catalina and María were only seven, yet more than a year had seen them no longer needing their horses tied to training ropes, or riding their mounts around a pole in the stable yard.

Grinning at Diego, Beatriz clicked her tongue to her mount in encouragement, her eyes still on Catalina. The girl now cantered Isa in wide rings around the yard. Catalina's smile of deep pleasure caused her cheeks to flush and her eyes to shine. Always, riding added to her natural prettiness.

Diego patted María's mare. Nickering, the horse nosed his shoulder, greeting him with affection. He laughed, giving the mare another pat. "I see you've made good friends with Bela, little doña. I thought you would. You go well with her. She ate the grass of your birthplace as a foal, and the best of your father's stallions was her sire."

"Not Hector?" María looked more closely at the animal. "Do you know her mother?"

Planting his calloused hands on his hips, Diego barked out a laugh. "What other mare would it be but the queen's favourite, gifted to her by your good father?"

María almost danced with excitement. Diego winked and smiled again at Beatriz. "Up you go." He gave María a leg up onto her mount.

Beatriz pulled down at the sides of her gown, ensuring her lower legs and ankles remained hidden, keeping her eyes on her two charges. María watched from her horse as Catalina reined in her mount, coming to a halt next to the waiting Diego. The horse-master rubbed the mare's ears while murmuring love words to her. He nodded at Catalina. Grinning again, the lines around his eyes crinkled and deepened. "As I thought, Isa's a good match for you, my infanta. You and she possess a similar spirit. She is loyal, brave and always protects those she loves."

Juan trotted his stallion over to Catalina. "Where to today, my sister?"

After a moment, Catalina smiled anew. "Our good horse-master Diego has given me a demanding horse. Brother, what if we go for a demanding ride today?"

A demanding ride? Beatriz sighed again. It promised to be another day when she would have little time for her books or study.

Away from the stables and prying eyes, Beatriz slowed her horse to an unhurried canter, trying to keep behind María, the prince's companions and well behind Juan and his sister, allowing them to be alone together. Three of Prince Juan's large hounds bounded past her.

Prince Juan half-wheeled his mount, looking across the green fields. Catalina did likewise, her ribboned sunhat slipping off her head, bouncing against her back. Juan pointed over to a low, green hill, a good ride from the earthen track they now followed. Holding her reins in one hand, Catalina stood up, balancing in her stirrups. She shielded her eyes and gave him a quick nod. The pair galloped off the road, heading across the fields to the hill, the prince's dogs barked and followed after them.

One of Prince Juan's companions swore. Another yelled, "Follow him." Horses neighed, protesting as men kicked them into a gallop. Hooves pounded the earth, stirring and flicking up dust and dirt.

Beatriz's frightened horse snorted and half reared, circling one way and then the other. By the time she had calmed it, she found herself left well in the wake of the other riders. She dug in her heels. Up ahead, a dust cloud was the only sign of her companions. *How fast they move across the fields!* Harder this time, she dug in her heels again and surged ahead with greater power. The valley dipped and a path opened up before her, long years of man and beast cutting the way clear.

A short distance away, horses and riders gathered close together. The race seemingly over, Beatriz saw why upon reaching her party. Dismounted from their horses, the prince stood protectively at the back of his sister and María. He held two snarling dogs by the leather of their jewelled collars while Catalina waited for an old woman to finish drinking from her flask. Nearby, a young woman, hair hidden under a matron's veil, her tiny frame showing the swell of pregnancy, sat on the edge of a wagon's broken wheel. Semi-shaded by the loaded cart, she wiped her wet mouth with her sleeve. Her worried eyes, large and blue, stayed on the men and their horses. Tied to the cart, a mule pulled tight its rope, backwards and forwards in a half-circle, hee-hawing at the sight of strangers.

Beatriz rode close to Catalina's mount and slipped off her horse too. Getting her land legs back and grabbing her horse's reins, she hurried over to her infanta.

"Do you need food?" Catalina asked the women.

"God bless you, child," the older woman said. "There's plenty for us to eat, just nothing left for us to quench our thirst. Our drinking jars broke when the cart fell into the ditch."

Concern fluttered over Catalina's face, darkening her eyes. Giving his dogs to his page, Juan came to her side. He tossed back his black fur cloak, freeing one shoulder. "You say your men went to the village for a new wheel?"

The young woman stared at the prince, her mouth wordlessly opening and shutting. Gazing fully at her, Beatriz realised her youth. Her skin, eyes and mouth, even the shape of the face seemed unformed and childlike. She seemed no more than a maid of thirteen, not much younger than Prince Juan himself. "My man, he –"

With the suddenness of an angry snake, one of the prince's companions jerked his head to another and hissed, "Don't they know whom they address? Why do we waste our time here?"

Fear widened the whites of the girl's eyes. Someone spat, the explosion of sound breaking into the brief silence. Diego de Deza, Juan's tutor, came to the prince's side, speaking swift, soft Latin meant only for him. Beatriz listened, disturbed. "You think this wise, Your Highness? Our blessed queen, your most prudent and noble mother, gave the Jews a chance to do right by our land. These ones have clearly chosen exile. It is not for us to meddle."

Men shifted and muttered angrily. The prince glanced over his shoulder and frowned, gesturing for them to desist. "Go, leave us." Loud grumbles swelled before another dark glance from Prince Juan caused his companions' protests to tamper off into silence. A few men shrugged and laughed. Behind Beatriz, one man murmured, "It is good he cares. A good king he'll be one day."

Two companions broke away from the group and returned to their horses. The rest soon followed. A flurry of vaulting feet, grunts and groans interwove with that of horse neighs and wickers, hooves shifting in the dry earth, as the prince's companions and his small troop of guards remounted. One of the older men gave a jerk of his head. He whistled, wheeling his horse around. His fellows trailed after, moving farther away. The clearing now filled with a smaller number, Beatriz clasped María's hand and Prince Juan again addressed the girl.

"I promise you my sister and I only want to help. You were saying?"

"My son went, my good lord. We were with others, but they feared to wait for us when the wagon broke. This path took us too close to the alcázar of the queen and none of our company could help us, for none possessed a spare wheel." Fingernails broken and dirty, the old woman twisted her gnarled, bare hands. "They wanted us to leave all our belongings and walk behind them, but this is all we have. Young lord, I am old, and my son's wife is weary and ill with child. We cannot carry much."

Catalina stepped in closer. "Tell us what my brother and I can do. Our mother teaches us the meaning of charity."

The old woman gave an almost toothless smile. "God bless her good heart, and you and your noble brother. Sweet children you both are, that I can see. A shame others do not teach their children like your lady mother."

Fidgeting, Prince Juan fingered the dagger tucked in his belt and the sun glinted off the rubies embedded in its hilt. He studied his feet before gazing again at the women. "Are you Jews?"

The girl cowered, and moaned softly. The old woman tightened her mouth. "Be calm, Raquel, and don't carry on! You're overly taxed, that's why you are having some pain. The babe's months away yet."

The woman held out her other sleeve. Sewn upon it was the badge all Jews wore.

"My poor dead husband called us God's elect." Her face

crumbled. "God's accursed more like. I give thanks that death came for him before he saw his whole life's work sold for little more than a song and his wife and son driven from their homes, with nowhere to go. It would break his heart to see his first grandchild born in the open, as is now like to happen."

The girl rested her head on the woman's shoulder.

One of the prince's companions brought his horse closer to us. "My lord prince, more Jews approach."

The woman's eyes opened wide, her face blanched grey. Juan's eyes met hers. His mouth pursed and he nodded, holding out hands palms up, as if showing them empty of weapons. Beatriz's heart missed a beat. *He came in peace? The prince came in peace? Is this what he is trying to say?*

Bewildered by his action, she felt cast adrift in dense fog. When Juan and the old woman gazed silently at one another, Beatriz felt more than simply adrift. All the tales of sailing to the end of the world became all at once true. Tottering on its edge, she couldn't see what lay beyond it, but she knew, whatever it was, something slithered and hissed, hissed of everything in this world that was evil.

Trembling, Beatriz shook herself, mentally stepping away from her dark thoughts. She returned to the bright, hot day, only to be reminded of the reason for the darkness. She gazed at the path winding and cutting its way up the hill. Some distance away two young men and a far older one strode fast towards them. The two younger men dragged behind them a frame made of tree limbs with a wheel and saddlebags roped to it.

Hand to her belly, the girl lumbered weakly to her feet. Her face lost all colour. She moaned louder this time, half bending forward. The other woman's eyes narrowed in concern. Getting her breath again, the girl straightened and rubbed the sides of her belly. "David," she called.

Beatriz stared at the girl's slender hips, remembering the queen's arguments one year ago when the king wanted to finalise Juana's marriage. "Do you want to give us cause for uncalled grief?

Husband, she is barely flowered. Speak to your mother if you need to, but I don't need a midwife to tell me we'd see our Juana dead within the year if we give her to her husband now. She's still only a child. Have you noticed her hips? Narrow like our son's."

Just like this girl in front of her, who now shielded her eyes with her right hand. Beatriz sucked in her top lip, disquieted. Her eyes searched the track. A young man hollered, trying to enunciate his words over the distance. One man waved. They quickened their stride, almost to a run. The girl stepped forward as if to go to them, but the woman grabbed her back.

"Wait! They're almost here. I beg you, Raquel, let us not have any more mishaps we can avoid by patience."

The girl bowed her head like a censured child, returning to her mother-in-law's side. Once there, she squeezed shut her eyes and groaned again. The older woman's mouth pursing into fine wrinkles, she looped her arm around the young girl's shoulders, hugging her. She looked towards their menfolk, swallowing hard.

"See, Raquel. I told you all will be well. David would never abandon us. And look! He brings back my brother and his son." She glanced at the prince, her head dipping in acknowledgement. "My lord prince, I thank and bless you for all your help. God will remember your charity. But please leave us now. Go in good conscience." A smile burst across her lined face, hinting at the once handsome woman of long ago. "My son returns, and we must be on our way."

Catalina stood, shaking dust and leaves off the bottoms of her skirts. She gazed at her brother, but he refused to meet her questing eyes. Wringing her hands, she faced the old woman. "You don't want us to find you a place to give you shelter? Your son's wife looks in sore need of it."

The girl's eyes opened, her pupils so large they made her eyes seem black. Her tears welling, she bit her lower lip.

Juan took his sister's arm. "Come away, Catalina. Their men are almost here. I promised our lady mother I would have us both home before it becomes too hot. We best go."

Confusion clouded Catalina's eyes. "My brother, the girl's in pain!"

Prince Juan looked helplessly at the woman. She smiled gently, then lowered her gaze to Catalina. "Good Doña, we cannot stay. Our broken wagon has forced us to tarry overlong. By nightfall, we must journey as far as we can while we still have our donkey –" She glanced at the beast pulling up grass near the cart. "At the border we must give him up, too, God help us..."

Another groan came from the girl. Breathing hard, her face frightened, she crumbled against the cart's frame. Beatriz saw her stare ahead, her youth leaching away to nothingness. The woman gripped the girl's shoulder and turned to Prince Juan. His eyes glimmered bright in his white face.

"My lord prince, take your sister away. We'll look after our own, but I beg you, take your men and the two little maids from here now. Our fates rest in the hand of the good God."

Only a short distance away their men strode toward them. Seeing fear stamped on their faces, Beatriz tightened her grip on María's hand and stepped over to Catalina. Sunlight turned tears on the girl's eyelashes into tiny diamonds. Taking her hand, Beatriz walked with the girls back to their horses. She gazed at the two women and then more searchingly at Juan. He marched swiftly away from his small sister, his back rod-straight and his hands at his sides in tight fists. A grey, large cloud covered the sun, dimming the colour of the day.

"I don't understand," Catalina whispered.

Beatriz licked her dry lips. "Your mother may know the reason for it."

She looked back. The woman crooned, cradling the girl's head on her lap. The girl writhed and moaned, her legs continually bending, unbending. In the dark earth, rivulets of blood gushed from underneath the girl's skirts. Utterly chilled despite the afternoon's heat, Beatriz felt touched by a finger of death. She gazed at the girl. No – death touched not her.

Beatriz met Catalina's terrified eyes. Si – childhood ends so quickly. One moment a rabbit bounces and leaps, unaware, free, heading for the safety of its hole, weaving a streak of amber life through the long, green grass. The next moment, it is only torn flesh, blood and bone. Just a memory of blithe beauty glimpsed and then, like a falling star, gone forever. Beatriz took the child's arm and quickened her pace to their horses. Nothing remained of the day's joy.

14

The beginning of health is to know the disease
~ Castilian proverb

Riding with María behind Catalina, Beatriz pondered about Prince Juan's behaviour. Meeting those poor Jews had left him unnaturally silent and brooding. The change altered him so much from his usual companionable self. Juan rode slouched in the saddle, as if a great weight burdened his spirit. Catalina questioned him, trying to untangle her knot of bewilderment. Over and over she asked her brother for answers until he swung around, blue eyes blazing, and snapped, "This is none of your concern." Savagely, he dug his heels hard into his horse, making it protest and half-rear before it bounded away, leaving those behind in the wake of its dust. Soon, only two of his companions remained with them, the rest galloping after their prince. In silence, they herded Beatriz and her two small charges back the way they came such a short time ago.

At the entrance of the alcázar, Beatriz saw Juana and her sister María. Juana, white-faced and eyes glittering, stalked up and down the hallway. Their dueña stood some distance away, as if she sought to stay away from the infanta. The infanta María watched on, her face tense and unhappy.

Seeing them enter the alcázar, Juana rushed over. "Why did you not tell me you were going riding with Juan?"

Catalina blinked. "You didn't tell me when you went with him yesterday."

Juana grabbed her sister's arm, shaking Catalina so hard her wide sun hat, with its loosened ribbons, fell to the ground. Her fine dark hair loosening from its net, Juana wiped tears from her eyes. "And I would have gone today too, if you sent me word. What right have you to ride alone with him? He is closer to me than you."

Their eyes locked. Whatever Catalina saw there made her lower her head. She attempted to free herself from her sister's hold. "Stop it, you're hurting me."

Flinging Catalina away, Juana burst into passionate tears and ran in the direction of her bedchamber.

Taking the hand of one charge, Beatriz hurried over to the other. Catalina rubbed her arm and wiped her eyes. Beatriz wound her arm around her in sympathy. Nearby, the infanta María fanned out her fingers on either side of her wide girdle, staring after Juana. She stepped towards them, picking up Catalina's hat. Frowning, she handed the hat back to her sister, her long fingers fluttering up and down Catalina's arm, as if not daring to touch. Hooding her eyes, she heaved a long, sad sigh.

"Mi chiquitina..." She sighed again, and eyed her sister. "Juana sometimes thinks Juan belongs only to her and that he should never give any mind to his other sisters; especially on a day when our father lashes her with his tongue. She does not mean it, my sister. She strikes out only because she is hurting." María touched Catalina's wet cheek. "Do you want me to tell Mother?"

Catalina lifted and dropped her shoulders. "I don't know..."

María shuffled her slippered feet and frowned. Disquiet darkened her eyes. "When Father shouts at her like today, calling our sister unworthy of both him and our royal lady mother, Juana turns into another person. Sister, it might be best to tell her when you next ride with Juan. While Juana loves him dearly, as we all do, she fears making him angry too. Thus, she accepts it when Juan tells her she's not included." María frowned and bit her bottom lip. "I will go to her now. I'll get her to apologise to you."

Juan rarely asked his sister María to accompany him on his daily ride. Less pretty than her sisters, and often taken for granted by many – sometimes even by her own mother – María shone with an inner sweetness and truly deserved her nickname of Joy. Bestowed with common sense, content with her lot in life, her calmness offered others a green oasis of peace in the midst of a family made up of emotive and complicated individuals.

Catalina stood on tiptoes, kissing her sister's cheek. "Thank you. I'll remember. Is Mother busy?"

Starting down the corridor, the infanta chuckled over her shoulder. "Mother is always busy, but she sees us even so."

Catalina chewed her thumb, watching María stride away. "Is this a good time, do you think?"

Beatriz pushed back strands of hair from her forehead. "I cannot say. No time is ever a good time when you are a queen –"

Catalina took her hand. "But Mother will speak to me."

Beatriz nodded, taking Catalina and María's hands. They slipped through the stone arch into the Court of the Lions, edging close to the narrow path of water dividing the court. Twelve stone lions supported alabaster basins, into which crystal jets of water poured and sparkled.

East, west, south and north, triangles of well-tended flowerbeds marked the corners of the courtyard. Fronds from various climbing plants festooned their own nimble design. Slender columns of the purest white marble supported archways of open filigree. Delicate fretwork covered the walls.

Wherever Beatriz looked, light dappled and water sparkled in a constant exchange between one and the other, the exquisite art of nature adding to the fine art as man had ever wrought. The Alhambra, Heaven reflected on Earth. Surely little in their mortal world compared with the beauty found here?

Beatriz's pace slowed, drawn again by the seductive beauty of this place. Catalina grabbed her, heading into the Hall of the Two Sisters, going straight to its secret staircase taking them to the queen's chamber in the highest tower.

Out of breath by the time she entered, Beatriz covered her surprise at finding Prince Juan also there. He sat at his mother's feet, in front of her high-backed chair, arms around one bent leg, leaning his chin upon his well-formed knee. Seeing Catalina, he blanched, straightened his shoulders, looking up at the queen. "Mother, I tried to tell her it was none of her concern. Still, my sister must know everything. Isn't that right, mi chiquitina?"

Stepping out of the grey shadows in a window embrasure, Princess Isabel padded over to the rear of her mother's chair, garbed in one of the black habitos she wore, day after day. The coarse fabric left behind patches of red, irritated skin. Hollows pushed deep into her cheeks and dark rings circled her huge eyes. Some days, especially when she fasted overlong, her grief ate away at her – soul and flesh. Those days the princess seemed a beautiful rose placed in a dark place, wilting for lack of sun and water. Then they needed to beware her thorns.

Mouth hard, nose pinched, Isabel glared at Beatriz. "Go. My sister must speak to the queen. Alone."

Beatriz faltered. She felt struck. Once she had thought of Isabel as a friend.

Starting to leave, Beatriz saw the queen shake her head at her, gesturing to her to halt, her grim eyes on her youngest daughter. "Latina will stay, Isabel," the queen said. "She can take Catalina back to her chamber once I finish speaking with her."

Looking at her youngest daughter, the queen's face wore almost the same expression as when she had scolded Gonzalo, one of her most powerful grandees. "Stop squandering all the honour you earned through your victories by misgoverning," she had told him. The queen's words reduced him to abjection and fervent apology.

As if fighting against a sea rip, Queen Isabel's confessor, Hernando de Talavera, trudged his way through the deep gloom of the recesses bordering the queen's chamber. His head popped out from the cowl of his dark monk's mantle. Beatriz took hold of María and led her back a few steps. The grim atmosphere in the room entangled her tighter in its net. She sought refuge in humour, remembering the turtles Prince Juan had received from his father on his last birthday. Re-emerging to the world after being frightened, their heads popped out of their shells in almost the same manner as the queen's confessor. But her refuge crumbled when she noticed the red eyes of the cardinal. Mouth trembling, tears still dripped down his winkled, hollowed cheeks. Bowing very low, the priest fell to his knees, clutching to his breast his heavy, gold crucifix, a recent gift from Queen Isabel. "My noble queen, pray, I beg you. This a great sin and an act of infamy. I agree with

Abravanel, your grace, what you and the lord king now do risks divine punishment. Your Majesty, 'tis not too late, I beg you, withdraw the order."

The queen rounded on her priest. Beatriz shivered at seeing her white, stark face.

"Dare you question us, my lord cardinal?" She spoke a voice Beatriz rarely heard from her – soft but threatening, underlined with steel. "Did you not once advise me to be a model to my subjects in the service of God? I remember your words, even if you do not. I need your prayers and support, confessor, not your ill-considered doubts. God gave me this crown, and I mean to do what I believe is right."

Queen Isabel swung a scorching glance at Beatriz. "Bad enough that Latina argues with me too."

Beatriz looked down at the floor, feeling like a roped felon. She gazed over her shoulder at the arches opening to views of the palace grounds. Up high, engraved in the delicate stone-work, were the words: *I am in this garden, an eye filled with joy.* In this sunlit room, there was nothing of joy.

"My queen," pleaded the cardinal, "I once also told you that you were an eagle, placed on the peak of honours and sublime dignities." The priest choked and wiped his hand across his mouth. "Never would I believe the eagle capable of ripping and tearing her kingdom to shreds."

The queen lifted her chin. "I vowed to my first confessor, Torquemada, to devote myself to the extirpation of heresy. I must do what I must. Enough, I say. I have heard enough." Furious, her eyes glittering like aquamarine stones, Queen Isabel rounded on Beatriz. "I've changed my mind. Go with María and I will send my daughter back to you once I speak to her. Leave us."

Relieved at the queen's dismissal, Beatriz re-clasped María's hand and curtseyed as she backed to the door. Before she closed it behind her, she made another curtsey, a curtsey that almost buckled when she saw Catalina's wide, scared eyes. She couldn't smile at her, couldn't offer her any comfort. She could do nothing but leave her all alone to face whatever this was, what the priest called an act of infamy.

Trembling outside the chamber door, Beatriz found herself weeping with María. Drying her own tears, she took the child in her arms, giving her the comfort that she couldn't give to her other charge. Sweating now in the mounting heat, she led María to the infanta's bedchamber, and they waited for her. María too upset for lessons, Beatriz took up a book to read while the child took up her sewing.

For once even Aristotle could not hold Beatriz's interest, and her threads of thought unravelled. So much stayed knotted and tangled like the uneven stitches María now needed to unpick and redo. The hours passed, the bright afternoon light growing dim and grey, as day approached night.

Drawing the curtains on the remains of the day, Beatriz lit the candles in the room. She sat on the red velvet-covered stool closest to the unused fireplace, near María. From the open wicker basket at her feet, the child picked up a small canvas frame. She rummaged in her basket, and then settled back on the stool and sewed, more clumsily than ever. She dropped the frame to the floor and took out from the basket a small square of saffron silk. Traced on the silk there was a small, wine-red butterfly, with half of one wing still unstitched. María started sewing again and gave a cry of dismay when she stabbed her finger, soiling the embroidery with blood. The wide, terrified eyes of the girl they met today flashed in Beatriz's mind, a terrified child-woman feeling birth pangs upon her. She remembered the prince almost breaking down before them. How the old woman had looked at him – full of... knowing... forgiveness... compassion... pity.

María sewed a loop and pulled too hard, puckering up the scrap of saffron silk. The butterfly wing close to ruin, the child looked about to burst into tears. She tossed the silk onto the already abandoned canvas. The silver needle spun in the air, a filament of candlelight caught it and glittered it with light.

The child picked up the precious piece of silk again and

smoothed it out on her lap. *Such awkward stitching for a girl with a mother and grandmother who sewed with such great skill.* Beatriz almost smiled at the girl's look of tragic despair. María was yet to learn that to capture beauty was the work of a lifetime. She too yearned to hold beauty in her hands, make it stay for more than just a heartbeat, a breath of time.

The eyes of the old woman flashed in Beatriz's mind. They merged with Catalina's, the gaze turned towards her when she closed the door of her mother's chamber. She trembled, chilled, the afternoon's heat all gone. She knelt on the floor and threw kindling into the fire's hearth and started to ready it for lighting. She heard the door open and close. Catalina leaned against the door, her eyes and hair lit by the light of candles.

The child released a moan, odd and ragged as if contained over-long, and ran over to Beatriz and into her waiting arms. María came to join them. "You've been so long!" she said. Beatriz shook her head at her, hoping she would not ask any questions. The distress on Catalina's face slammed the door upon that.

Catalina reached out and clasped María's hand. Beatriz studied their interlaced fingers – chubby and thin, one hand with broken fingernails, showing evidence of morning gardening, the other the well-kept hand of royalty, both hands still those of children. She sighed.

"I've been praying with my mother. We all were." Catalina swallowed, chewing at her bottom lip.

María stared, her eyes wide in her pale face. Time for prayer came for the girls from morning to night, but they had never prayed away a whole afternoon. Lowering her eyes, Catalina pulled at her riding gown, straightening its folds.

"I am not allowed to ride with Juan until Mother tells me." She shook her head a little as if to clear it. "I am not allowed to go riding. I mean, we're not. We're to stay inside, unless told otherwise."

María blinked. "But why? Did we do something wrong?"

"Not us. We've done no wrong..."

"Then why can we not ride?"

"We're in danger from the Jews..."

The two girls looked up at Beatriz. They looked more lost than ever. Beatriz rubbed the side of her face, uncertain of what to say. "Did the queen tell you this" she asked Catalina.

"Si." Her grip tightened on Beatriz's hand, and her eyes fell. "They are bad people. They have done bad things, evil things..."

Beatriz shivered, and the words of a poem beat like a heartbeat in her mind. A poem written by a Jew:

> Hand of its clouds, winter wrote a letter
> Upon the garden, in purple and blue.

Upon the garden, in purple and blue.... Now she feared what happened this day would shadow winter's clouds upon these two young lives. For ever.

Yet again haunted by the girl and her mother-in-law, Beatriz remembered the old woman's compassion, her tender care for the child-woman. She remembered the girl's terror.

"Those people we saw today? Truly them?" María asked.

Catalina's mouth trembled. "Perchance, not them, but their people bear the guilt of wrong doing..."

María blinked and shook her hand. "What have they done?"

Catalina swallowed again, her eyes travelling around the room before returning to stare down at the hand clasped by her friend. Once again, her hand tightened on Beatriz's.

"I don't want to speak of it."

"But," María injected, "we vowed to tell each other everything! Everything!"

Beatriz felt it was time to interrupt. "Did the queen tell you not to speak? If she did, you must do what she says."

Catalina rubbed at her eyes. "No, Mother said nothing about that."

"Then please tell us," María said.

Beatriz shivered at what she saw in Catalina's frightened eyes.

"Why do you always want to know?" the child said.

María wound her arms around her and hugged her tight. "Because I love you."

Catalina let go of their hands and stepped away from them. When she faced them again, tears ran down her face. "The Jews crucified a baby! An innocent boy! Cut out his heart and asked the Devil to kill us all. The Jews desire our deaths – the death of Christians."

Beatriz felt sick. Putting her arm around the horrified María, she whispered, "By all... who said this?"

"Mother." Her eyes challenged Beatriz. "Do you doubt her word?"

Hand of its clouds, winter wrote a letter
Upon the garden, in purple and blue.

The garden, their childhood. The two girls looked dazed, as if their whole world had darkened, and been ripped apart.

Beatriz remembered her grandfather, son of a converto descended from the great Samuel ibn Nagrella himself. Her mother's great-grandfather stayed a Jew to the day he died, as did so many of his kin. Her kin. Jews. And not too many generations away Catalina's own father and mother lay claim to sharing the blood of a converto. Learning lessons of history in their school-room, they often delighted to own these men as kin. Sometimes, even the queen spoke of them to her daughters, telling stories that fuelled their pride.

Rubbing the tears from her face, María spoke. "If the queen told you this, then it must be true. But all the Jews? How can it be all the Jews, Catalina?"

Returning to the stool, Catalina sniffed. "Mother said she gave the Jews three months to become convertos. That time has ended, and now all the Jews not Christian must go.

"That old woman and her family were leaving Castilla, as my mother commanded. Surely if they were truly good people, they would convert and stay. Mother says those people we saw today not only have the blood of Jesús on their hands, but that of the child's. She thinks only of her kingdom's safety. That boy was her subject, and Jews murdered him."

"My mother says there are bad people everywhere, calling themselves Jews, Moors or Christian. Just because a few are bad doesn't mean all are," María pleaded.

Catalina appeared deaf to her friend. "The Jews refuse to turn from their evil life. They refuse to see Jesús Christ as their Messiah. Mother says as long as she allows Jews to stay, she's endangering the unity of her kingdom, failing her duty to her subjects and service to God. God made her queen, and her conscience tells her she must clean Castilla of... this contamination. Father thinks likewise. God stirs them to do what is right for all."

She spoke a lesson learnt by rote. For the third time today, Beatriz saw in her mind the virgin-faced girl, labouring far too early with her child. Kept silent because of her loyalty to the queen, she wanted to weep. She felt the prescience of death, casting its shroud upon her, the girls, the winter clouds that shadowed them all and made their world black.

"Contamination... What do you mean?" María asked

Catalina sniffed again, gnawing at her mouth. Another milk tooth came loose. Catalina's eyes continued their restless search around the room. It seemed peace eluded her. Beatriz felt sickened. Surely a child of seven should not be burdened with such things? "The Jews are a stain on Castilla and my father's kingdom. God wants us to rid ourselves of them – my mother told me so. Please, let's not talk of this any more."

She fell on her knees, pulling María down alongside her. "Pray. Pray with me. For our sins."

Beatriz could not look away from the child's tear-streaked face as Catalina said one of her mother's most loved prayers. "I praise the Virgin Mother and her son Jesús. Vehemently I mourn my sins, constantly hoping in Jesús."

15

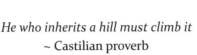

He who inherits a hill must climb it
~ Castilian proverb

The days following, Beatriz found Catalina glum and silent, not even responding when it came to her studies. For hours the child prayed in her mother's private chapel, leaving Beatriz with María as her sole scholar. Miserable too, María longed to go home to her own mother. With darkness surrounding them – a shroud of miasma hiding some nameless horror – suffocating and ill, Beatriz decided to grab their sunhats and take María out into the garden and wait for Catalina there.

Encouraging María to do the same, Beatriz fell to her knees and started clearing the weeds from the herb garden. An hour sped by before a shadow fell over them. Beatriz straightened, rested her dirty hands on her lap and peered up at Catalina. Beside her María gave a yelp of joy, going to embrace her friend.

"What happened to today's lesson?" Catalina asked, narrowing her eyes against the morning's glaring light. Not waiting for an answer, she sank down to her knees and picked up a spare hand fork. "Let me help you."

Catalina cocked her head, and pointed to a small shrub. "What's that?"

Beatriz dug into the earth. "Sage. It's used in salads and sauces. And to protect us from restless spirits, and even for wisdom."

Catalina inhaled a deep breath and sighed. "I pray to be wise."

Beatriz jabbed deeper around the rosemary bunch, careful to avoid its spiky branches, tidying the patch of earth in front of her. "Time will give you that wish," she said.

"Mother is so unhappy."

Beatriz gave a vicious tug to a healthy dandelion growing overtop a wilting feverfew, and tossed it to the pile mounting at her side. "I must speak to the queen about the good sisters here. By all the good saints, either they possess a great need for diuretics or they neglect this garden. The dandelions win the victory here." With a sigh, she sat back on her haunches, contemplating Catalina. "You know your mother's position is not one to encourage happiness?"

Beatriz carefully eased up a small seedling of angelica too near to the comfrey and replanted it farther away so it would not fight for ground as it matured and grew its tall stalk. She perused the garden, naming the herbs. Yarrow, the awful tasting horehound – what she used to becalm Juan's coughs – rue, rosemary, balm – to attract the bees – and the low, grey-green leaf of creeping thyme. "Si, a ruler's life is not an easy one," Catalina murmured.

"You don't know the half of it, child. Times like these dagger the queen's good heart." Beatriz pulled out another dandelion. "Child, I do not mind dandelions. As I have told you, boiled in water and left aside to sit for a time, they make a useful drink that helps us void our bladders." She grinned at both Catalina and María. "The French call dandelion not only Lion's teeth but also Piss in Bed – a good name too. They do their job that well. But this plant needs controlling otherwise they'll take over an entire garden. If I left this any longer, I fear all the precious herbs used for doctoring would be in a bad state. Already, dandelions draw to themselves all the moisture in the earth."

Catalina planted her hands on the warm, rich earth. "You talk of other than simply dandelions, Latina..."

Beatriz grinned at her bright student, yanking another weed out from the earth to add to her pile. "More things grow in the garden than the gardener sows or desires. Child, a good ruler is a little like being a good gardener. Gardeners are often called on for decisions that bring them pain. Not long ago at my home at Salamanca, I gave permission to cut down a dozen good trees in my orange grove to give the remainder a better chance for a longer and more productive life."

Catalina absorbed her words while the eyes of the old mother flashed into Beatriz's mind. What real harm did she hold for them?

The words she spoke to Catalina seemed so hollow – so wrong.

Beatriz rubbed her face. *Do not cry, do not cry.* How many times she had spoken to the queen in recent times? Reminding her of the golden age, when Christian, Moor and Jew all worked together for the advancement of all. It was not perfect, nothing ever is, but it showed what could be done. "God Himself tells us a kingdom divided against itself cannot stand," she said, trying to remind herself, as well as offer some comfort to Catalina. "Your mother has tried hard to solve her kingdom's troubles ever since she first came to the throne. Now she is ill and worn out. She fears for your brother, Prince Juan. She wants him to inherit a strong and unified kingdom."

"So she commands the Jews to become Christian or else leave Castilla."

"Believe me, 'twas not an easy thing for her to do. The queen realises she is indebted to many Jews. From the first days of her rule, powerful Jews formed an important part of her government. She knows the debt she and Castilla owes to them, especially men like her finance ministers, Abraham Seneor and Isaac Abrabanel. She begged them – so many times – to convert. Some Jews have – the loyal Andrés Cabrera for one. It is my thought that being the governor-general of Segovia and married to Doña Beatriz de Bobadilla helped here. The queen rewarded him richly. She would have done the same for the other Jews, if only they converted."

Catalina bit her lower lip. Beatriz lifted her eyebrows and heaved a sigh. "Your question, child?"

The girl looked all around, as if making certain there were no others in the garden. "Do you think she's right to do this?"

Beatriz attended to the herbs for a moment, hoping to hide her sudden tears. "Your mother believes herself right, that God Himself means for her to do this. You know God's will is the stone on which her whole life is built." Beatriz pulled out another weed, another, and another. "For your mother, and for so many others, the divine right of monarchy is as real as this garden we see here. To doubt it places doubt upon her entire rule. But I see the woman behind the queen and know, even if she refuses to own to it, how this daggers her brave heart."

Straightening up again, Beatriz heaved another sigh and rubbed her hands from the top of her thighs to her knees. "My whole life revolves around questions." She reached for Catalina's hand. "I trust you with the truth. I want to speak to you as I would to one full-grown. Infanta, my heart tells me that only time and God will tell us whether our queen judged right for her kingdom.

"But I give thanks to our Almighty God. I'll never be forced into a position like my queen. In my life I can expect to cast out just weeds and other unwanted plants from a garden such as this. I can sleep at night and, if not, a hot elixir of Valerian will soon put me to right. Not so with your mother. She sleeps hardly at all."

Weeks plodded by, and the royal family remained at the Alhambra for the hottest weeks of summer. Despite the sunlit season, recent events still darkened the infanta's spirits. Catalina's capacity for joy was such that she usually surmounted her sadness during the day, but her nightmares increased at night. Beatriz tried to keep her occupied with new books, but it seemed her nightmares began to keep her company during the day too. Even her companion María could not console her. Depressed, Beatriz felt as changed as both girls.

One day, Beatriz brought Catalina and María to one of their favourite places, the seats set near the fountains in the Hall of the Lions. For a time, Catalina just sat, saying nothing and staring out ahead. Sighing, Beatriz read again the lines engraved around the fountain. Hoping to raise a smile from Catalina, she read the poem aloud. Like the water pouring down in the huge marble bowl, her words flowed in musical rhythm:

*In appearance water and marble seem to confuse
themselves, not knowing which of each is flowing.*

Do you not see that the water spills into the basin

But its drains hide it immediately?

*It is a lover whose eyelids brim with tears,
tears which hide in fear of a betrayer.*

Catalina groaned, as if the poem tore down her fragile defences. Beatriz turned. She clasped Catalina's hand when she saw her sorrowful face. "Speak child. Tell me what disturbs you," she said.

Catalina lifted her chin, sucking in her top lip. She shook her head as if in sudden anger. "I cannot tell you..."

Beatriz gazed all around – only wide-eyed, listening María and the growing shadows kept them company. Beatriz squeezed Catalina's hand. "You can." She called María to her side. "Child, go to my chamber and get the book on my table. We might as well do our lesson here."

María gone, Beatriz turned back to the infanta. "Tell me what troubles you."

The blue shadows under her eyes speaking of her broken nights, Catalina took a long breath through her nose, and lowered her gaze. "My father is a liar," she muttered, before clamping her mouth shut, screwing up her face, as if she tasted something vile.

Beatriz rubbed the side of her head. *So she knows. But what lie does she speak of?* She wondered if this intelligent child finally acknowledged her father's mistresses. How could she not? At court, his bastards outnumbered those of his children born in wedlock. Beatriz shivered. She would rather not think about the king, ever. But she caught Catalina's restless, unhappy gaze, and took a deep breath before posing her next question. "Are you talking about your father's women?"

Catalina winced. "No. 'Tis more than that, Teacher," she whispered. Bowing her head, she gnawed back and forth at her thumb knuckle.

"More? What more, child?"

Shielding her face with a hand, Catalina shook her head, making a tortured sound. "My father is a liar." She gazed up with desperation, her eyes begging Beatriz to say otherwise. Beatriz looked away, fighting a temptation to lie herself, but unable to. "Why do you say this, mi chiquitina?

Without meaning to, Beatriz called the girl the name used by the royal family. As the child's tutor, she avoided using it. Catalina didn't notice Beatriz's slip of the tongue. Perchance it no longer mattered, and she didn't care.

"It is not because of God he wants the Jews gone. My father wants the Jews' gold."

This did not surprise Beatriz. "That could not be your mother's reason," she said quietly.

Catalina shook her head. "My mother does this because she believes it's God's will, but not my father." Catalina snatched Beatriz's hand. "He must have good reason. Perchance he believes he does do it for God too, if pushing the Jews out makes his kingdom richer and stronger. 'Tis right that they do this for my brother – one kingdom is hard enough to rule, let alone two."

"It could be that..." Beatriz chewed over what she knew of the king. Si, he hated the Jews. Si, wealth was important to him. He loved the power it gave to him. Whilst the queen built her whole life on serving God, the king built his on gold. No, she didn't think King Ferdinand used religion for any other reason than as an excuse to achieve his own ends. But looking at Catalina, seeing how the child trembled, Beatriz stayed silent.

Not many days after this, an awful event caused Catalina to lock away her doubts about her father.

"Catalina!" With only one attendant behind her, Princess Isabel burst into the school-room. "Catalina!" Princess Isabel rarely raised her voice, but now she almost screamed. The princess looked white, her huge eyes wide with fear.

Catalina bounded up, her haste toppling over her stool. Wood resounded against the floor, the sound punctuating a moment of silence.

"Come." Princess Isabel struggled to catch her breath. "'Tis Father... they have bought him to his chamber..." Isabel closed her eyes, her mouth moving as if in silent prayer, before looking again at her youngest sister. "An assassin tried to kill him. He is alive..." Princess Isabel raised her hand to rub at wet eyes. "Sister, our father is gravely wounded. Mother wants us with her. We must go."

Deciding her place was with Catalina, Beatriz told María to stay in the library and practice her writing, Beatriz followed after Catalina and Isabel. The closer they came to the royal apartments, the closer to turmoil. Men scurried about and ran down the long corridor. Passing one of the royal physicians, Beatriz glanced into the silver bowl he carried. A blood soaked white doublet lay within it.

Outside the door of the king's bedchamber, a crowd of courtiers stood close together. Seeing the daughters of the queen, they bowed and cleared a pathway to the closed doorway of the king's most private room.

Beatriz gazed over her shoulder. *Should I go back?* She wished she could but, despite her hatred for the king, she couldn't forsake Catalina. Following them, she closed the door after the princesses and froze. Beside the unconscious king the queen knelt holding his hand while her children huddled in a frightened knot behind her.

Arms up to his elbows covered in blood, Guadalupe, the king's favourite and most trusted physician, bent over the bed, tying the bandage firmly across the padding on the king's right shoulder and chest. A smaller, similar padding covered his neck. Blood seeped through the cloths. Guadalupe stood to his full height, rubbing his face with blood-spattered hands. "The wound's serious, my queen. Four inches long and almost as deep. But I don't believe it has touched the nerve and spine."

The queen, keeping her eyes on the king's face, whispered, "I must pray." She clasped her hands. "Dear God, it is true kings die by accident like others. We believe we are ready to face death, but trials like this teach otherwise. God, in your mercy, do not let it be time for your servant, my husband, to be taken from us. God, do not take him from me..."

In the following days the queen and her children stayed by the king. His fever worsened until the day it gripped him utterly. Beatriz remained in the school-room. Never had she felt so conflicted. She did not care if she left the king's physicians without the benefit of her expertise and advice. When she tried to pray with the court, knowing the crisis had come at last, the words were ash and meaningless in her mouth. She wanted to curl up on her bed and hide from the world.

Like most mornings the dawn song of birds woke Beatriz to a new day. For a time she lay in bed, fearing what this day would bring. Dressing, Beatriz stepped lightly to Catalina's chamber. Disturbed at seeing only María sleeping in the bed with Catalina's side untouched, she made her way back to the king's apartments.

A courtier outside the king's chambers told her the news. Hours before, King Ferdinand's fever had finally broken and he had asked for food. All the royal family remained with him.

She entered the large, inner chamber next to the king's bedchamber. Before she reached the door of the king's most private room, she paused, hearing the pure voice of Prince Juan close by, singing like an angel:

> Glorious king, true light and clarity,
> Almighty God, Lord, if it please You,
> Be a faithful aid to my companion,
> Because I have not seen him since the night came,
> And soon it will be dawn.

Beatriz looked towards the room's embrasure. A haze of golden light enveloping both their forms, the prince sat with his sister Isabel across the other side of the room in the deep window seat. Isabel gazed out the window, her long, golden hair uncovered, knees drawn up, as her brother, his head lowered, played his vihuela and sang. They were so engrossed in their own private worlds they didn't notice Beatriz across the room. Like a bee to pollen the prince's beautiful voice drew her in. She leaned against the wall, letting the dark shadows cloak her, listening to the prince:

Fair companion, are you sleeping or awake?
Don't sleep any longer, but softly rouse yourself,
For in the east I see the star arisen
Which brings on the day, I know it well,
And soon it will be dawn.

Fair companion, I call you with singing:
Don't sleep any longer, because I hear the bird sing
Which goes to seek the day through the woods,
And I fear that the jealous one may attack you,
And soon it will be dawn.

Prince Juan looked out at the breaking day with his sister. "I wish my songs were as good. To write one song to last down the years, as this song has, is to have immortality."

"Father will be soon well enough for you to sing to him." Isabel spoke automatically, as if not really attending to his words.

Juan lowered his head and let out an odd sound. He put the vihuela down beside him, his hands gripping his upper legs. "Well or unwell, Father has never liked me singing to him."

Isabel swung around. "Is that important when we praise God for giving back our father? What is a song, brother, long lasting or otherwise, compared to Father's life? At least this hasn't proven to be a death-watch like when I lost Alfonso."

Juan reached and clasped her hand. "Isabel, you mistake my meaning. It goes without saying, I thank God for our father's life. Perchance I have true and better reason to thank Him. For days I have feared I might be called to take Father's throne."

Isabel turned back to the window. "And if you were so called? Fear or not, 'tis your place to take up our Father's crown. 'Tis your duty. Just thank God that you've more time to ready yourself for it."

Juan picked up his vihuela and stared at it. "What if I am never ready for it?"

The prince looked drawn, pale, fearful. Beatriz began to steal away, going closer to the bedchamber of the king. All the time Beatriz kept her eyes on the prince, hoping his sister would offer a word of comfort and chase his sadness away. Isabel did not move, but kept looking out the window.

My love,

Pray, forgive my evil writing – my hand cramps from an afternoon spent translating a book I discovered in the library. A very difficult task it proved, too. The book is old and written in poor ink – some of the pages are almost impossible to read. But it is a valuable book, all about disorders of the blood. It is far too important not to try to save.

We have moved to another alcázar *– one better suited for King Ferdinand's convalescence. He recovers slowly. Queen Isabel told me she feels like she has been to Hell and back. She prays daily for her family to be spared more grief. She does not think she could withstand any harder trials.*

Like many men forced to remain inactive, the king is often short-tempered with his family. The other day he muttered angrily, "Isabel. I am not Lazarus. Do not treat me as if I have been raised from the dead!" He was angrier still when she replied, "To see you suffering, my husband, was more than I could bear. I deserved to suffer in your place... I would have, if God had allowed." Forgive me, love. I know you respect the king, but I wish he could look beyond himself and see how ill his wife is – and the great distress and fear of his children...

Beatriz lifted her head. On her table, the candle flame flickered and danced in a draught, and wax dripped down the length of the thick candle. She sighed. Catalina was an utterly altered child since the threat of death touched her father. Normally a child who claimed happiness in the school-room, now she just came and attended silently to her books. She never brought up again that her father was a liar.

16

How beauteous is this garden where the flowers of the earth vie with the stars of heaven! What can compare with the vase of yon alabaster fountain, filled with crystal water? Nothing but the moon in her fullness, shining in the midst of an unclouded sky!

~ Arabic inscription on the walls of the Alhambra

Beatriz drooped and panted for breath, the heat of the day stifling her in the school-room. Seeing the pale faces of Catalina and María, she decided to end their Latin lesson, packing up their books, quills and writing equipment.

"Pray, could you not tell us a story?" entreated Catalina. Locking up her moveable desk, Beatriz thought longingly of an afternoon siesta. All she wanted was something to eat, and then to fall into bed, whiling away at least one hour of summer heat in slumber. But still she laughed. "Do I need to ask which one?"

Catalina's eyes lit up, her tiny feet jigging on the tiles before doing a dancer's turn, with one arm flung up, the other across her waist. Beatriz gave a sleepy laugh followed by a longer yawn, envying again the children's boundless energy after hours of study, and pleased to see Catalina's zest for learning making her happy and zestful in other ways.

María interjected. "Please, my princess, could it be my favourite story this time? The one about the three princesses locked in the tower?" Since listening to stories meant keeping their hands busy in other ways, María skipped to collect their embroidery frames from their exile at the side of the closed door.

Catalina tapped her mouth with a bent index finger. "All right, my choice of story for another time. But remember, my turn next. Shall we take our embroidery to the Hall of the Two Sisters?"

Beatriz forced herself to stop yawning. "A most fitting place for storytelling." She gathered up the books about Alexander the Great and Charlemagne from the table. Tossing back her head, she laughed. "So we go from the tale of the king gifting his beloved wife a field of almond snow to that of a faithful daughter. Perchance my next lesson should not be history but give thought to the use of metaphors in fable." She took care to place the books in their rightful places on the library shelves. When she faced the girls again, she smiled at them teasingly. "Did I say I agreed to this?"

Catalina and María laughed, and Catalina grinned. "Good teacher, have you ever refused us a story?"

Beatriz planted her long-fingered hands on her narrow hips and pretended to think. "Now, give me a moment to cast my mind back." Catalina and María exchanged looks, grinning at one another. Drumming ink-stained fingers on the soft folds of the black velvet habito, she pursed her lips, as if preparing to whistle. "I have been your teacher for three years. Surely there has been one time when I told you girls no?"

Chuckling with mirth, Catalina shook her head. "Never! And for that, Latina, we're both grateful. No other compares with you as a storyteller. We never get enough of your stories. They're a perfect reward after a hard morning's lesson, si, María?"

María nodded vigorously, turning begging eyes upon Beatriz.

Beatriz tilted her head to one side, fighting laughter. "You never get enough? I would have never guessed! But with praise like that from you, my infanta, Doña Catalina, one day Queen of England, how can I refuse?"

From the library, Beatriz walked with the girls to the Hall of the Two Sisters. Soon, the murmur of water fountains melded with the soft pad of slippered feet upon the tiles of paved coloured marble. The cheerful chime of running water returned Beatriz's thoughts to the Moors, awed anew by the creation wrought by their skills and labours. Here, as in so many of their alcázars, they created a paradise on Earth, rendering beauty from word to reality.

Water came down from the surrounding high mountains to the

River Xenil. Building the Alhambra, the Moors had drawn from myriad tiny streams to make a system of aqueducts throughout Granada. Another alcázar of gardens and fountains and the most glorious alcázar in all Castilla, high-ceiling chambers, honey-combed walls and archways melded together water, light and shadow, rendering the Alhambra a place of wonder, a place to nurture their very souls.

Beatriz eyed the inscriptions on the nearest wall: "There is no conqueror but God" and "Your God is one God". Similar sentiments echoed upon the other walls too. Everywhere she looked the walls of the Alhambra gave voice to man's reaching out to God, man's love of God. The words built a bridge of man's faith to a God of love and seemed as real and solid as the tangible stones that built the Alhambra. Years of long study had brought her to the belief the Moors worshipped the same God as Christians. Heavy of heart, she sighed. What right did they have to believe the Moors wrong? Did God really belong only to those who called themselves Catholic? A cold finger smote her. If she ever spoke her thoughts she knew what people would call her: Wicked! Evil! Sinner! Blasphemer! Repent, or you'll end in Hell.

The light showered upon her and she felt disembodied, as if her spirit broke free from her body and she became one with the haze of light, seemingly veiling the air itself. She shook her head and returned to her body, back into the moment. She had no sense of evil here, rather the Alhambra deepened her awareness of God. Slow, reflective weeks at this citadel of the Moors made her feel whole.

She remembered her father telling her of his grandfather, a son of a learned rabbi, himself a descendant of the great Samuel ibn Nagella. Converting to Christian faith in young manhood, he had told his grandson that God was God whatever name man – whether Jew, Christian or Moor – gave Him. Many roads journey to the same destination, to God. Gazing around Beatriz pondered this, wondering whether men able to create such beauty truly deserved condemnation. The Alhambra sang a song of love and praise to the inner life of man, and spoke of eternity. Many times, walking along this same way, through the shadows of the arches, Beatriz sensed the watching ghosts of Moors, as if they held her presence somehow accountable. Perchance, this was the truth. She belonged to a people who had robbed this beauty from others. What gave them the right, when the Moors had wrought this beauty with their own hands, hearts and souls? Her people lived here only upon sufferance. They had no right to call this home. Beatriz felt a darkness falling on her spirit – a darkness as black as crow wings. In her mind flashed the memory of crows picking at death's leavings on the edge of battle. She shivered, her heart as cold as the marble chilling her feet through her thin slippers.

Around the Hall of the Two Sisters exquisite tiles decorated the lower walls. Each one a work of art in its own right, some bore the escutcheons of former Moorish rulers. Above the tiles, interwoven with rich gilding and lapis lazuli gemstones, stuccowork formed large plates of arabesques. On the plates was written text from the Koran or verses from Moorish poetry. Sometimes she read the words out loud to the girls. She prayed that Catalina would one day understand:

> My heart has become capable of every form:
> it is a pasture for gazelles
> and a convent for Christian monks,
> and a temple for idols and the pilgrim's Kaa'ba,
> and the tables of the Torah and the book of the Quran.
> I follow the religion of Love.

Beatriz brushed tears from her eyes. All she ever wanted was to understand. She gazed up at the cupola. Gentle golden light imbued the Hall of the Two Sisters and rendered it restful, but it was a serenity her conscience refused. No matter where she looked, voices of the former owners spoke from the walls of the alcázar, proclaiming loudly, *What you take, you never own.* To live in such ill-gotten beauty, tarnished by years of war and destruction, so often stole away her peace.

She led the girls to the far side of the chamber. They sat on a low ottoman, directly below an inner balcony belonging once to the harem. She gazed up, once more disturbed by fleeting shadows. Phantoms lingered there, up in the balcony – ghosts of beautiful, jewelled women, with slender wrists, ankles and waists encircled by chains of gold.

Half shutting her eyes, she imagined them gathered on the balcony, brushing and braiding each other's hair, threading tiny jewels in their long dark or fair tresses. One ebony-haired woman turned her way. Spreading out long, henna-stained fingers, the woman's deep-set, dark eyes stared down, her mouth clamped shut in a thin, straight line. Beatriz blinked, and saw a black skull, eye sockets embedded with fiery jewels. Hatred touched her soul. She blinked away the vision and trembled.

The girls waiting for their tale, Beatriz shut the door on her thoughts and lounged back on the cushions of her ottoman, closing her eyes. "Years ago, there lived in Granada a king named Mohamed El Hayzari, meaning Mohamed the Left-handed. His people named him thus because he used his left hand rather than his right, or perchance because he always conducted his life the wrong way around and was continually in some kind of trouble."

"Your sister Juana is left-handed, too," María whispered to Catalina. Frowning in annoyance, Catalina shushed her.

Beatriz opened her eyes. "Shall I go on, María?"

The rebuked child wiggled in discomfort. "Forgive me, Teacher. I will be silent."

Beatriz smiled, all lightness again. "I am but teasing, little doña. Now, where was I? Si, he was a brave king and managed to keep himself upon his throne no matter the trouble he brought on himself and his people. And not forgetting us Christians. When Mohamed was an old king, he rode with his people in the foothills of Elvira. It was spring and even the old find it difficult to stay always within stone walls..."

As she told the story, she found herself drawn to the cupola. Light. There's always light. She looked at the girls. Si, light. Both the girls were that. Lights piercing through the darkness of her life.

17

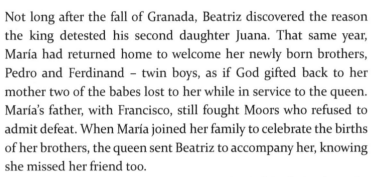

We do not easily suspect evil of those
whom we love most.
~ Peter Abelard

Not long after the fall of Granada, Beatriz discovered the reason the king detested his second daughter Juana. That same year, María had returned home to welcome her newly born brothers, Pedro and Ferdinand – twin boys, as if God gifted back to her mother two of the babes lost to her while in service to the queen. María's father, with Francisco, still fought Moors who refused to admit defeat. When María joined her family to celebrate the births of her brothers, the queen sent Beatriz to accompany her, knowing she missed her friend too.

She came for another reason. Queen Isabel had also brought forth twins into the world and almost died in doing so. The first twin, her daughter María, came into the world easily, but not so her sister. It took two days of dreadful agony before the queen, near to death, brought forth her dead babe. Queen Isabel, remembering that experience and how close her cousin came to dying three years ago, wanted Beatriz to assure her all was well and remained well for her cousin.

Arriving home, little María found her mother and grandmother ready with gifts for her – for the most part, additions for her clothes chest, gowns or undergarments to replace those outgrown since the child's last visit home. Largely, the clothes were once worn by her older sisters – made anew by a new collar, girdle or sleeves – but amongst the gifts were two garments made especially for her by her mother and grandmother. María's grandmother gave her a chemise, one so sheer Beatriz wondered if she had made it from silk. Seeing the fine, skilful embroidery at neck and hem, she thought it fit for the queen or her daughters.

María gasped with happiness when she opened her mother's

gift. Josefa had cut down one of her favourite court gowns to her daughter's size, making it a smaller copy of the original, yet leaving seams for room for the child to grow. The last cords tied on the gown, María turned to her mother's mirror. Beatriz recalled Josefa in this gown, her long, thick, black hair adorned with pearls, hanging in a plait down her back, one of the few times she ever did so, going against her usual choice of keeping her hair veiled under the toca. Black hair, dark eyes, olive skin, all melded with the red velvet gown and made her a paean of beauty. Now, Beatriz saw the same promise in Josefa's daughter.

Day-by-day, Josefa recovered her strength. Beatriz and María spent much of their time in her chamber, keeping her company while she lay abed, wet-nurses now attending to the needs of her sons. Early one morning, María asked what was often in Beatriz's mind. "Mamá, why does the king hate Juana?"

Working on a new chemise for the queen, Josefa stitched with care, her needlework a labour of love, readying it for when Beatriz and María returned to court. Her dark eyes rose again, considered her daughter, then fell to focus on the seam. Shifting closer to the candle near the bed, Josefa squinted at her sewing, leaning against the pillows.

"Do you think it hate?" she murmured.

Shrugging, María thoughtfully traced the thick lines of black embroidery on the scarlet brocade covering her mother's bed. "The king's cruel to her, Mamá."

Beatriz lifted her eyes from her own slow sewing, watching Josefa's needle dart almost as fast as a hummingbird in search of nectar. Her friend's needle flew in and out of the silk chemise, in and out of the sheer material, the white fabric so fine she saw Josefa's hand moving underneath it, every stitch tiny and neat. Beatriz shook her head, overwhelmed by the speed with which she sewed the seam. Her friend came to the end of her thread and sorted through her cards, seeking the same colour. "I am growing careless in my old age. Where did I put it?"

María picked up the card from the edge of the bed and handed it to her mother. Josefa beamed a bright smile that restored youth to her pale face.

"Thank you, hija. You asked about the king and the infanta." Josefa considered her daughter. "We shouldn't question the rights and wrongs of the family we serve."

María nodded, but grinned teasingly at her mother. "But you told me to keep my eyes and ears open to serve them better." Smoothing out the brocade of her mother's bed, María appeared all at once saddened. "Sometimes, my princess cries at night because of her sister. I don't know what to do."

Threading a needle, Josefa glanced at María, her eyes full of compassion. "From the time you toddled around my feet, you found something to mother – a kitten, a rabbit, and let's not forget all those half-dead mice you saved from our kitchen's cats – and then you were only scratched for your trouble. I'm not too certain if it wise to also wish to mother the infanta."

Not waiting for her daughter to answer, Josefa rubbed the side of her head. "Child, life is full of unanswered questions. Men and women are the same in this – none of us ever find all the answers we seek. Methinks, I agree here with the priests, only by suffering do we truly gain understanding. But suffering also means casting aside innocence about life. I do not wish that for you yet."

María clasped her mother's hand. "I see it in your face – you know the answer. Tell me, I beg you."

Josefa frowned, bringing her dark brows together that they almost seemed one. "I do know." She pursed her mouth, her eyes darkening. "A simple thing, my María, and a great misfortune for the infanta. Juana inherited too much likeness to the king's own mother."

María stared, startled. "The king speaks well of his mother. I have heard him many times. He speaks words of love."

Not looking at her daughter, Josefa lifted her chin and shook her head a little before exhaling a longer breath. "Santa María, must I really explain?"

"Please, Mamá."

Josefa raised pained eyes. "What can I do with a child who asks such questions?" She sighed again, and leaned closer. "This is something you really must know?"

María stood there, a knuckle at her mouth. "I think so, Mamá," she said slowly.

Josefa smiled at her daughter tenderly. "You're right. You should know the truth. Words, hija. Beware of words. Just because the king speaks, that does not mean he speaks the truth. Juana is too alike her grandmother, in looks and intelligence. The king can hardly bear it. He stifles her, perchance because it seems to him he finally has power over his mother. You are right to say he is cruel. In the right soil, Juana could grow into the best of both her parents. As it is, her own father twists her spirit into deformity. I fear for her."

Beatriz dropped her sewing in her lap, staring at Josefa, horrified at her friend's words. Also floundering, María swallowed, saying what Beatriz was thinking. "That's not fair. She is not his mother!"

Josefa twisted her heavy gold thimble around her thumb. One of the presents Beatriz had brought for Josefa from the queen, the arrows of Isabel's regalia engraved the thimble's circumference.

"We know that. But I do not think the king cannot stop himself recoiling from the constant reminder that Juana presents to him. It is hard for a man, especially a man like the king, to know he will never measure up to his own mother, her strength and intelligence makes him seem small. He is intelligent, but good, sound cloth does not compare to cloth of gold. He has few of his mother's gifts to call his own, then he marries a wife also more gifted than him... With his hijas, the king ensures he keeps an upper hand and they remain well and truly in their proper place. Perchance, child, the king deserves our pity and our prayers."

"But, Mamá, he is cruel... and always to Juana. Always to her!"

Josefa reached for her daughter's hand. "Si, I know, my child. Remember, I saw it for myself when I lived at court."

María shook her head, snatching back her hand. "Why does the queen not stop it? She could if she wanted to. Juana cowers whenever her father looks at her."

Josefa's well-shaped brows came together again before she resumed stitching. Moments passed, and then she lifted dark eyes brimming with sadness. "The queen cannot."

Blinking, María scratched her head. "Mamá, you become cross with Papa when he is angry with us for no good reason."

"By God's good grace, your father and I agree too well for that to happen often. But I am not the queen. Queen Isabel must present a united front with her husband – not only for the reason of their family, but also for the well-being of their kingdoms." Josefa took a deep breath. "Know this well, my hija, great woe falls upon a house divided. An enemy within is more dangerous than an enemy without." She glanced at her daughter. "Do you understand my meaning?"

María nodded, the explanation continuing to pour forth from her mother without her needle stopping once. "If people ever saw cracks in their relationship, my hija, that would be enough to plant the seeds of rebellion in men's minds. Always the queen remembers the road she must walk to ensure the survival of her marriage. So much depends on it.

"I know the queen's heart desires not to sacrifice her children for any cause, not even to safeguard her unity with the king, but she always has to think of the greater good. She first must be queen. For that, 'tis the mind that must rule over the heart. Believe me, she tries hard to be a good mother to all her children."

"You speak the truth, Josefa," Beatriz said quietly, moving to the table close to the draped window.

Josefa threw up her hand to clasp the side of her head. "Good Madonna, help me, you've that look in your eyes. Pray, not another of your vile concoctions you want me to drink?"

Beatriz laughed, holding up a wide neck urine flask. "And here I thought I pleased you by putting honey into all your medicines. Your complexion's far too pale for my liking, Josefa. I would like to see your urine."

Josefa settled against the pillows, her gaze rising to the ceiling. "By all the good Saints in Heaven! I am only pale because you refuse me permission to leave this chamber. I grow stronger with every new day."

Beatriz laughed. "Because you follow my instructions." She placed the urine flask on the chest near her friend's bed. "There's no hurry, but just give me a fresh sample when you next void."

Josefa grimaced. "I don't know what you expect my urine to tell you."

"Nothing, I hope. But many years of peering into urine flasks and using my nose and eyes has taught me a great deal." She smiled, glancing at María. "One day, I hope to share with your daughter some of my hard-earned knowledge."

"Me, Latina?" the child piped.

Beatriz lifted up the child's chin with her ink-stained fingers, and smiled. "Your eyes are round as twin plates."

Gathering her sewing on her lap, Josefa studied her daughter before turning back to Beatriz. "You know María's tender heart. We may be wrong, Beatriz. She may not be the wisest choice for this. She hates the sight of blood."

María's eyes darted from Beatriz to her mother. "Blood? I don't understand."

Josefa returned to her sewing, her needle neatening the neckline of the chemise, and spoke softly. "Latina wants you to learn from her to be a healer, and I have agreed."

María blinked, and her mouth fell open. She gazed at Beatriz and her mother, bewildered.

Glancing at Josefa, Beatriz laughed. "Child, why the surprise? Your mother and grandmother are both skilled healers. They have already taught you a great deal, more than you know. But, si, I plan to teach you. When the infanta leaves for England, it will relieve the queen's mind to know you safeguard the Princess Catalina with such skills. "

Josefa's dark eyes became deep wells of anguish. She gazed long at her daughter before glancing back at Beatriz. "I do not wish to think of this – my youngest hija forever gone from me, far away from her family, alone and exiled in a strange land..."

Beatriz sat on the edge of the bed and clasped her friend's thin hand. "You know the day will come."

Josefa tossed her head back as if combating something unseen. "But not yet for many years." She spoke so quietly it forced Beatriz to lean closer. "Too soon she will be gone from here, and I will see my child again only when the good God and the queen permit. Let me enjoy her while I can without remembering there will come a time when she is gone from me in this life..."

Beatriz stilled, her thoughts caught between one moment and the next. She stood, going to the chest with a selection of her glass medicine bottles. She straightened them in a row, exhaled a deep breath and pulled at her girdle. Turning to Josefa, compassion filled her heart. "Change is one of life's realities, and farewell is just a part of it, the long and the short." Beatriz gazed at little María. The child seemed all ears and eyes. "Like you and the queen, I do my best to prepare the children to deal with change. That's all we can do."

María turned back to her mother. "Mamá, but what of the infanta Juana? The queen must help her."

Beatriz eyed her friend. Josefa gnawed with worry at her lower lip, turning it cherry red, but gave a brief nod. Beatriz rested a hand on María's shoulder. "She cannot. The queen shamed the king once and she promised him never again."

Her face bewildered, María raised her thumb to her mouth. Josefa glanced at her daughter and pulled the thumb away. "Beatriz, tell her," she murmured, returning to her sewing.

Stepping into the light streaming from the un-shuttered window, Beatriz picked up one of the medicine bottles, put it down, picked up another, put that down. Rubbing the side of her face, she sighed. "You know the queen's word is sacred to her, si?"

The child nodded.

"What I tell you happened when your mother and I were younger than you... I heard it from my father so many times, sometimes I see it in my mind as if I witnessed it myself."

"You speak for me too." Josefa shrugged. "It's such an important story in our good queen's reign, likely we're not alone in this."

Beatriz grabbed a stool near the bed and sat down. She clasped María's hand. "You know our king and queen are cousins, si?"

María nodded. "Mamá told me."

"Did she tell you that the king also had the right to claim the crown of Castilla?"

Shaking her head, the child seemed to ponder this. "But the queen is queen..."

"Si, the queen is queen, thank our good God for His great mercy, but the king offers no thanks to God for it. When King Enrique, her brother, died, our queen found herself alone, her husband gone to aid his father in his wars. As soon as she knew of the king's death, she acted without hesitation, seizing the throne in her own right. King Ferdinand, still yet a prince of Aragon, was with his father when word came to him of the death of the King of Castilla. By the time he joined his wife, she had already had her coronation, a magnificent coronation when all the nobles of Castilla recognised her as queen."

Josefa spoke. "Our queen rode a white horse given to her by your grandfather; your father's own favourite war stallion comes from the same bloodlines. Mounted on his horse before her, don Gutierre de Càrdenas held forth an upright naked sword, the ancient symbol of the ruling monarch's judicial power over all. Si, the power of life and death, set in a young woman's hands." She shook her head in wry amusement before cutting the thread from the chemise with her teeth. "Furious, the king arrived back from his father's wars, ready for another kind of battle. Your grandmother attended Queen Isabel then. She told me he hurled at her the words of homage he owed to her as queen like ringing stones, asking through stiff lips to be alone with her. Once alone, the shouting began.

"Mother said all the court would have heard the king's anger if there had not been two chambers before the Queen Isabel's bedchamber. Your grandmother, alone and close by in the next chamber, feared for the queen's safety. The king was that angry."

Discomforted, Beatriz crossed her arms, pressing her fingers into her forearms. "The king likes not to be crossed..."

Josefa's head snapped up. "Nor does the queen, Beatriz."

Beatriz met her friend's eyes, feeling as if she had been slapped. "I did everything to keep him at a distance." Brushing away tears, she lowered her head. "I have no power in this. Everything I do works against me, Josefa."

"Why are you crying, Teacher?" María asked.

Josefa stared at Beatriz. "By the sword – the fields have eyes and woods have ears." She lifted her chin and looked at her daughter. "Your teacher weeps for a matter that does not concern you, María."

Beatriz swallowed and then spoke quickly. "María, do you remember what we discussed before we left court? 'Man is active, full of movement, creative in politics, business and culture. The male shapes and moulds society and the world. Woman, on the other hand, is passive. She stays at home, as is her nature. She is matter waiting to be formed by the active male principle.'"

"Aristotle's Politics!" María squealed with delight, looking over to her mother for her approval.

"Si, we spoke about the power of such works, and the great power they have upon our poor female lives." Beatriz crossed her arms again. "Sometimes, I think I am drawn to Aristotle's writings because it gives me much cause for dispute and argument." She laughed a little. "If only to myself. But think, child. What must it have been like for the queen to seize her rights when men have had such thoughts and still have such thoughts? And not only men! Most women, lacking the education to know any better, submit wholeheartedly to them too. When the queen married her cousin, I feel certain he believed he strengthened his own claim to the Castilian crown, not that his wife would see her marriage to the Prince of Aragon strengthening her stronger claim, and decide to act upon it quickly when the opportunity presented itself."

"But the queen is the rightful ruler..." María looked bewildered.

"Si, we see it that way now, only because we know what kind of queen she is, but at the beginning of her reign, nothing yet was proven except the queen's great determination and ability to draw the right men of power to her. Even as a young woman, many knew she possessed a lion's heart. She needed that and more to convince her husband she did what was right."

Josefa rested her sewing on her lap. "The king knows that now, I am sure of it. He respects her more with every passing year even if his passion for her is no more. He is a good king in that regard – able to recognise that he is stronger because of their partnership."

María shook her head, gazing at her mother and then at Beatriz. "But the infanta Juana? I don't understand why the queen cannot help her."

Beatriz leaned closer to the child. "Believe me, I speak only truth when I say she does all she can. But the queen's marriage ran afoul of rocks when she sailed ahead and seized her throne without her husband, without waiting for him, and not wanting to wait for him. She gained a kingdom, but almost at the cost of her marriage. It took months before he calmed down and saw reason. By then, she promised him he would always have the final say when it came to their children."

Josefa started sewing again – this time, beginning an edging of red arrows around the queen's chemise. She spoke without looking up. "Our good queen keeps her promises to those she loves, even when it causes her pain."

Later that day, Beatriz was alone with her friend. "You must stop the king," Josefa said.

"Don't you think if I knew a way, I would?"

"Amiga, if it was me, I'd leave court. While you stay there, you are far too close to the fire for your own safety."

Eyeing her friend, Beatriz sat on a stool near the bed. She rested an elbow on its edge and cradled the side of her face. A miasma of morning light stripped Josefa of all colour.

"Why should I go? I've done no wrong. In any case, both the queen and Francisco would want to know why. They would not understand me leaving when they know how much I love teaching María and the infanta." Beatriz shook her head. "And how can I tell Queen Isabel the reason? I never want her to know – it would kill me. 'Tis bad enough that he always threatens to tell the queen the truth about me." She laughed bitterly. "A truth he forced on me."

"He lusts for you more because he knows you have no lust for him. It crazes him, causing him to burn for you even more."

Beatriz rubbed her wet eyes. "You think I don't know this? When he raped me the first time, his threats and strength backed me against a wall, and I mean a wall, until I could do no other but submit. He has made me into his whore, Josefa, except it is I who pays. I the one to live with shame."

"End it, amiga."

Beatriz clasped Josefa's proffered hand. "'Tis not as simple as that. I wish it was."

"We are women, si? You're intelligent. Don't tell me at your age you do not know how to make a man stop lusting for you."

Beatriz shrugged, defeated. "I am a woman, si... I curse that almost every day of my life. But what of his threats? How can I ignore them? What if he follows through with them?"

"Threats? What threats?"

"Si, his threats to remove me from teaching the infantas, prevent me from teaching at the university. These positions are everything to me, Josefa. God forgive me for my weakness, but take away those two things, and you might as well take my life too. He took my body, my virginity, and I prayed he'd leave me alone. It wasn't enough. Whenever he wants to pull the string, he reminds me he has the power to strip everything from me, and this puppet must dance. I thank God I am not his only woman. Most of the time he finds another mouse to play with, and he leaves me alone. Thank God too I have never conceived his child."

Josefa sniffed. "My amiga, have you thought to speak to the queen's confessor? 'Tis possible he might help you."

"Si, I've thought of this."

"Then why not go to him?"

"A simple answer: Hernando de Talavera does not like me. I asked him why and he told me bluntly I am a weak woman, greedy for knowledge, one of the greediest he has had the misfortune to ever meet in his long life. He disapproves of me so much, I hesitate to give him true cause."

Josefa tightened her grip. "Si, like so many men cut from that cloth, he never forgets we are hijas of Eve, but I am surprised you have taken upon yourself his disapproval of all women. Do not let yourself be hurt by this. You should know the queen is the only female he allows himself to like and respect. Still, Beatriz, the father is a good priest, and I believe he would help you, if he can." Josefa spluttered out a strange laugh. "The good father has a tender heart when it comes to sinners. The more we sin, the more he loves."

Beatriz tried to smile. "I will think more of it, amiga. My father knew Talavera well when they taught together at Salamacha. They were good friends. He remembers me from when I was but an infant, in my mother's arms – more memory of her than I am blessed to remember. My father told me Talavera gave him much comfort when she succumbed to the plague."

"Surely that gives you even more cause to go to him for help?"

Round and round, Beatriz traced with her index finger a spiral on the bedcover. Unchecked, her tears fell, spattering their pattern as if following the finger's wake.

"What is it, Beatriz?" asked Josefa.

Beatriz raised her hand and wiped her face. "I'm not sure if knowing him from childhood would help me here. I remember too well the many harsh words he and my father had over my education. He believed my father was very wrong and misguided in his desire to teach me as he did."

"The good father would not have been alone in this. Very few women are brought up to be prodigies of Latin."

Bitter, Beatriz gazed at her friend. "Even you expressed strong disapproval of this."

Josefa heaved a sigh, shaking her head slowly. "'Tis not that I disapprove... I have told you this before too. I believe women walk a hard enough road without walking a road where there are pits at every step. As my mother often said to me, since we cannot get what we like, let us then like what we can get. Tell me truthfully, Beatriz. Do you think you'd have this awful hole dug for you, as you do now, if your father had not set your feet on this journey to become a scholar and professor of the university?"

Beatriz pondered Josefa. "Si, I am in an awful hole, as you say. But, Josefa, I know there are more terrible and darker holes. I will always be grateful to my father for giving me the key to escape ignorance, even if it only came from his great need to console himself after losing my mother."

Josefa placed her hand over Beatriz's. She gave her a wry smile. "Escape ignorance? You know many ignorant women, si?"

"Josefa, you mistake my meaning." Beatriz stared at the coverlet of Josefa's bed. "All of us must walk our own roads, but 'tis wrong to prevent women from walking so many roads just because we're women. Even Plato said, 'Nothing can be more absurd than the practice of men and women not following the same pursuits with all their strengths and with one mind, for thus, the state instead of being whole is reduced to half.' I so agree. Our world cuts off its nose to spite its own face by insisting the only purpose for women is to bear children and perpetuate the human race, as also said Plato. Surely 'tis far too hard a view to forever blame women for Eve's sin."

Josefa frowned. "But, Eve's sin brought death to the world and condemned women to suffer."

"Perchance you can see it that way. But our Lord Jesús welcomed women as his followers. Whenever I feel defeated, I keep that in mind and remind myself that the good lord knew women possess minds as well as hearts and encouraged them to use them. If our saviour believes this, then it must be right. That's why I believe learning for the young to be so important. For not only do most of us then discover the road we are meant to walk, but good learning also hands a child a light to guide them all their lives. Just because a child is female, does it mean she should walk in the dark?"

"Si, I understand, Beatriz. But perchance my feet are more on the ground than yours. I am not at all certain that learning, as you give my María and the queen's hijas, will make their lives any easier."

Beatriz laughed. "Easier? My good Josefa, have I ever said learning makes living any easier? But to be taught to think is to be taught to truly live."

Josefa lifted her dark eyes. "And I believe he who knows how to live, knows enough. 'Twas not until I was a grown woman that I began to have the learning you speak of. 'Twas not because I doubted the fullness of my life, but because the queen asked me to learn alongside her."

"Do you regret it, amiga?" Beatriz asked.

As if weighing her answer, Josefa slowly shook her head. "No... I appreciate having now the words to describe so much that once eluded me like a mirage eludes us in the desert. But still, my amiga, I remember the prayer of the good Saint Francis, 'Lord, grant me the serenity to accept the things I cannot change.'"

Beatriz laughed. "Perchance you, Josefa, are the wisest of us two. I cannot tell what must be changed and what must be accepted as unchangeable. I just charge ahead into the dark, carrying my little bit of knowledge before fear gains an upper hand, pulling me back. But despite the winds of life often pushing me the wrong way, I am farther along the road than I was when I first started my journey."

Rubbing her forehead, Josefa sighed. "And we are no further along than when we began this conversation, to no good purpose, amiga. You must find a way out of this cesspool before the dam breaks and carries you away with it. I fear so much for you."

Beatriz reached for her friend's restless hand. "Don't. I tell you truly, talking of bulls is not the same as being in the bullring. Life has taught me well how to survive my dance with my particular bull. Even if I must humiliate myself to do so, I will extricate myself from the mire before the flood comes."

18

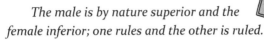

The male is by nature superior and the female inferior; one rules and the other is ruled.

~ Aristotle: *The Politics*

"I require and charge you both, as you will answer at the dreadful day of judgment when the secrets of all hearts shall be disclosed, that if either of you know any impediment, why you may not be lawfully joined together in holy matrimony, that you confess it. For you be well-assured, that so many as be coupled together otherwise than God's word doth allow are not joined together by God, neither is their matrimony lawful."

Sunlight struck Beatriz's indigo wedding dress as the priest's words drummed in her ears. Clutching at her cloak to cover her gown, she looked aside at Francisco and consoled herself. *One of us is happy. Pray God, Francisco would always be this happy. Let the ceremony end before I run away.*

Standing near the church door with Francisco, his grown children and a few of his friends as witnesses to their wedding, she once more confronted her uncertainty about marrying him. Si, she loved him, but could marriage change her life just like Francisco's artillery changed the landscape of the war? *Pray God, I am barren.* She stared at the elderly priest and then at Francisco. *Did I speak that out loud?* Swallowing, trying to slow her breathing, her rising panic became difficult to contain. *Surely Francisco's three children means he would not miss having more?*

"Will you have this woman to be your wedded wife, to live together after God's ordinance in the holy estate of matrimony? Will you love her, comfort her, honour and keep her, in sickness and in health, and forsaking all others, keep you only unto her, so long as you both shall live?"

Francisco's smile after he said his firm "I will" began to calm her. He doted on her, was proud of her. He promised to place nothing in her way to prevent her from keeping her position at court, and the university. He would not make that promise to her unless he meant it. His years of patience, waiting to marry her, surely proved he was a man of his word.

"Will you have this man to be your wedded husband, to live together after God's ordinance in the holy estate of matrimony? Will you obey him, and serve him, love, honour and keep him, in sickness and in health, and forsaking all others, keep you only unto him, so long as you both shall live?"

"I will," Beatriz murmured. Gazing at Francisco, she swallowed, speaking the words louder. Wedding Francisco offered the best solution to her problem of the king. The king admired Francisco. He was not likely to pursue a woman married to a man he called friend.

The rest of the ceremony seemed a dream. It still felt like a dream when they feasted with his family and friends at Francisco's home. The little she forced herself to eat lacked taste and made her nauseous. Hiding her disinterest in the festivities, her eyes kept returning to her wedding ring. A plain band of heavy gold, it fitted tightly around her finger. *Don't be a fool. The ring is not already leaving its mark on you.*

It was after midnight before she was alone with Francisco in his candlelit bedchamber. The night was cold and the fire in the hearth burned sluggishly. Francisco, now in his shirt and hose, went to the fireplace to stir it back into life. The embers glowed red and he carefully arranged twigs before placing a small log onto flames. Mindlessly, Beatriz began to undo the cords of the low neck of her gown. Glancing up, Francisco grinned, rose from the fireplace and came over to her. "Let me do it, love."

Standing with him so close, watching his busy fingers, Beatriz felt a lump in her throat. Francisco was a good man. A good, good man.

Her untied gown fell to the ground. She shivered in her thin shift, and crossed her arms over her chest. The neck of her shift was so loose it threatened to drop from her shoulders and expose her breasts. Francisco grinned again. "We are married, love," he said.

Gently, he took her arms away from her body and the shift fell almost to her waist. Cold air puckered her breasts with goose bumps before Francisco's warm hands cupped them. She stood there, gazing at him, aware of her partial nakedness, his hands on her body. He pulled her into his arms, kissing her mouth, first one side, then the other, his tender lips slowly claiming hers. *Thank God, thank God, the king never sought to possess my mouth. Don't think of the king. Don't let him destroy your wedding night. Just think of Francisco. It is time to experience what it is really like between a man and woman.*

Francisco released her, loosening the drawstrings of her shift so it dropped to the floor from her naked body. He studied her for a long moment, and Beatriz raised her hands to her hot cheeks. As if she weighed nothing, Francisco gathered her in his arms and carried her to the nearby bed.

He put her down gently on the bed and pulled his shirt over his head. Stepping out of his hose, he almost bounded on the bed beside her. Lying on his side, keeping a little distance between them, he turned her to face him. Francisco traced a finger from her temple to the side of her mouth. "My beautiful wife," he said, before kissing her again. This time, she kissed him back, first experimentally, then with greater confidence. He tasted of honey, and a hint of good wine. When his tongue went into her mouth, she drew her head away in surprise and looked at him, lifting an eyebrow. "You've never done that before," she said.

"If I had, I would have found the years of restraint too hard. You didn't like it?"

"I don't know." She moved her face closer to him. "Pray do it again and let me decide."

Kissing him again, she found her mouth opening to his. The feeling of his tongue in her mouth stirred her. Without thinking, closing her eyes, she began to do the same to him. Her heart drubbed fast in her ears.

Francisco pushed her back down on the bed. He must have felt her tense up because he smiled, caressing her face again. "Don't worry. I have waited too long for this day to spoil it now by hurrying. We have tonight, tomorrow night, all the nights of our lives. I want you to want me as much as I want you."

Francisco stroked from her cheekbone to her neck, his finger following an unseen line to her breast. Smiling, he traced its large areola, and her nipple hardened. Francisco lowered his head and kissed her breast, before sucking the nipple softly. She moaned a little, a strange feeling beginning to course and pull in her woman parts, making her move closer to him. He gazed up at her, grinning like a youth. "You like that, love?"

Trying to chase away her shyness, she smiled back and reached up to touch his face. "And what do you like, Francisco?"

He smiled again. "That answer can wait for another night. We have weeks before us for you to learn what I like." He cradled tenderly the side her face with his broad hand. "Tonight... tonight let me show you men do not always hurt. I want you to know true lovemaking is about mutual pleasure, not pain. I want tonight to forever cast from you the memory of being ill-used."

She placed her hand over his mouth. "Shhh – do not speak of it." Her hand going behind his head, she pulled him closer to kiss him. Her mouth seemed to dissolve into his. She felt his hand go between her thighs and opened them up to him. She froze when his fingers slipped into her, but became relaxed and loose-limbed at his gentle touch. She laid back, letting his skilled fingers give her sensations she had never known before.

"Is this the sin the priests warn against?" she murmured, her blood coursing with sweetness and delight.

Francisco laughed. "The priests can go hang. I will never call loving my wife a sin." His lips went to the side of her neck, kissing from just under her jaw to where neck and shoulder joined. She gave a moan, and he kept kissing and sucking gently at her neck until she embodied pure pleasure. His erect penis pressed into her side when his gentle fingers entered her again, this time with greater ease. Aware of wetness between her thighs, she tossed her head back, shut her eyes and moaned.

"Are you ready for me, love?"

She turned, met his eyes, and took a deep breath. Unable to speak, she nodded.

Francisco shifted his body over hers, and opened up her thighs to kneel between them. Skin touching skin, she felt a moment of surprise at his hairiness but, unlike her past experiences, he only hurt a little as he eased himself into her body. She wound her arms around him, her hands caressing his back muscles. He began to move, and she found herself moving with him. A flash of memory. Strong, vice-like hands tearing at her clothes, refusing to let go, forcing, hurting, debasing. *Hear me. I deny you now. You will not destroy this moment. You are nothing to me. Nothing.*

She began to move rhythmically with Francisco, her pleasure intensifying. Beatriz felt swept on a wave taking her beyond the constraints of physical flesh to where Francisco and she fused, as one.

A lull in the flare ups of fighting between Christians and Moslems meant Francisco expected to stay at court for several months. Beatriz still tutored Catalina and María in the mornings, but now spent most of her afternoons with Francisco. Often, they would go into the countryside. Her hands already ink-stained from teaching, she dirtied her hands even more by helping him experiment with small parcels of gunpowder and small hand weapons he had designed. She had designed something too, thick woollen hats with ear muffs to protect their hearing. Francisco had burst out laughing at seeing them.

"I'm not too certain if I can wear these at the battle-front," he told her. "But I'll wear them here for you."

Their nights were also happy times – when they washed from their bodies the grime and smell of sulphur, and Beatriz began to welcome marriage and the love she shared with her husband. Mornings, she returned to the school-room to share with Catalina and María what she and Francisco had learnt that day from setting off their explosions. There was another reason she roamed far with Francisco from court. Francisco remained at court because the king remained too. Beatriz prayed her marriage would finally end the king's eyes falling on her with lust, but lived in terror lest she discover otherwise.

Birds chorused a morning ode to spring, the silver wash of a young day spilled out into the hall – pooling a path of light, one leading Beatriz to the outside garden. Alone this morning – Catalina, accompanied by María, commanded by the queen to talk with her after their early morning devotions – Beatriz wandered into the courtyard. There, wide archways encased her in a thousand shades of green shadow. Everywhere butterflies flittered and drifted around the flowering vines. Festooning blossoms, coloured pale to deep and bold, adorned a garden already glorying in the first weeks of spring.

Beatriz stepped deeper into the garden, her movements breaking apart the silver light. A few butterflies flew close to her face, the wings of one tickling her nose in passing. A haze of showering light rendered them into flying, living sapphires, their wings edged with bright rubies. Laughing with simple joy, Beatriz spun around, watching their beauty vanish into the dark recesses edging the garden. She stood there, her palms upraised, grieving again for beauty lost. She wanted to rail and weep at her empty hands. *How long must I wait to see them filled?* Then she scolded herself. She had so much more than most women she knew.

A man's laughter frightened her, and she stepped back into the dark shadows, breathing a sigh of relief when she saw, seated on the far edge of the wide rectangular pool, the man called the Italian. His form half in shadow and the other half in light, he lifted a hand and beckoned to her. "Good morrow, Latina. Come. Come and speak to me."

Curious, but also cautious, Beatriz padded closer to him. She kept her gaze fixed on him, stopping when only half a dozen steps separated them.

The man laughed again. Stretching out his long, thin legs, he considered her. "Strange, isn't it, that I have been back at court for months now, and this is the first time we have really met? I remember seeing you with the youngest daughter of the queen, the day the Muslim king came out of the gates of this beautiful alcázar for the last time. The day the banners of Castilla and Aragon were lifted high on its towers. The day the queen made yet another promise to me. I hear you are the tutor of the youngest infanta."

Beatriz smiled. "Si, since before she was five."

He tossed back his head as if surprised, the moment casting dark shadows on his face. A man in his forties, there also seemed an air of youth around him. He peered at Beatriz more closely. "You know my name?"

Treading on the dry leaves beneath her feet, Beatriz listened to their crackle, and then looked at him, remembering seeing him with the queen before the fall of Granada. "Si, I know your name."

Cristóbal Colón rocked a little, rubbing the heels of his hands on the sides of his black tights, where leg joined body. He took off his black velvet cap and put it beside him, scratching the thinning, reddish-white hair on top of his head. "You have an advantage over me. The La Latina is all I know of you. May I ask you for the honour of your real name?"

"Doña Beatriz Ramirez, recently known as Doña Beatriz Galindo."

Cristóbal Colón considered her again.

"Is your husband Francisco Ramirez? He who serves the queen as one of the men in charge of the gunpowder?"

Beatriz smiled. "The queen calls my husband one of the bravest men she knows. He left two days ago to return to his work."

Cristóbal Colón boomed out laughter, slapping his legs with a resounding smack.

"Why do you laugh, senor? I speak the truth."

A wry look settled on Cristóbal Colón's face. He rocked again before he spoke, crossing arms over chest. "Forgive me. The laughter wasn't directed at your good and most esteemed husband. No, I laugh at myself. Heed my words of warning, Doña. The queen is good in feeding us what we want to hear. Perchance she means what she says for your husband, but for myself, I am no longer so sure. There have been far too many promises made and not kept, all mixed with too much honey." Cristóbal Colón gazed around the courtyard.

A fragrant place of peace, the arched entrance and the blossoming vine mirrored itself on the quivering pool of water. The drift and flutter of hundreds of butterflies were captured too on the forever-changing water's surface. Cristóbal Colón shook himself, as if ridding himself of his own visions.

"'Tis time for me to leave this place. I have wasted too many years waiting for the queen to make up her mind and keep her promises." He shifted in what seemed to be anger. "Look at me now. Cast aside for yet another morning with excuses, the queen too busy to see me. Si, left to audience with her child's tutor. By God's good name!" Moved into sudden action, he lumbered up to tower over Beatriz. "But all is not wasted. This morning has served to clear my mind about what I should now do. Others in France or Genoa will listen to me. I shall leave for Códoba today." Picking up his cap, Cristóbal Colón turned and bowed. "Farewell, Doña Beatriz Ramirez and thank you. I doubt we'll meet again."

Beatriz stood there, watching him stride away. Oblivious to their beauty, his passing unsettled a crowd of butterflies amongst the flowers flurried into the air, they flitted and interwove a dance around him in the morning light.

Later that morning, Beatriz resumed her Latin lesson with Catalina and María. She selected for Catalina a tract of Aristotle while watching María struggle with Galen. The child squirmed beside the infanta and sighed.

Beatriz placed her quill into the inkpot and turned her full attention to the child. "You have a question, María?"

María pushed the open book away from her. "Too many. He writes of the three principal members – heart, brain and liver – but I cannot understand his explanation about how they control everything in our body."

Beatriz smiled. "You are reading *On Natural Facilities*, si?"

María folded her arms, her face puckering her annoyance. "Of course, Teacher! You told me to."

Catalina, pressed against María's side, piped up, "But Aristotle says 'tis the heart controlling all."

Beatriz clapped and burst out laughing. "First, my student and now the princess." She turned to Catalina. "Aristotle is firstly a philosopher, my young scholar. Philosophers spout theories like the Earth awaking to spring – whether they're right or wrong... that's for you decide. You're free to spout theories in their stead. I would be very disappointed if you didn't.

"María's tract, on the other hand, comes from Galen, a physician from hundreds of years ago. Again, life will teach her to agree with his theories or not." She smiled at the girls. "Believe me, they are only theories. Stepping-stones flung out by men and women from humanity's own journey, for their children to stumble across in search of truth. But I think Galen might be flinging out the right stones. Healers work so much in the dark, we need help to find stones, some substance to set our feet upon."

María scratched her scalp underneath her roundlet. Pulling the book back under her nose, the pages opened to a complicated anatomical drawing inspired by Galen's teachings, the child looked ready to weep. She looked up at Beatriz. "There is so much to learn, Latina. I'll never know it all."

Beatriz twisted on her stool, leaning towards the child. "Do you think I do? I don't – none of us do. But think, and look back at the many hurdles you have now behind you. You've gone over so many since our first days together. Child, let the hurdles behind you now encourage you to go forward. One day, I promise you, you'll thank God you didn't give up. You might even thank me."

The doubt on María's face made Beatriz smile in reassurance. "You learn here the difference between life and death. The queen has every confidence in you, as does your mother. And I, of course, possess no doubt you'll one day be a skilful healer."

María glanced at Catalina, murmuring quietly: "Teacher, is it true the queen feeds us what we want to hear?"

Beatriz stared at her, hearing again the words of Cristóbal Colón. "Who said this to you?"

María lowered her head. "Forgive me, I heard you speaking to Cristóbal Colón in the garden. I did not mean to, but the queen told me to go back to you."

Catalina lifted her gaze from the book, a frown puckered between her brows. "What do you speak of?"

María swallowed in her confusion. "I heard Latina talk with Cristóbal Colón this morning. He told her he has had enough of waiting and will leave the court today."

Beatriz cocked her head to one side, tracing a circle on the polished wood of the table.

She inserted a triangle within the circle, crossed both circle and triangle with a determined line straight through the middle before she stopped doodling and instead drummed the table with two ink-stained fingers. "Cristóbal Colón is a man who wants his own way – and now, not tomorrow." Her gaze fell back on María. "Child, do you think he told the truth? Or was just venting out his frustration?"

María sat straighter, her eyes shining with delight. Beatriz hid her smile, pleased that her question made the child so happy. Scratching her head, María licked her top lip. "He said the words as if he meant them, Latina."

Beatriz remembered the man in the garden, a seated man turned into one of action, disturbing the garden's tranquillity and its butterflies by his sudden departure. She sighed, thinking the child was likely right. She gazed over María's head and rubbed the back of her hand across her mouth. Coming to a decision she stood, the wood of her chair screeching its protest against paved tile, flinging her trailing skirts over one arm.

"The queen needs to know this," Beatriz said. "Keep to your lesson while I tell this news to Santángel. Only yesterday he told me the queen is thinking seriously to sponsor Cristóbal Colón in his quest."

Catalina glanced at María with a shrug of her shoulders, and returned, without speaking, to her book.

Beatriz returned to the school-room near the time they usually ended their morning lesson.

"Did you find Santángel?" María asked her.

"Si, in the queen's chamber." Beatriz swallowed. "The king was there, too, playing chess with Fonseca." She felt her cheeks flush with heat. "The Count of Tendilla, Ponce de León and Gonsalvo of Cordoba watched on while Santángel spoke to the queen alone. You know how serious a game of chess is to the king – I did not dare at first to speak, but then the queen herself directed a question to him about Cristóbal Colón. She wanted the king's thoughts on the matter." She smiled. "Fonseca took advantage of the king's distraction, made his move, saying, 'Your Highness's queen has acted like a rash navigator. She has come too close to the abyss and the black hand is about to seize her.'"

Fascinated by the story, Catalina put down her book, and even María leaned closer. "What did the king say?"

Beatriz shrugged. "What do you think the king said when he came close to losing? He asked the Devil to take the Genoese. But by then I had told the queen what you told me. Once the king had won the game, she told him there would be no great risk in granting Cristóbal Colón his desire. When the king agreed, the queen summoned a page and told him to mount his horse and ride until he overtook Cristóbal Colón, and tell him she had appointed him Admiral of the Ocean."

Time passed. In summer of every year, Beatriz attended her duties at the University of Salamanca. Gone for over two months, she missed Catalina and María, and her husband, although he was often not at court, but at the battlefield. The long weeks at Salamanca returned her to her two charges full of zest and fire. Distracted with writing new treatises, she sat the girls down and read her work to them, treating them like true scholars. She knew this was true for Catalina, but María often struggled with boredom, especially when they detoured into areas of no interest to her. But Catalina was still determined her friend would learn, whether she liked it or not. Sometimes, Beatriz thought María's Latin and knowledge improved simply because of that, rather than because of her skills as a teacher.

Now that the girls were older and able to read and write Latin and their mother tongue with ease, Beatriz handed over some of Catalina's learning to the Italian Geraldini brothers, scholars of high calibre who the queen employed to teach her children.

Catalina enjoyed the younger Geraldini's lessons. One day, Beatriz found them at a table spreading out a large map, Geraldini's black eyes flashing in excitement. "Princess, this is what we knew of the world yesterday, but today?" He stood tall, waving dismissively over the parchment. "Princess, the return of Cristóbal Colón changes the world as we know it. This map is worthless now. Remember this day always, for 'tis not every day man discovers a new world and transforms the old forever." He barked out a laugh. "Thank the good God the noble queen, your mother, honoured me by allowing me to speak to her of my countryman."

Less than one year ago, Cristóbal Colón had sailed to what many believed promised certain doom. Most called him loco, but from the day of his return, Geraldini never let them forget he was one of those to gain the queen's ear, helping Cristóbal Colón obtain what he most desired – the money for his ships. When he returned, he more than paid his debt to his royal patron. He opened the door to a new world of unbelievable wealth.

That very morning, wagons full of treasure struggled their way to the old alcázar at Barcelona, perched high over the city. The donkeys' high-pitched screams, men whipping then to pull them up the steep road, ripped apart the quietness of dawn, and heralded later events. Not long after noon, the queen and king commanded the court to their presence chamber.

Unusual smells greeted Beatriz when she entered the chamber – sweet, rich and spicy, thick and heady, all wafting towards her. Set against the walls, squawking monkeys threw themselves against the wooden frames of their cages whilst jet-eyed, rainbow-coloured birds, their bright colours putting the colours of the court to shame, cawed incessantly and competed with cries of excitement from men and women.

The royal family gathered below the dais of the queen and king. Her widow weeds making her slenderness painful to see, even the Princess Isabel seemed full of wonder as her mother relished the tangible harvest of Cristóbal Colón's voyage, strange animals, strange food for her to taste, and much, much gold.

Six silent, strange men, strange men with red skin, caught Beatriz's eye. Bathed in golden sunlight streaming through the colonnaded arches, the men wore nothing more than scanty loin cloths and painted skin. Wild looking, lithe and wiry, the men had heavy gold rings in their ears and nostrils, feathers and ornaments decorated their long black hair that gleamed with oil. They appeared forlorn, frightened, alien, but still unshakeably proud.

Grinning, Catalina took María's arm and pointed to the men, and María laughed. Beatriz could only see the men's great unease and almost tangible fear. She looked again at the girls. They were so young – so young they forgot that one day they would be just like these men – these men fated to die far from their homes, in exile.

My sweet Francisco,

Has the news come to you about Cristóbal Colón? Imagine, my love, a discovery of a new world. Two weeks ago, he returned to court, bringing with him great bounty. Birds, treasures from a strange land, even food stuff. The queen gifted me with a necklace from the treasure chests. Its wooden beads, smooth and polished, stained deeper than the colour of blood, reflected back my face like tiny mirrors. My student María received a similar necklace. The older infantas each took into their possession the best of the caged birds, while the infanta Catalina was given a very young monkey. It clung to her as if to its mother, while Catalina cooed and sung to it.

The animal soon became a great nuisance. It was only in the princess's care a day when it snatched María's necklace from the small chest in their bedchamber. Hearing shrieks coming from the infanta's room, I rushed in to discover the animal whipping the beads this way and that way. I tried to rescue the beads for María, but the string snapped, and the beads flew far and wide.

The next thing I knew, the monkey had scurried up the bed-head, and started swinging on the bed-hangings. It screamed like one possessed by demons. Poor María scrambled on the floor, gathering the beads together. The animal must have thought it was game. Dropping to the floor beside her, the animal fought with her for the beads. It became a race between them to see who could pick up the most. At last, the race over, the monkey scurried to the bed to innocently groom itself. María disliked the animal as much as me. I did not envy the girl sharing a bed with not only the infanta, but also her new pet and its fleas.

Day after day, the animal disrupted my lessons. When Catalina answered her mother's summons, María became the animal's lone attendant. Thank God we could call servants to clean up its messes.

Catalina loved the small monkey and took pleasure in its antics. What else could I do but bite my tongue and care for the animal as well?

María found it cold and dead in its basket one morning, no more than ten days after the princess claimed it for her pet. How I regret all my ill thoughts about the animal. How I wish the annoying urchin was returned to life and back in Catalina's arms...

Remembering the death of Catalina's monkey made Beatriz wonder later whether Juana acted wisest of the four sisters about her wild pet. After Cristóbal Colón's return to court, the king found Juana laughing and dancing with her two female blackamoor slaves – and banished her to her rooms until the next day. The king always told her she was far too free with her slaves, but they were her truest companions beside her sisters and brother. Without her siblings and slaves, Juana would have been very alone at court. The king's constant distaste for Juana caused others at the court to shy away from her. Even her mother's attendants did not serve her with the same devotion they offered to the other royal children. Many feared to befriend her because they feared the king.

Summoned to her mother the next day, Catalina gave a sudden cry of dismay in the school-room. Coming to stand beside her, Beatriz glanced down at the open volume of *The Consolation of Philosophy* on the table, reading: "But now is the time for the physician's art, rather than for complaining." Beatriz gazed at Catalina and recited: "Are you the man who was nourished upon the milk of my learning, brought up with my food until you had won your way to the power of a manly soul? Surely I had given you such weapons as would keep you safe, and your strength unconquered..."

Catalina grinned at her before looking crestfallen. She snatched the book from the table. "Latina, this must go back to Juana. Her new tutor, Doctor Miranda, gave it to her for her study and I've kept it too long. I am forbidden to see my sister. Could you please take it for me?"

Beatriz heaved a sigh. If she were Juana's tutor, she would just locate another copy of the book from the queen's well-stocked library. After borrowing it from her sister, Catalina hadn't stopped talking about it or reading its pages aloud. Already, the girl knew passages from the book off by heart. Like many before her, Boethius's doctrine spoke to her. Catalina wanted to believe she also had the capability to survive the ill winds of fortune, and often talked about how God used fate as a tool to shape them. Of all the queen's daughters, Catalina was the one to truly love knowledge for knowledge's sake. Her intellect grew apace with her age and more.

Knocking on the heavy wooden door of Juana's bedchamber, Beatriz heard no answer. She opened the door. Deeper in the large chamber, the inner doors opened wide to the balcony. Padding inside the room, she saw Juana looking out on deep valleys awash with pale oceans of mist. Dawn's light tempered the girl's form in soft light.

The wind blew stronger and whined, twirling Juana's long, dark hair, up and down, the thin strands of her tresses slithering snakes around her white face like Medusa. The wind's power pulled taut the folds of Juan's red habito, accentuating tiny waist and maiden breasts, lifting the gown skirts to reveal narrow, naked feet. Between her breasts, hanging on a black ribbon, a red ruby flashed and winked with light. Passed down many generations, her grandmother had given the ruby to Juana on her twelfth birthday.

Juana's air of grief halted Beatriz halfway into the chamber. The girl opened the golden cage of her small parrot. Beating rainbow wings against the cage, the bird squawked.

"'Tis wrong to keep beauty caged, 'tis wrong to cage living things," she said, stroking its feathers. Calmed by her touch, the bird perched on her hand, fluttering a little. Tenderly, she drew it out of the cage. The parrot ruffled feathers and fluttered wings.

Juana let out a cut-off sob.

"I can no longer bear to see you so unhappy. God gave you the gift of flight..." she flung out her hand in half an arch, "... be free and fly."

Flying a short burst, the parrot first settled on the half wall of the balcony. Juana rushed towards it, weeping with heart-broken abandon, waving her hands. The small bird spread its wings and flew away.

Juana sobbed, clinging to the lace stone rail of her balcony. In the skies, a small bird flapped its rainbow wings higher and higher until, at last, it disappeared from view. Beatriz stepped softly back to the door, not wanting the infanta to see her, desiring to intrude no more. Her heart sad, she left the room still holding the book. Its return could wait for another time.

19

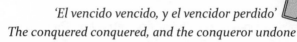

'El vencido vencido, y el vencidor perdido'
The conquered conquered, and the conqueror undone

~ Castilian proverb

The midday sun beat down without mercy. Light-headed, Beatriz wiped the dripping sweat from her brow, sweltering in her heavy clothes. Her mule sidestepped upon the uneven, sun-parched ground, rocking her violently in the saddle-chair. She tightened her hold on the reins, and heeled the mule to canter to sounder ground. She bit back a curse and then another. The wind gusted strong on the summer-seared banks of the River Tagus, blowing dust into her eyes, offering no relief from the heat.

Juana, the last of the royal family to do so, rode her mule to the other side of the wide river. Waiting for her own turn to cross, impatient for their journey to come to an end and finally to arrive at Alcántara, Beatriz noticed Juana's pale, tense face, and recognised the girl shared her impatience too. The infanta reached halfway across the river. She stiffened in the saddle-chair and swung her mule whip to hit its flank, as if urging her mule to greater speed. Beatriz's heart almost stopped when the animal stumbled into stronger currents. Deep water swished and splashed at the bottom of Juana's saddle-chair. Swaying on her panicked mount, she looked down, then back towards her parents. Juana straightened up in her saddle-chair and tried to regain control of her mule. That very moment, the situation worsened.

"Mother of God!" gasped Juana's dueña. Mounted next to Beatriz, the woman watched the infanta, horrified. Out of the river's safe depths, Juana's mount had lost its footing. It staggered, stumbling again, throwing the infanta head first into the deep water. For a terrifying moment, she vanished from view. In the rush of water, her dark mantle billowed like an overblown rose, with its petals about to drop.

Voices shouted out from both sides of the river. Beatriz's young mount surged forward, threatening to bolt. It took all her strength, and two stable boys snatching its bridle, to keep the terrified mule from hurling itself from the bank into the river.

Beatriz swung her gaze back to the river. Juana, her veil and mantle lost in the currents, now clung for dear life to her saddle-chair, angled and tottering on the mule's back. Her huge frightened eyes rendered her a child again, rather than a fifteen-year-old princess preparing to leave her family to become a consort of a prince. The rolling-eyed mule appeared too shocked to move, other than to give way, slow step by slow step, to the pull of the currents. A swirling torrent of water rushed and smacked around its body.

On the other side of the river the queen and king galloped their mounts back toward the water's edge, their three remaining daughters and son close behind them. Catalina bowed forward in her saddle-chair, a hand fanning across the lower part of her face, watching her sister struggle frantically in the river.

Too far away for Beatriz to hear, the queen spoke and gestured to King Ferdinand. Motionless, he seemed to watch some play-acting, rather than the life and death struggle of his own daughter. Turning from her husband, the queen twisted on her mule and lifted a hand. In answer, a stable boy broke from the crowd of men and women of the court and rushed to her side. The queen spoke a command and the boy whipped his mule, charging into the river, hollering out a cry fit for the battlefield.

On the two banks of the river, silence settled over the crowd of courtiers. Everyone watched the youth head toward the infanta. Time stilled, and it seemed to Beatriz that they all took roles in a painting, people in various stances, frozen together, locked in a moment, a breath, that might yet unfreeze to the reality of grief and loss.

The youth wrapped a rope around his waist and attached it to his own mule, and then swam the short but dangerous distance to

Juana. He seized the bridle of her baying mule, tugging with all his strength and that of his mule towards safer river depths. Cheers echoed from both river banks. A few more heart-stopping moments, and Juana and her mule came close enough to the other bank for a group of courtiers to go in after her. They carried the fainted Juana from the water.

The queen rushed to her daughter's side while the king rode over to speak to the stable boy. Later that day at Alcántara, the court coming to rest like a stork to its nest, Beatriz heard the king rewarded the stable boy by promoting him to keeper of the silver.

Female voices murmured close by. Hastily making her way back to the queen, Beatriz turned into the hallway and almost ran into Juana, half-in and half-out of her chamber's doorway. Fully recovered from her near drowning three days ago, she huddled with her blackamoor slave over an open scroll. Seeing Beatriz, the slave's head ducked as if a whip threatened her. Christened Catalina by the queen, in honour of her daughter, the Moor took the parchment from Juana, fast closing it before Beatriz saw more than a few well-drawn astrology symbols.

Juana smoothed down her gown, visibly relaxing, and clasped her hands before her. "'Tis but our La Latina. There's no need to worry," she said quietly to her slave. The slave Catalina licked her lips, holding the scroll tight to her breasts, underneath crossed-over arms. Her thin shoulders shook as she glanced around. The terror on her face rendered her far older than just fourteen.

Footsteps echoed down the corridor. Juana grabbed Beatriz's arm, her fingers digging so deep Beatriz yelped with pain. She pulled Beatriz through her doorway. Catalina followed, shutting the chamber's door behind her. Closing her eyes, she leaned against it, the parchment still held to her chest.

"Don't worry, Latina keeps our secrets." Juana glared at Beatriz. "She knows what would happen if she did not."

Beatriz stared at the roll of parchment in the slave's arms. "What is it, Infanta?" As soon as Beatriz spoke the words, she wanted to call them back, wanting to go. For the first time in her life, the infanta frightened her.

Juana took the parchment from the slave "Did you see anything?"

Beatriz shook her head. "Symbols of the zodiac, that's all." The slave released a long, held-in breath. Juana glanced at her. Taking the scroll from her, Juana turned to Beatriz in decision. "I trust you to say nothing of this. If you betray my trust, you'd be responsible for whatever happens – my slave being whipped for one."

Beatriz gazed at the closed door, and then back at Juana. She lifted her chin. "I don't want your secrets, Infanta. Keep them." She curtseyed. "With your permission, I must go to the queen."

Juana took Beatriz's arm again, but gently this time. Her tight smile offered her an apology. "Forgive me, but I do no wrong here." When she glanced at the slave, Beatriz wondered whether to believe her.

With a deep breath, Juana whispered close to Beatriz's ear, "My father has always forbidden me to cast my own horoscope, but coming so close to death the other day, I asked my slave to do it for me. So, I haven't disobeyed the king, my father, have I? My slave did it for me, not I."

Beatriz stared at her in horror, knowing what the king would think. She hoped for Juana's sake the king stayed unaware of that parchment in the slave's hands. Not only did she risk punishment for her slave, but she risked it for herself too. "He forbade you to do this?" Beatriz gazed at the slave. She held the parchment to her as if it somehow protected her. "Why? There's no harm in looking at the alignment of our birth stars. All do it."

Juana lowered her eyes and shrugged. "I know not the reason why my father commanded this, only that he has." She nodded to her slave. "Open the door. Latina will not betray me."

Dearest One,

Pray forgive me for the delay in replying to your last letter, but much has happened since last time I wrote. We have had important visitors at the queen's court. A weary group of Englishmen arrived almost a month ago. After their first welcome, they barely had a day's rest before torchbearers brought them to stand before the king and queen in the great hall. I stood near the royal children, while other attendants spread out at distance from the dais of the queen and king. How the eyes of the men widened at the sight of our two monarchs in their jewels and rich clothes. Upon the dais, sitting close together on their thrones, the queen and king were garbed in cloth of gold edged with sable. Cloth of gold hung behind them too, quartered with the arms of Castile and Aragon and the words of their motto: Tanto monta, monta tanto – Isabel como Ferdinand, *as much as the one is worth so much is the other – Isabel as Ferdinand.*

The queen draped a black velvet cloak, edged with gold and rubies, over her golden gown. With every movement, the queen's jewels shimmered and flashed in torch and candle-light. That night the English fell on their knees and bowed low, greeting Queen Isabel and her husband as "kings". I could not help smiling when my infanta lifted her head with pride.

Much feasting, costly entertainments and long, private meetings with the king and queen followed over the coming days. There is news of more unrest in England. With the support of the Scottish king, the young man claiming to be Richard IV invaded England with his army. He was little welcomed by the English and soon was pushed back into Scotland.

In recent days, the Duke of Milan has written to the queen, asking her and the king to broach Scotland and negotiate with them a peace with England. When the men departed, they took back with them not only gifts for their royal family, but also what the King of England desired: a new treaty for Catalina's marriage.

The infanta Catalina is now formally betrothed. Catalina stood in her mother's presence chamber, and appealed to the papal delegate to allow her to wed before reaching legal age. She then wed England's prince and heir by proxy. Si, still only in her tenth year, my princess's life now belongs to England, and a prince she has never seen...

Their backs slouched against the wall, Catalina and María sat on the wooden bench in the library, listening intently. "How Sir Tristram and La Beale Isoud came unto England," Beatriz read, "and how Sir Lancelot's brought them to Joyous Gard. Then La Beale Isoud and Sir Tristram took their vessel and came by water into this land. And so they were not in this land four days but there came a cry of a jousts and tournament that King Arthur let make –"

Hearing Juana call out to her sister, Beatriz stopped reading. Even so, María's gaze adhered to the illumination of Beale Isoud and Sir Tristram and a dreamy look settled on her young face. The knight and his ladylove was so vibrantly painted, the picture seemed lit from within by myriad candles. *No wonder they name such things illuminations.* The girls had asked her to read to them the story of Isoud and Tristram. She pushed down her discomfort. Perhaps she should have chosen something to help them deal with real life, rather than see them take to heart stories of courtly love.

Catalina glanced aside at her friend. "You need not come." Laughter bubbled in her voice.

"No, no, I'll attend you," María said. Beatriz smiled, shutting the precious book. At ten, the girls strived to act adult.

With her usual impatience, Juana stepped out of the open doorway and into the sunlit corridor. Beatriz studied Juana. White-washed walls on either side seemingly caging the girl, Juana's fine black hair was precisely parted down the middle, arranged so carefully, so tautly, conflicted with the flashing, midnight blue eyes and a passionate mouth. Not yet sixteen, Juana was the fairest of all the queen's four daughters. Aware of it, she held this knowledge to her as a shield, sometimes acting condescendingly to her less beautiful sisters. The other royal daughters, content with their own measure of beauty and rarely victim to their father's darker side, understood. The four sisters loved one another. Sharing these last days together, Juana readying to leave her mother's court and sail across winter seas for her new life in Flanders, the sisters seemed closer than ever.

María shuffled her over-large feet away from her skirts, her black, tight slippers doing little to disguise their true size. She looked at Juana with jealousy. Beatriz could not help wondering if María was remembering the painting in the book. The artist had depicted the knight's ladylove with tiny, graceful feet, so alike to Juana's. The infanta, on the threshold of young womanhood, made Catalina and María but pale moon slips set against the bright noonday sun. Juana's zenith was here and now, whilst they still lingered in their dayspring. Beatriz thanked God for it.

"Hurry!" Juana called, looking back over her shoulder. "Mother wants to walk with us while the fair weather lasts."

Stretching like a waking cat, Beatriz arose a trice after her two students, returning the book to the table in the school-room. She set it carefully between the other two volumes telling of King Arthur's court. A well-thumbed volume of *El Cid* rightly crowned the three books.

Down the corridor she saw the two infantas and María, waiting for her to catch up. Standing side-by-side, Juana towered over Catalina. Tiny in size... gazing at her small princess, answering her wide smile with her own, Beatriz couldn't deny Catalina was surely that. But she made up for her lack of height in many ways. Already greatness blazed its promise around her – a promise beyond the fleeting beauty of soon corrupted flesh. Si, Juana may be the noon-day sun, but already a new star rose in the dawn's horizon and shone.

A ribbon of unending gold, the sandy beach stretched and curved towards the land-locked embrace of smoke-blue mountains. The setting sun dyed the sea pink and orange. Luminous, it shimmered and swelled, the white froth, streaked and flecked by the sun, going in and out, in and out, onto the beach. Seabirds flying out to sea changed from white to orange to pink and finally to spots of darkness on the horizon before disappearing from sight.

Despite the evening's chill, Beatriz walked barefoot, holding up her habito from the packed, wet sand. The infantas had also kicked off their slippers. Catalina and María walked together, hand-in-hand. Far behind, her grumbles no longer heard, the infanta María's newly appointed dueña carried the girl's silk slippers, protecting them from ruin. Exchanging a quick look with one another, Catalina raced against María de Salinas. Despite her shorter legs, Catalina made it difficult for María to win.

Catalina swung around and grabbed María's hand. Holding up their gowns, the girls danced around and round, making a circle in the sand. María laughed and laughed. Letting go of Catalina, she collapsed on the ground. Half-lying on the sand, rubbing her belly, María gazed up at the clouds and pointed. "Look. A galleon sails in the heavens."

Catalina sat beside her friend, drawing up her knees. Her eyes scanned the skies. "No longer a galleon, see. The wind breaks it apart and turns it into two angels." Her eyes shone. "'Twas a ship of God you saw."

María looked at the clouds, and then glanced first at Catalina and then Beatriz. Shyly, she grinned. "Let me try a poem." She looked back at the clouds, gnawed her lower lip for a moment. "All right. Tell me what you think:

> Scattered clouds,
> Wisps of cloud
> White, billowing clouds
> Pregnant cloud,
> Life-giving clouds.
> Thin streaks of cloud,
> Banner cloud,
> Shape-forming cloud,
> Storytelling clouds.
> Clouds made golden,
> By bright sunlight
> When the Sun
> Beats against
> Dense grey veils
> Of cloud."

Catalina giggled. "Far better than your last attempt. We might yet call you a poet." The girls helped one another up, still searching the skies. Beatriz knew it distracted them from what happened now, upon this beach.

A fair way ahead, her arm threaded through her daughter's, the queen walked and talked with Juana. Loosened and lifted by wind, the infanta's ebony locks gleamed with the blue shine of a crow's wing. The low murmur of their voices drifted to them whenever the brisk, chilling wind dropped or the surf pulled back to a quieter roar.

Early next morning, if the weather continued to be good, Juana and a large party from her mother and father's courts would board the ships now waiting in the royal bay of Laredo, the ships that waited to take Juana to her marriage to Philip of Flanders. Before the infanta boarded her ship, the queen would bid the girl farewell, leaving her second daughter to face her future.

"Come," Catalina said. She pulled María along for another race, their feet sinking into the sand. They faltered when Juana crumbled against her mother. The wind carried to them her unconstrained sobs. Holding her daughter, grief carved upon the queen a stillness none dared near.

Catalina and María clasped hands, looking back the way they had come. Water filled their small footprints, making tiny pools reflecting back the vivid colours of the setting sun.

A few steps away, Prince Juan, the gloaming burnishing his tousled hair gold, coughed behind his hand. Standing with his sisters Isabel and María, Juan, like his two sisters, gazed out at sea, pretending unawareness of Juana and their mother's grief.

Overlooking the bay, upon sandy hills, tall tufts of green grass growing here and there, the family guards stood at watch, archery bows at the ready. Beatriz wondered what they thought, watching this drama enacted on the beach. Queen Isabel held her daughter as if she would never let her go.

Catalina dropped María's hand and looked at Beatriz as if for reassurance. "My mother's afraid. I have never seen her so afraid." She picked up a shell from the yellow sand, tossing it out towards the surf. The white shell arched far in the air before disappearing into the water. Dark storm clouds on the horizon-edged sea and crimson cloud ribbons streaked the sky.

"'Tis being forced to send your sister at the beginning of winter," Beatriz said, gazing again at the ocean.

María spoke the words she dared not voice. "They say the sea crossing is not for the weak-hearted."

Catalina laughed as if discomforted. "Juana isn't weak-hearted. Father says Juana's heart rules her head. She is a slave to her emotions. That's Juana's weakness, my father says." She gazed at Beatriz. Clearly guilty for saying so much, Catalina blustered out, "If only he was here to lift mother's heart. Alas, his soldiers have great need of him."

Beatriz gazed at the grieving daughter and mother and pondered Catalina's words. No more did the child express doubts about her father's motives. It had taken the king many months to recover from the attempted assassination, that and his frequent absences returned him, unquestioningly, to Catalina's loving heart. Far better, Beatriz thought, the king remained with his soldiers. She could easily imagine his black-froth fury at both his wife and daughter for their public display of emotions. On the eve of her departure, Juana especially did not deserve his contempt for her unchecked tears.

Staring down at the sand squeezing through her toes, Beatriz's thoughts pounded in her mind like the surf on this beach. The queen was so alone, so miserable – bereft of the comfort of the man who held her heart in the palm of his hand. He failed her as he did his daughters. Beatriz glanced up at Juan, still struggling to stop coughing. He even failed the prince, giving him a poor example of manhood to follow. Rather than uncompromising, so often pitiless kingship, King Ferdinand would be better to show the prince a loving, compassionate and noble heart. But how could he do this when he lacked those very qualities?

Wretched for the queen but helpless too, Beatriz stepped away from the royal family, picked up two scallop shells from the sand, and studied them. So alike, yet so different, each one shaped by the elements to their own special uniqueness.

She slipped the more perfect shell into the hidden pocket of her gown, and traced the fan of the other, beauty etched in simplicity, humbled at the art wrought by God. It was no wonder pilgrims of Santiago took the shell for their symbol. Not only did Christians love the shell, but once pagans did too. The scallop shell, coupled with the sea, symbolised eternity and rebirth.

Beatriz held the shell up to the light. Watching the translucent fan draw in the colours from the lowering sun, she wondered if she could do a painting of it. She walked slowly alongside the sea, looking at the meandering trail of shells marking the tide of the surf. Why just one? Why not a whole border of shells? White shells emblazoned by light.

In her mind, Beatriz saw her painting take shape, the canvas edged with scallop shells, all of them unique. She looked back at

Catalina, seeing her beside Prince Juan, his arm protectively around her. Like the shells, her students too were unique. She made her way back to them, hearing the prince speak: "Is it any surprise our mother's heart breaks? She is worried she sends Juana into danger or worse. But she is queen. 'Tis her duty to let her go, as she will do with all of us."

Without warning, Princess Isabel strode towards the sea, the trailing hem of her black habito becoming drenched by the outgoing tide. She gazed all around, as if seeking a way to escape. She looked aside at her siblings, her huge eyes welling with tears. "Soon, it will be my turn again."

For the last five years, Isabel had devoted herself wholly to God. For five years, she clung onto the hope of taking the veil, despite the continual refusal of her mother and father. Isabel gazed at the sky, closed her eyes, and swallowed. The pulse in her neck beat hard and fast, like a caged, wild bird. She opened tormented, haunted eyes. In spite of the passing years, she had never stopped sorrowing over the loss of Prince Alfonso. It was a grief darkening and eating away at her spirit.

Beatriz clasped the shell in her fist, its sharp edge almost cut into her flesh, and a cold finger stilled her heart. She thought of Francisco. He was so far from her, living day-by-day a life flirting with danger and death. Loving always carried with it such burden, the danger it could destroy as well as give joy. She remembered her father once telling her that love was a two-edged sword. He had never recovered from losing his wife, and died only months after Beatriz left their home. But he also told her when you love – really loved – it becomes part of your whole being, something you never lose. Surely, that was true?

Princess Isabel stepped further into the surf. For a moment, Beatriz feared she wanted the sea to sweep her away. "No more I say! I don't want this duty." Isabel's words were like a scream that competed with the surf.

Prince Juan reached out and enfolded her hands with his own. Coughing, he pulled her back to drier sand. "Sister, sister. Please, I beg you, don't let grief destroy you. Leave this darkness, Isabel, I beg you, and take joy in life."

Tears fell down Isabel's cheeks and dripped onto her neck. She inhaled a deep, ragged breath and shook her head. "Juan, you don't know. You've no notion of how I fight every day to live – and how I hate it when Father and Mother remind me of my duty to marry again. One marriage is all I want, and Alfonso my only husband. I don't want to be ever unfaithful to him – even in memory. I sicken at the thought of another man touching me." Isabel bent her head. "Our lord father tells me Portugal has again said no to María. I'm to marry Alfonso's cousin. Father refuses to listen to me... refuses to give me more time." Isabel closed her eyes tight, wrapping her arms around her body. The coarse black habito, pulled tight about her form, revealed Isabel's years spent in fasting and vigils. Her body was simply taut skin over far too slender bones.

Isabel muttered, her voice tear-drenched, "Castilian princesses never cry without good cause. They do their duty. Duty!" With a savage cry, she opened her eyes and kicked at the sand. "How I hate that word! Hate it, hate it, hate it!"

She whirled back into the surf, stumbling to her knees. The foam licked, eddying froth around her skirts.

Juan lost all colour and left Catalina standing alone, taking his older sister in his arms. Waves splashed their lower bodies, soaking the silk and velvets of the prince's rich robes and Isabel's chosen nun-like gown. They took no notice. Juan, coughing, hugged his sister tight, his own eyes awash with tears. "Hush, sweet Isabel. You who have so often been like a second mother to us four coming after. I wish I could give you true comfort. I cannot. You are the eldest child of our parents. Look into your heart and tell me you never knew this day would come."

Her face hidden in his doublet, Isabel clutched at him like one drowning and spoke with a muffled voice. "I prayed so hard, so hard every day, for this cup to be taken from me."

Beatriz trembled, her heart full of pity, unable to take her eyes away. Isabel had so hoped her parents would relent and allow her to become a nun. Perchance the hope had increased because the queen, who loved her daughter dearly, stalled her husband whenever he suggested it was time for Isabel to face again the marriage bed of diplomacy.

Juan shook his sister gently, helping her to her feet. "Think what your marriage will do – again unite Portugal and our parents' kingdoms. Our parents worked hard and sacrificed much to make their two kingdoms united and strong. You wedding Portugal's king is but another of our mother's sacrifices."

"Mother's sacrifice, Juan?" Isabel laughed with bitterness. "What about me? Brother, it is I who our mother sacrifices." She gazed towards Juana and her mother, and then back at her two sisters who stood nearby, listening, still as statues. "All her daughters are! We are the lambs our parents sacrifice upon the altar of power. Sometimes I wonder if the profession of our parents' love is but the Judas sheep leading us to our fate." Isabel shut her eyes, as if struggling for composure. Catalina's companion, María, edged closer to Catalina's side, clasping her hand.

"I knew Alfonso and loved him. Loved him, Juan! Do you know what that means? I still love Alfonso. My heart belongs to him. Only to him! His cousin Manuel – I barely know him. And I don't want to know him! I curl up inside and die a little whenever I think about another marriage."

Juan gazed towards his mother and his other sister. Smaller in the distance, they walked hand-in-hand, leaving a trail of footsteps behind them. Grimacing, he glanced back over the long way they had walked this evening, to the other side of the harbour where a fleet from the king's navy, two carracks and one hundred caravels and more, rocked in the bay. Even at this distance the wind carried to them the complaint of wood groaning in the sea and sailor songs. Tightening his embrace on his sister, Juan kissed the top of her head, cushioning his chin there. Beatriz gnawed her bottom lip, concerned about the Prince. He was so pale. Taught from birth to take his burden of responsibilities seriously, in recent years

Prince Juan was less inclined to venture out to ride with his sisters. Ritual cloaked almost every moment of his life. From morning to night, it choked his spirit, leaving him increasingly rigid in public and stripped of every ounce of spontaneity. Royalty robbed him of a true season of youth, leaving him far older than his years.

"Sweet sister, Juana goes to a man she has never met. As will María and Catalina. I too wed a stranger, who comes with the return of our father's ships." He turned his face, coughed again, and shrugged. "'Tis the destiny of princes. Look to our parents – they wed only days after meeting one another for the first time. Yet they love truly. We must hope for the same for ourselves. Hope eases our journey in this world. I beg you, Isabel, try to hope, try to believe you can be happy again."

20

And I beg you to be served
By the present treatise
Very perfect infanta,
Furnished with virtues
And prudent at a very tender age;
In much you follow the shining
Great Queen of Castile
Who is the fountain of virtues.

~ Pedro Marcuello's ode to Juana

Beatriz sat in the embrasure with Catalina and her sisters, all of them watching the queen read the letter, the dry parchment crackling as it moved in her eager hands. Concentration scored a frown between her greying, thin eyebrows. Lifting her eyes from the letter, relief lessened the worry lines on her face, and Queen Isabel smiled. "All's well with Juana. Thanks be to God."

The king strode across to his wife, taking the letter. Closing the weak eye inflicted by a cast, he skimmed the page with his good eye. He glanced aside at the queen, his poor eye blinking, readjusting to light.

"More pleasing news, wife. The fleet lost only two of its vessels crossing a winter sea. All is as I hoped, and expected. The ship carrying our hija had the best captain to ensure she arrived safely in Flanders." His eye squinting again, the king smiled and pointed out a line. "Note here, Juana writes they praise her beauty."

Queen Isabel held his arm, glancing back at the message. "And her suitability for motherhood." She swallowed and looked away from the missive, her mouth clenching shut.

The king, his eyes and mouth no longer merry, placed his hand overtop the one on his arm. The queen's fingers clutched his, keeping his hand imprisoned. He frowned.

209

"Why so glum, Isabel? Be easy. There's no better mother than you, and Juana is your hija. With little time, she will prove these words right."

Any suggestion of healthy colour fled from the queen's face. "Husband, I have told you this before. Juana reminds me too much of my dear mother. She lost her mind after my brother's birth. I am fearful, my lord. What if the same fate awaits Juana? I pray to God we did right to send her so far from us. She needs love and understanding. What if she finds that lacking in Flanders?"

Carefully the king folded the parchment in half, setting it upon the table beside him. "Pray, forget it, wife. You worry overmuch for her – for all our children. What will be will be. Making yourself ill isn't going to help matters. Think of the stronger ties we've gained by sending Juana to Flanders. Very soon our son's wife comes, and the ties will be stronger yet. Smile. 'Tis long since I've seen you smile, my Isabel."

The queen leaned on him. Her beautiful green/blue eyes liquid pools, she offered him a tremulous smile. "I am becoming out of practice, my lord. 'Tis good and well I have the company of our children. You're away far too often, and for other causes than ruling our kingdoms and leading our armies. My lord, I beg you, stay at my side..."

Eye to eye with his wife, the king kissed her slack cheek.

"You know I want that too. I am your slave, now and always. But you know our service to God means there's much to do. We're so close to achieving our dream of two united kingdoms for Juan to rule after us. With God's help, the day will soon come when I never need to leave your side again."

"I pray God that day is close at hand, Ferdinand." Espaliered against the king, the queen crossed herself.

Beatriz looked across at the queen's hands, troubled. She wore no rings – gout swelled her fingers to almost double their natural size.

"And our eldest? Is she now ready to show the face of a willing bride? We cannot stall the Portuguese for much longer. Their patience wears thin, as does mine. We have allowed her five years of widowhood – surely that is enough time for Isabel to put the past behind her. The girl gets no younger."

Queen Isabel's anguish shadowed her eyes. She lifted her chin. "Isabel knows her duty. I pray to God we do right in this too. My heart hurts every time I see my daughter's unhappiness."

Shrugging, King Ferdinand removed himself from his clinging wife. For a breath, she stood alone, holding out empty arms, before wrapping her arms around herself.

"You make too much of it. Marriage and children is what she needs."

Queen Isabel gazed at the king, her brow knotting into a brief scowl. "I pray God you are right, husband," she muttered. Seemingly without any awareness, she dug her heavy crucifix into her breast.

The king turned from his wife and strode to the table, opening another letter. Reading it, his eyes widened, his face loosening and greying to sudden ugliness. His mouth clenched shut and hardened into a thin line. Beatriz met Catalina's wide eyes as the queen rushed to her husband's side. "What is it?"

King Ferdinand folded the letter and put it back on the table. He covered it with his hand. "'Tis no matter. Just a letter from Juana's confessor."

The queen held out her palm, "Let me read it."

They stood there gazing at one another, battling out wills, whilst all in the room watched. King Ferdinand passed the letter to her, glancing across at Beatriz and his silent daughters. "Leave us," he commanded.

Hurrying after Catalina, Beatriz left the room just as the queen gasped. She looked back over her shoulder. Queen Isabel sat on her chair as if her legs suddenly lost all strength, one hand clasped behind her bowed head.

King Ferdinand rested his hand on her shoulder. "I tell you 'tis no matter, Isabel. The girl is safely wed now."

A terrible, raw sob tore from the queen and the letter fluttered to the ground. "Juana. Oh, my Juana! Why can you never think before you act?"

Early the next day the story came to Beatriz. Not from the king and queen – if they still spoke of it, they did it behind closed doors, well away from other ears. But the infanta María overheard the gossip of her mother's women. Distressed, she whispered what she had learnt to Catalina, and Catalina brought the tale to the school-room.

"Do you think your sister has the right of it? How could Philip bed Juana within just one hour of meeting her and before the final wedding vows?" María de Salinas looked a picture of confusion.

The day already warm, Catalina wiped at her sweating face. Sunlight coloured her cream habito saffron and rose, and transmuted her hair to gold. "All speak of it. Your lady mother's so discomforted I think there must be truth in the story. They also say this is what Juana and Philip wanted, and the clerics blessed their marriage," she said.

"But the final wedding ceremony wasn't until the next day. They named it an act of love... of great passion..."

Catalina gazed aside at her friend. "You believe that? My sister says Juana arrived in Flanders very ill. You know what she is like then. Speak one word to her and she growls. Philip and Juana don't even speak the same language. Si, she reads French well, but her spoken French is... impossible. She does not understand the language when people speak too fast."

Beatriz stared at her. "What are you trying to say, princess?"

Catalina swallowed, glancing first at Beatriz, and then at María. "I don't believe this of my sister. Mother thinks she should have used her woman's wit to make him wait until at least the next day and the proper ceremony. But think you, what woman's wit has Juana in this? My sister's not yet sixteen and gently brought up. Now Juana is surrounded by strangers. What choice did she have but to do what Prince Philip wanted? Did she even know what would happen when he took her to the next room – without even the priest coming with them to bless the bed?" She swallowed again. "Seems to me... seems more... like rape..."

She murmured the last words under her breath. Beatriz studied her. In this school-room, she did not avoid telling the girls terrible events from history when royal women had met the refusal of virgin martyrdom, tossing in unbridled legends of lustful Greeks for good measure. Still, she would have expected twelve-year-old maids to shy away from saying the very word. Beatriz shifted with discomfort on her chair, staring at the high ceiling. The gold swirls decorating it made her head spin.

She closed her eyes and saw Juana sobbing like a child in her mother's arms the morning before she boarded the ship taking her to Flanders. Catalina was right. How would Juana have known what Phillip intended? Ah, how she pitied Juana. She no longer had her mother's protection. Her fate was now in the hands of her husband.

"Mother says it hurts the first time, and for some time after," María muttered.

Now Beatriz stared at the blushing María, glancing with apprehension at the wide-eyed Catalina. "She has spoken to you of such matters?" she asked.

María looked at Beatriz in silence.

"María – please answer me."

The young maid squirmed. "My sister wed last year. Mother told Isabel."

"You never spoke of it to me," Catalina said.

Blushing again, María eyed Catalina. "I thought you knew."

"How would I, María?"

"The queen? Your eldest sister?" María offered. The maid glanced at Beatriz. "Latina?"

Catalina reddened now and shook her head. "I could never ask my mother. I can talk to her about so many things, but my tongue ties into knots whenever I think of asking her about what happens abed between a man and a woman. And now she spends all her free time in prayer. How can I ask her?"

"What about the Princess Isabel?"

"Oh María! When I asked Isabel, she bolted from the room. Later, my sister suggested I borrow Juan's copy of Julius Caesar commentaries – written, she said, in very pure Castilian. Like I should strive to be. She told me to exercise my mind by attending to my studies and confess to the priest about thinking of such matters."

María giggled while Beatriz turned away her smile.

"And did you?" María asked.

"Did I what?"

"You know what I mean. Why borrow your brother's book when a copy is in this library? Did you confess to the priest?"

"Of course. He told me to fast and pray with Isabel for God's help to keep a clean and chaste mind." Catalina looked across at Beatriz. "Teacher, could María please tell me what her sister said."

Beatriz looked out of the un-shuttered window. The sky was blue, cloudless. A bird winged to land on a nearby tree and sang its courting song as the tree's green leaves trembled in the breeze. She felt like laughing – in minutes the conversation had gone from disaster to comedy. "We all would need to confess then."

"We confess always. At least this would give us something new to tell the priests," Catalina argued.

Beatriz met María's eyes and they both laughed.

"All right. How about if I leave you two girls alone for a time while I go back to my chamber to find that copy of the Commentaries. I borrowed it from the library yesterday." Beatriz grinned at the two girls. "If there are any areas of confusion, I am certain in my role as your tutor I am allowed to provide answers." Beatriz left the room, not heading to her chamber but to the garden. She heard the call of spring.

Two weeks later, Beatriz hurried with Catalina and María in answer to the queen's summons. They entered the curtained-drawn chamber, one lone candle guttering and smoking in a high sconce. Her daughters Isabel and María trying to comfort her, Queen Isabel wept by a cold, unswept fireplace.

Closing the door behind them, Beatriz took María's arm, leading her deeper into the chamber and farther away from the queen and her daughters. Stepping with María into the window's embrasure, she whispered close to the girl's ear. "We'll stay. Catalina might yet need us."

The infantas María and Catalina now knelt by the queen's side. Isabel gripped her mother's shoulders, her pale face pinched, her eyes flashing with annoyance. "What has Juana done this time?"

The queen sniffed, blowing her nose. She leaned against the intricate carving of the chair's high back. "Not Juana, 'tis nought to do with my Juana..."

Dressed in hunting clothes, Prince Juan broke into the room, his blue eyes searching for his mother. Beatriz started, gulping back a bubble of laughter. Struck in various poses, the prince's men took one look at the scene within. The closest man unfroze and shut the door fast between him and the royal family.

"What's wrong?" Juan cried, his long legs bringing him to his mother in no time. Queen Isabel reached out her arms to him, her eyes welling with tears. "Son, my Angel."

Falling to his knees, he took her hand, gazing up at his older sister. Expressionlessly, Isabel shrugged. The younger infantas nestled closer to their mother, holding her tighter.

Hooking a finger under his belt, Juan frowned. Unnoticed next to María, Beatriz almost forgot the queen's sorrow for a moment. For the first time she saw Juan as a grown man.

"Mamá, you're frightening us. I beg you, what has happened?"

"My beloved mother..." The queen pulled Catalina and María closer. "She's dead."

"Mamá!" Isabel gasped, the younger infantas looking up in shock. Prince Juan massaged his mother's hand. Beatriz could easily guess his thoughts. The younger royals dreaded the times when the queen visited her sixty-eight-year-old mother. The queen's mother's black moods and sudden bouts of inconsolable weeping frightened them. Living a life of enforced isolation, their grandmother only recognised her daughter, gazing at her grandchildren with glazed bewilderment. The old queen knew them somehow connected to her, but Beatriz had long stopped counting the times she called Prince Juan by the name of her own long dead son.

For months the queen's mother loosened her hold on life, no longer wanting to eat or drink. On her last visit, Queen Isabel sat down beside her mother and fed her with her own hands. Perchance, Beatriz thought, the queen's mother's death should be regarded as a blessing.

Prince Juan kissed his mother's hand. "Mamá, no more weeping. Your mother is now at peace, and with God," he comforted.

Red rash splotching her face, Queen Isabel flailed out her hands, snatching at Juan and Isabel's clothes. "Si. With God, and my poor, poor brother, Alfonso. God bless both their souls." Queen Isabel gazed at her eldest daughter. "I named you for her. Despite everything, every day we were together I knew her love. She called Alfonso and me her gifts from God – as you five are to me."

The queen crumbled, her sobs tearing from her as if something broke irrevocably within her. Her four children tightened their knot around her, helpless to stem her wild grief.

21

How beautiful it is to do nothing,
and then rest afterward

~ Castilian proverb

My love,

I beg your forgiveness, but I write to you with a sad heart. Everyone is sad. No – not everyone – those who hate the queen no doubt gloat at the signs of the queen's weakness, her woman's tears. They do not pity her for the loss of her mother.

Once I would have said there was no one more certain of her actions than our queen. No more. She is often lost, and disturbed by little things. She worries all the time about her children. Every morning, she goes to visit her mother's tomb. On her return, I see she has cried.

The king seeks to distract her by the plans to celebrate the arrival of Prince Juan's bride...

All night the snow fell heavily at Burgos. By dawn, the flurries lessened and a messenger rode in before the snow fell again at the palace of the Constable de Velasco, where now stayed the king and queen. Soon, all the court knew his message. Her sea journey safely over, Prince Juan's bride and her party slowly rode to Toranzo. King Ferdinand and his son broke their fast and set off to meet them, accompanied by a strong gathering representing both the nobility of Aragon and Castilla.

Beatriz stood outside with Catalina and María, watching them prepare to depart. María drew her thick fur mantle around her thin body. As yet she still had the body of a child. "How will they find her, I wonder?"

With the lightness of a dancer, Catalina stepped quickly backwards and forth, making it a game to keep warm. She shrugged. "As well as can be expected after such a rough sea crossing." Catalina's laughter sounded grim. "The messenger praised the princess, she kept up everyone's spirits, but it must have been truly terrible. Mother told me my new sister came to shore bearing upon her a verse she had written when she thought they were all doomed to a watery grave."

"A verse? She wrote a verse?" María stared at her, amazement widening her eyes like saucers in her face.

Catalina giggled. "Not just a verse, but her own epitaph." She closed her eyes, screwing up her face in concentration. "'Here lies Margot, the willing bride. Twice married, but virgin when she died.' My new sister has a good sense of humour. And she's brave. She wrote that despite her terror. Mother told me my brother's bride was so certain she was going to die she tied the verse to her hand with a purse of gold for her burial."

Beatriz smiled at the story, gazing again at the king and prince. Juan brought his mount alongside his father's. Gay and eager, and now fully grown at nineteen, Juan's leanness was noticeable when compared to his shorter, stockier warrior father. Even from their distance the definition of the king's leg and arm muscles was apparent. Prince Juan tossed back his head, laughing at something the king said. King Ferdinand looked at his son as if seeing him anew, joining in his laughter. Prince Juan was joyful that day – going to his bride.

Margot, fickle the ways of kings, was an unexpected bride for Prince Juan. The girl had spent most of her childhood in France, learning to be its queen, but the man she called her husband, Charles VII, cast her aside for a far bigger prize. He married Anne of Brittany instead. The shift of power to the side of the French caused a sudden scramble by her father and Queen Isabel and King Ferdinand to balance it, and Margot boarded a ship to wed Castilla and Aragon's golden prince.

Beatriz shivered with cold despite her thick, fur mantle, beating leather-gloved hands together. Overhead, luminous clouds readied to burst forth more snow upon the already thick layer covering the ground. The long cavalcade, king, prince, grandee, soldiers and slave became smaller in the distance, as the snow's bright, reflective light hurt and watered her eyes.

"Prince Juan at last to marry," María murmured distractedly. Troubled, Beatriz glanced aside at her. *Not her, too?* So many maids at court dreamt of becoming Juan's beloved, if only for a single day, a single hour. The unwed girls at court wept jealous tears on hearing of his approaching wedding. Handsome, noble and gifted, Prince Juan sang with a voice to make any maiden swoon. Plucking the strings of his harp, he strummed the cords of the hearts of many young girls to hopeless misery. Shadow, he called María. He cared for her as his cousin, but nothing more. Surely she had not allowed herself to hope for his love?

The years fell away, and Beatriz remembered the first time she too had loved without hope. She had been only thirteen when she awoke from a dream of bewildering desire, a dream when she had been naked with the boy, alone in a white bed, their bodies, a confusion of limbs, writhing together in a mysterious, rhythmical dance, coursing her with sweetness as thick as honey, and awaking her to guilt. Terrible, terrible guilt, trepidation and shame. Her heart beating fast, she had swung out of bed and fallen to her knees to pray.

Beatriz gazed at Catalina and María. The girls were almost the same age when desire first fired her heart and body. María's eyes stayed locked on the prince. Beatriz gazed at her with pity. Twelve was very young for María to face Prince Juan embodied a dream of love and only that. Beatriz had no doubt that, for the girl, it would stay an illusion, a wisp, a daydream, a vapour dissipating like a morning frost in the harshness of cold reality. It is well to dream of love, above all at only twelve, but the grail of one's heart often proves something else entirely. Her sweet, green passion for the prince was likely but the forerunner of the love one day to come, the love to flourish like a pomegranate tree, bearing fruit both bitter and sweet.

Threading her arm through her friend's, Catalina sang softly the words from a song about Montserrat:

Resplendent star on the mountain.
Like a sunbeam miraculously glowing,
All joyous people
Come together
Rich and poor
Young and old
Climb the mountain
To see with their own eyes
And return from it
Filled with grace.

Beatriz went back to fetch the bucket she had left earlier at the entrance of the alcázar. Holding the rope of the bucket in one hand, she clutched her dress with the other to keep it from the snow. Already the sodden bottoms of her gown and mantle showed the ill effects of the winter day. A ruby and sapphire brooch, pinning together her mantle, sparkled in a haze of silver light. A gust of strong wind flapped open her cloak, revealing the gown of rich brocade with a pattern of red thread. About to enter the alcázar, Beatriz saw just inside the building a knot of servants waiting for Catalina's return. They grumbled, pounding their hands and feet for warmth.

"Princess! Doña María!" Beatriz called. "Come quickly. If you're not careful, you'll find yourselves with colds on the morrow."

Catalina dimpled with amusement. María laughed, stamping her feet in her own dance against the cold. "What about you, Latina? You're more wet than us!"

Beatriz glanced at her dragging skirts, yanking them up from the steps and holding them away from her honey-brown leather boots.

"By all the good Saints, you're right." She shrugged her shoulders, shaking off flakes of snow. María glanced at the packed snow in her bucket, and then back at Beatriz. Dimpling again with quiet laughter, Catalina picked up her skirts and padded back inside. Beatriz and María followed her. Servants rushed all around, relieving them of their mantles. Beatriz passed the bucket to one of the women, murmuring low her instructions. The servant nodded, hurrying towards the private chambers, while other servants sped off with their damp mantles, disappearing in the opposite direction. María gazed at Catalina. Their eyes mirrored unbridled curiosity.

Without need to hasten elsewhere, Beatriz took the girls to the hall's fire. There, the three of them warmed their icy hands back to life. Catalina lowered herself onto a stool. She pulled up her thick layers of clothes to her ankles, directing her feet to the fire's heat. María seated herself beside her. María acted as her friend's body servant. She undid the laces of Catalina's wet boots, pulling them off with a plop. Twisting one side to the other, Beatriz studied her wet hem.

"Si, I wear one of my best gowns today, when we go out to stand in the snow." She sighed. "The queen gifted this to me only two months ago. I don't think she'd approve my lack of care." She held the hem of the wet brocade out to the warmth of the fire. The red threads of its drenched embroidery seemed rivulets of blood.

The firelight flickered on her hands and the heat began to make her feel drowsy. Yawning, she turned back to the girls. "To be truthful, I am glad we went out to watch the prince make his departure. It offered us a pleasant escape for a time and gave me the chance to gather what I need to test an idea."

María glanced askance at Catalina. "And what idea was this, Latina?"

"Si." Catalina laughed. "Pray, tell us the reason for the bucket of snow."

Beatriz pushed aside the two separate pieces of the brocade skirt from her legs and sighed, plucking at the layers of clothes underneath. "Saint Michael's sword – even my stockings are wet. I must go and change." She smiled at the girls. "Why don't you both come with me to my chambers and see what I do with my bucket of snow? Hopefully the snow hasn't all melted."

The girls exchanged a look and let loose a short ripple of laughter. Catalina broke into a wide, unrestrained smile. With Beatriz and her friend María, Catalina slackened the knots tied upon her by her position as a royal daughter. "Si, why not? It will give us both something to do while we wait for my brother's return."

Yanking off her own boots, Beatriz grabbed their slippers by the fire. With foresight, she had left them there to warm before venturing out on the cold morn.

Beatriz led the two girls to her chamber – conveniently not far from the queen's rooms. Valuing her opinion, morning and night, Queen Isabel would often call on her to speak over matters of state. The passing of years had made her one of the queen's most trusted advisors, rivalled only by the cardinal, the queen's confessor.

A roaring fire and half dozen or so lit candles gave the large, spacious room as much light as could be expected on a winter's day. The court had settled at this alcázar for all of winter – long enough for Beatriz to set up the room to her liking. A wide wooden screen, so dark it appeared black in the dim light of the far end of the room, was placed near a wall. A large bed, a table, a stacked bookshelf at one end, Francisco's second best vihuela, two stools set by the fireplace and a high-backed chair by the long table furnished the room. In the huge fireplace, over a thick bed of red-hot embers, a large steaming pot simmered.

Beatriz picked up the bucket of snow left at the side of the door and smiled, seeing the snow still packed tight and little melted. "María, please bring me my box from the table."

Beatriz pointed to the long, wooden box lying across the end of the table, its wood blended so well with the dark wood beneath it. María padded over to the table and picked the box up, bringing it to her. A sweet, musky fragrance from the box brought to Beatriz's mind hot summer days.

Beatriz pulled the cauldron away from the fire's flame on its hook. Simmering water lapped halfway up an empty metal bowl. She held out her open hands to María. "Pray give me the box." Releasing its sliding panel, Beatriz showed to the girls the rose petals filling the box almost to its brim.

"From my best roses this last summer," Beatriz said. She scattered rose petals in the simmering water, all around an empty inner bowl, and then picked up the cauldron's lid, placing it upside down on the pot. She gazed back at the two girls. "I thought this morning of another way to make rosewater. Now for my snow." Reaching for it, she scooped handfuls of snow until the concave of the lid became almost full, then swung the black cauldron back over the burning embers. "We wait now and see if this works."

Catalina peered at the snow filled lid. "Why the snow, Latina?"

Beatriz grinned. "Cause and effect." Taking a chair from the table, she half-lifted and half-dragged it closer to the fireplace. "I beg you, princess, please sit down here. With permission, María and I can make use of the stools. But I am in need of a change of clothes first. Once I do that, you both can ask me whatever questions you want."

Beatriz slipped behind the screen, tossing her wet garments over its top and ensuring the brocade gown hung straight. She chose a deep moss green velvet habito from her clothes chest and re-plaited her hair so it fell over her shoulder before covering it with a transparent toca. She strode back to the princess and María, and sat on the stool, holding her hands out to the fire.

"I must ask my servants to find a brazier for this room. Jesu', the day's so cold!"

Beatriz winced at her distorted reflection on the side of the cauldron. She looked pale and weary, her large eyes with dark rings beneath them. María must have caught her thought. The girl shook her finger at her, just as she did with the girls, on the rare occasion when she scolded them. "To get yourself in such a state, my good doña! I'm surprised at you! Did not the ancients say a healthy mind in a healthy body? Wasn't it enough to go outside to watch Prince Juan make his departure? Did you have to get a bucket of snow too?"

Beatriz laughed, turning aside to Catalina. "See, princess, my time spent with María is not wasted. Already she sounds like a healer, although a trifle disrespectful to her elder, and not forgetting the one who teaches her too."

Catalina grinned. "Blame the disrespect on me. I tell María to always speak her mind in private, but she has right to be concerned. You look none too well..."

Beatriz shrugged before swinging the cauldron under her gaze. The snow mostly by now melted, she scooped the water back into her bucket and grabbed a thick towel from the floor. When her hand hit the lid to raise it, the sudden movement caused the heavy lid to clang upon the floor. A few droplets of water left over from the snow dropped like rain on the floor. Liquid filled the metal bowl almost to the brim. Beatriz smacked her lips. "Rosewater, my young scholars. When the pot cools, I'll pour the water into flasks."

"And the snow? You haven't told us about the snow?" Catalina asked.

Beatriz turned to María. "Can you give the princess an answer, child?"

María blinked, shaking her head with such vigour her roundlet became lopsided.

Beatriz pursed her lips. "María, if you thought long about it, you'd know the reason."

Catalina giggled, fanning short fingers at her hips. Firelight twinkled the large ruby in her new thumb ring, a recent gift from the English king, given in the name of his son. "I don't think María wishes to think about anything today. Surely you know cold days turn her into a cat wanting only a warm spot near the fire? You had better just tell us."

Beatriz stretched out her hands again to the fire's heat. The cold of the day seemed to be seeping into her very bones. "A simple thing really, and most likely thought of before today," She shrugged again and faced the girls. "Perchance I may have read or heard of this already, but I cannot recall it. Perchance from Aristotle..." She grinned. "Putting snow on the inverted lid caused condensation to form inside the pot and then rained rosewater in the waiting pot."

All at once, Beatriz felt dizzy and ill. She put one hand on the swell of her belly, and the other over her mouth. "Pray, excuse me –" She hurried behind the screen, grabbed her chamber pot and vomited. Dry retching, she heard the girls speaking.

"She must be with child," María said. Beatriz retched again, overlaying it with a few choice words she had learnt from Francisco.

"With child?" Catalina asked. "Isn't she too old?"

Still dizzy and retching, Beatriz now fought back the urge to laugh.

"No, not too old," María said. "But didn't she tell us that she did not believe her marriage would see the blessing of children?"

Someone clapped, and the princess spoke. "'Tis like the story of Saint Elizabeth. How pleased she must be."

Still nauseous, Beatriz returned to the girls and sat on the stool again, avoiding the eyes of her students. An uneasy silence fell.

Catalina cleared her throat. "Does Don Francisco Ramirez know?"

Beatriz licked her dry lips. Francisco still served the queen, spending long weeks away from court fighting against the Moors who still resisted the queen's yoke. "No – he doesn't know. Can I beg you both to say nothing? To no one, please."

Catalina gazed aside at her. "Not even my mother?"

Beatriz reached for Catalina's hand, clasping it in both of hers. "Especially not to her, my princess." She licked her dry lips again. "I do not want to be the cause of giving the queen needless worry. She doesn't know, and I don't want her to. Not yet."

María blinked, and turned a look of bewilderment on Beatriz. "But she'll know sooner or later, si?"

Keeping hold of Catalina's hand, she now reached for María's "You must both promise not to say a word of this to the queen. I cannot tell you how important that is to me."

"But the queen will know –" María interjected.

Beatriz shook her head. "By all the saints in Heaven, not for a long while if I can help it," she muttered, as if vowing to God Himself. She gazed first at Catalina and then at María, feeling like a trapped animal, desperate for escape.

"Princess. Doña María, if the queen knew..." She swallowed hard, lifting her chin. "I am not certain if the queen would want me to continue as your tutor if she knew I'm with child." She pressed her fingers into her temples. "Pray help me hide it from the world a little longer." Beatriz glanced at them, her tears blurring her sight. "Have I your promise not to say a word to the queen, not to anyone? Let me have more time to work out how to convince the queen that I can stay at court and teach, without her thinking she needs to send me away from here to be a wife and mother."

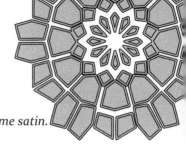

22

Have patience and the mulberry leaf will become satin.

~ Castilian proverb

Later that day, Beatriz made out the first hazy glimpse of the returning party as they crested a near hill. She pointed them out to Catalina. "Look! The princess rides between the king and prince."

Shielding her eyes, Catalina leaned on the balcony. "Is she pretty?"

Beatriz laughed, lounging beside her. "How can I tell? At this distance she could be Helen of Troy brought back to life. All I can tell you now is the honour bestowed on her by the king – she rides beside him – and that the princess rides like a true horsewoman."

Catalina bent forward for a better view. "I see them now."

The royal party close now, the girl between the prince and the king twisted in her saddle-chair, turning in the prince's direction. The gloaming light illumined her strawberry blonde hair and profiled her pert, turned-up nose. Prince Juan twisted in his saddle too. It seemed their movement towards each other strummed the notes of a song, echoing bird songs in spring. Beatriz grinned. "I think the prince and princess already like each other very much."

At her table in the library, Beatriz pretended to read a book. María and Catalina, sitting close together in the nearby window-seat, had clearly forgotten her presence – or perhaps they did not care if she heard them or not.

María read out loud: "Without permitting anyone else to lay a hand on him, the lady herself washed Salabaetto all over with soap scented with musk and cloves. She then had herself washed and rubbed down by the slaves. This done, the slaves brought two fine and very white sheets, so scented with roses that they seemed like roses; the slaves wrapped Salabaetto in one and the lady in the other and then carried them both on their shoulders to the bed."

Catalina leaned back, glancing out at the bright morning. Threads of bird songs looped an embroidery of sound, thick, thin, bold and sweet. The girl closed the book on her lap, chewing at her bottom lip. Beatriz knew that look – the child brimmed with questions she wanted answered. Cupping her cheek with a hand, she sighed. "Do you think our wedding nights will be like that?" María shifted restlessly, and the girls remained silent for a time.

Beatriz suspected their choice of reading and conversation was sparked by recent events at court. From their first meeting, when Margot's humorous dismay at the court musicians' overloud welcome had brought the prince to laughter, she gifted to Prince Juan happiness. Those who loved Juan thanked her for it. Si – the marriage of Prince Juan and Princess Margot was a great success. Since their wedding, Prince Juan gazed at his bride as if unable, si, unwilling, to draw his eyes away. They found every excuse to touch and caress the other, disappearing for hours into their private chambers at every possible opportunity.

Sitting crossed-legged, María moved deeper into the window-seat. "'Tis a long time before that day comes, for both you and me."

Catalina sighed, her words rushing out as if in pain. "Amiga, you know the English demand Mother stop delaying and send me to their country now?" Her eyes glowed with unshed tears.

María reached out and clasped her hand. "Si, but the queen plays them for more time. Why should this be any different than what happened with Isabel and Juana? The queen will not let you leave until you are at least fifteen."

Beatriz winced at Catalina's bitter laugh. "Father says differently. He's more than willing to see me go."

María released Catalina's hands. She gathered herself up in the corner of the window-seat, hugging her legs.

Beatriz listened to the birds twittering and chirping outside. *How happy and carefree they sounded.* How many times in her life had their song of joy to morning's glory lifted her heart and filled it with hope? What would she do if she were forced into a life of exile? She heaved a long breath and gazed at the girls. Should she remind them that Christ cared for the least of his creatures?

María settled her shoulders against the stone. "Has your mother allowed any of her hijas to leave her side before she knew them ready to do so?"

Rubbing her temple, Catalina averted her face to the shadows. "The day comes."

Beatriz blinked away sudden tears, relieved to see María lean towards Catalina and take her hand. "I say again the day is still a long way from today. Listen to the whistles of the larks, my princess, and please, like them, welcome the spring morn. Joy is here for the taking, amiga. Worrying about what will befall us in the future won't change it. Whatever will be will be. And my princess, whatever the future might bring, rose petals will adorn your wedding sheets." María giggled. "But not until your mother allows."

Catalina held María's hand in both of hers. "You will be there – you will come with me?"

"Do you doubt it?"

Catalina shrugged, a slight smile tugging at her lips. "I don't doubt it. But tell me true, is it what you want, really want?"

As if she made a vow, María placed her hand over their linked hands. "My life is with you. Don't you know that yet?"

"You haven't answered me. Is it what you want, María? You don't need to leave Castilla..."

María leaned towards her and spoke the words of Ruth. "Whithersoever thou shalt go, I will go: and where thou shalt dwell, I also will dwell. Thy people shall be my people, and thy God my God. The land that shall receive thee dying, in the same will I die." María rubbed at her eyes. "It is as simple as that. If you go, I go too. I cannot lose my sister. Not now, not ever."

The light from the window glittered on the tears on Catalina's thick eyelashes. "If you come to England, you'll likely marry an Englishman. Have you thought of this?"

María rolled her eyes. "An Englishman," she giggled. "I have thought of this. Can you promise me something?"

"You know if I can, I will."

"Promise me that I can choose my own husband. Grandee or English lord, I would like to think I could love him."

Catalina rested her head on her friend's shoulder and clasped her hand. "I promise, my sister. That's the least I can do for one who is willing to be my fellow exile."

Beatriz stared down at her book, and the page blurred. Blinking away her own tears she felt so helpless. All she had was books to help ready her students to leave their home, forever.

My love,

We have a son. He was born three days ago – a healthy, beautiful boy. The wet-nurse cannot believe how lusty he is – I tell her he takes after his father. Josefa looks after us very well. I am so blessed to have her as my friend. That she has agreed to take care of our boy when I return to court – I cannot say how grateful I am.

The queen is happy about this arrangement too. I cannot believe how I feared to tell her of my pregnancy. I thought it would be the end of my position at court. Strangely, like you, my love, she wants to support and help me continue to walk this road that is so different to so many women. Our baby is a miracle. He deserves a woman who will devote herself to him with full joy, not a mother who desires to devote her days to study and teaching. I own it a selfish devotion – but here at court and the university I can give more to the world than to a home. I am what I am, and it is too late to change that. You say you do not wish me to change. For that, I love you.

Every day I thank God for you, Francisco. And now there is another Francisco. Josefa will raise him well. She has even promised to do the same if we have more children. I cannot believe my good fortune.

When I left the court three weeks ago, Queen Isabel was dreading farewelling her eldest daughter, Isabel. As you know, my love, the queen blocked Isabel's new Portugal marriage for years. She played a hard game of chess against the king in his efforts to pressure her into agreeing to their eldest daughter resuming her position as a pawn to be moved for the sake of power. But the passing of five years has now shut the final door on both mother and daughter, leaving them no more excuses of avoidance

Once more Isabel retreated to the shell she had built around herself after her husband's death, ignoring the preparations for her wedding. She even cut her hair short again, as if proclaiming her unwillingness to marry, and her desire to take the veil of a religious order. Soon the season turned and time neared for Isabel to leave her mother's court for her new life in Portugal. The queen became increasingly desperate to see Isabel show some sign of happiness before her wedding.

"My hija, Manuel has done as you asked," Queen Isabel said. "He has commanded the Jews to convert or leave his kingdom. He has given them three months to do so."

Without expression, Isabel lifted her eyes from the altar cloth she was embroidering, glancing at her mother. Despite her extreme slenderness, her beauty at twenty-five seemed far greater than Beatriz's memory of her at twenty. Isabel's pale, thin face possessed the delicacy of a sorrowing angel. The young woman looked back at the embroidery. "Then in three months I wed."

A frown deeply furrowed between the queen's eyebrows. She watched her daughter add the final threads to a red cross. "You go to be queen, Isabel."

Isabel's head cast a shadow over her embroidery, dimming the colours of her intricate work. She sewed on for a few moments in silence.

"Si, Mamá, Manuel's queen." She pulled too hard at the red thread, puckering the material. Her fingers stilled over the ruined cross. "Do not fear, my mother and queen, I know my duty."

Queen Isabel winced. Catalina swung from the window-seat, as if to go to her mother. Beatriz grabbed her arm, shaking her head in warning. At Catalina's cross look, Beatriz stepped into the shadows beside her, whispering close to her ear, "This is between your mother and your sister."

Catalina drooped back onto the cushions, her eyes fixed on her mother and sister. The queen reached out to her oldest daughter, but Isabel, her head lowered, ignored her mother. Spoiling her embroidery even more, she jabbed and jabbed at the cross, ignoring her mother's trembling hand. Beatriz almost wept seeing Queen Isabel's fallen face. For a long moment, the queen's mouth seemed to struggle for firmness before she turned away from her daughter.

Beatriz recalled Josefa, María's mother, saying to her, "Princess Isabel is the daughter most precious to the queen, perchance because after her birth there was no other living child born to the king and queen for nearly eight years. By the time of the prince's birth, our queen more than simply doted on Isabel. Isabel became the glory of her mother's life. Whilst Juan is his mother's angel, his older sister reigns in her mother's heart like the Queen of Heaven."

But Queen Isabel was first a queen. Like Abraham sacrificing Isaac, she sacrificed Isabel's desires for what she believed right for her kingdom.

Summoned by the queen to her private chamber, Beatriz slipped into the shadows of the embrasure. Not far away two physicians knelt before the king and queen. "We advise a time of separation," one said.

Prince Juan, sitting on a large cushion at his parents' feet, jerked up to balance on one knee. His eyes fired with anger. The king rested a hand his son's shoulder, meeting his son's eyes, shaking his head. His hands clenched at his hips, the prince settled back onto the cushions.

"Let them be," the king laughed. "They are young. 'Tis only right the passion waxes strong between them. I remember too well how it was when I first wed you, wife."

Beatriz raised a hand, touching her hot cheek, feeling ill when she saw Queen Isabel's face. Her eyes glowed with love meant only for one man. For a moment, the ghost of a young woman settled upon her. The ghost still lingered when she beckoned Beatriz. "Good friend, what is your opinion? Are the physicians right to ask this?"

Beatriz gazed at the cowering physicians, and then at Prince Juan. There was no trace of the boy he once was, only a furious young man. She sighed, thinking of the vein of melancholy running deep in this family, and the link between body and mind. "My queen, your son loves his wife. For what my opinion is worth, I say a separation could cause him great unhappiness, and may do more harm than good."

The queen nodded decisively, turning back to the physicians. "What God joined together let no man rip asunder. There will be no more talk of separation. You're dismissed."

Fidgeting as if sitting upon sharp rocks rather than soft cushions, Prince Juan scowled, watching the men leave the room. Utterly mother now, the queen bent low to her son. "Did we do right, my Juan?"

"Mother, those men are fools!" The prince's blue eyes flashed in his pale face.

She gripped his shoulder. "'Tis true what they say. You've lost flesh since your wedding..."

The prince bounded up to his full height. "Mother! There's nothing wrong! The physicians have brought you worry every day of my life. I am fed milksops and forced to stay abed at the least sign of illness. I am a man, Mother. Pray, as God intended, let me act the man."

The king grinned with pride. "Listen to our son. Can we doubt this marriage is good for him? Juan is right. 'Tis time for our son to live his own life. How else will he learn to be king?"

The queen's mouth tightened. When she gazed down on her son, she seemed, to Beatriz, mouthing a silent prayer.

The three expected months to Isabel's wedding stretched to four. Time enough for all to grow to love the Archduchess Margot. That she loved the prince was apparent to everyone. She wanted to please him in every way. Margot was a good wife, a good daughter, a good sister, embracing Prince Juan's family as her own.

Outside the library, Beatriz listened to Margot's sweet, melodious voice and the soft notes from a vihuela:

> *"The time is troubled, but the time will clear;*
> *After rain fair weather is awaited:*
> *After strife and cruel contention*
> *Peace will arrive, misfortune cease to be,"*

sang the prince's wife.

Both vihuela and voice dwindled off when Beatriz entered the room, Margot and Juan sat with Catalina and María, the prince holding his vihuela as if he was about to play again.

"Come," Catalina said, smiling in welcome. "Join us." Gesturing to the space beside her on the bench, she turned to the princess. "Latina writes poetry too."

Bobbing a curtsey to the three of them, Beatriz laughed. "I don't think my poor verses compare with Princess. I've heard enough to recognise the better poet."

Margot smiled impishly, and her blue eyes twinkled. "You flatter me. But don't you agree any poetry sounds good when set to music?" She took her husband's arm and looked up at him. "This poem is still far from finished. I only have to scribble out a few words and my lord husband must make it a song."

The prince kissed her cheek and then, more lingeringly, her mouth. "And why not? Finished or not, your words are music to my ears."

Bestowing another kiss on him, Margot threaded her arm through his. "My sweet lord, you distract me from my task." Holding his face between her hands, the girl kissed him again. Her body seemed to melt into him. She sighed, and playfully pushed him away. "I must not forget your mother sent me here for a purpose. My sister Catalina must become fluent in French, and who better to teach her than I, once called Queen of France?"

The prince scowled. "Do you regret the loss of that title?"

Nestling into him again, Margot pealed with laughter. "You're jealous? How can I regret it when I am your queen, my King of Granada?" She took his face between her hands and showered it with kisses. "I love you, Juan. Love you, love you, love you." Her arms winding around his neck, she kissed his mouth. Prince Juan enclosed her in his arms and kissed her back, deep and long.

Catalina picked up a letter on the table. Ignoring her brother and sister-in-law, now whispering love words to one another, she stared at the parchment. "Elizabeth of England advises I come to England speaking flawless French. 'Tis the second most spoken language at their court. My mother asked my good sister to help me."

Beatriz looked at the embrace-locked two young lovers and laughed. "If the princess really wants to teach you, I think she best leave your brother elsewhere."

But as the months sped by, Margot rarely taught Catalina her French without the presence of Prince Juan. Despite her constant love games with her husband, she still managed to tutor Catalina, helping her improve her French. By the end of four months, Catalina's grasp of the language was one the English would find difficult to fault.

Beatriz was pleased to see this time also teaching María to lose her jealousy of Margot. The girl's sweetness, her impish sense of humour, her intelligence that sparred and grew equally with the prince's, helped the child let go of her dreams – whatever those dreams may have been – but she seemed to let go of childhood too. The girl appeared to have learned one of life's lessons: to accept with good grace what she could not change. To be happy that others could be truly happy – even when their happiness was not hers.

At Alcántara, close to the Portugal border, the queen and her court celebrated Isabel's wedding to the Portuguese king. Just a year older than his wife, King Manuel treated Isabel tenderly, gazing at her like one love-struck. The queen told Beatriz that the king had fallen in love with Isabel when he met her during her marriage to his cousin. After Alfonso's death, he never gave up hope that she would agree to marry him. His unhidden love gave the queen hope that Isabel might yet find again happiness as a wife.

> *My dear one,*
>
> *Princess Isabel will soon be Queen of Portugal. Her final days with her mother come hard on the heels of another farewell, one causing Queen Isabel less pain, if not less worry. Prince Juan and his now pregnant wife have been cut loose from his mother's court to set up their own in the city I call home: Salamanca. If only the desire for greater independence was the only reason for this decision. Alas, Prince Juan has been once more struck down by a serious malady. Whilst he is mercifully recovered from his illness, the queen wishes him in the care of his former tutor. Diego de Deza is a man both trusted by the queen and her son, a man who Prince Juan can never mislead about when he sickens and knows how to deal with the prince in such times.*
>
> *Thus, on the slow, long journey to Alcántara, the royal courts detoured to Salamanca and we*

remained there for two weeks. The queen and king were greeted with joy, the citizens of Salamanca happy and proud they chose their city for Prince Juan's court. The city's celebrations showed no sign of abating when the king and queen and their courts farewelled Prince Juan and his wife...

God have mercy, the stop of one heartbeat turns joy into sorrow in a blink of an eye. That day Queen Isabel, the unending celebrations for her daughter's wedding proving too much for her failing health, dozed in bed. As was often her custom when the queen sickened, Beatriz brought Catalina and María to the queen's chamber after their morning of study, and they took turns reading to Queen Isabel, or playing chess or sewing together. Beatriz was not certain if the queen really desired their company, but Catalina always found a way to comfort her mother.

Whilst the queen slept on this day, Beatriz read her book and Catalina and María embroidered, talking softly to one another. Their conversation stopped when the king entered the chamber, hurrying to Queen Isabel's side, oddly followed by Cisneros, the queen's confessor, and Guadalupe, her most favoured physician.

"Isabel."

The queen awoke, starting at her husband's voice. Catalina and María gazed at one another. Beatriz could see they, like her, wondered what was afoot.

Queen Isabel half rose from her pillows. She rubbed her eyes, straightening with difficulty. Her eyes widening at sight of her confessor, she turned to her husband. "What is it?"

The king almost spat the hateful words: "A messenger's come from our son's wife... Margot... She says Juan's dying!"

Catalina dropped her sewing onto the floor. Beatriz stared at it, mocked by the almost finished summer's garden, the silks chosen for their bright beauty to celebrate abundant life. Beatriz picked it up, pricking her finger on an unseen needle. The sharp, sudden pain brought tears to her eyes – or was it from hearing the king's words? They pierced her heart far more than a simple needle.

"Ferdinand," Queen Isabel cleared her throat, "there's some mistake."

The king shook his head, his shoulders slumping in defeat. Sitting on the edge of her bed he gazed at his wife. "The messenger also brought word from Juan's physician. He says the same."

Queen Isabel opened and shut her mouth. For a moment she seemed deprived of all speech. "How can this be so, Ferdinand?" she asked at last. "Juan was well when we left him."

King Ferdinand laid his broad hand over his wife's. Like a claw of an old woman, the queen's hand curled and trembled beneath his. The king sighed, took his hand away, rubbing at the top of his leg hose with the heel of his palm. "For not long after, my Isabel. Our son refused to listen to the entreaties of his physician. He begged Juan not to further exhaust himself by following day revels with night-long banquets. Knowing our son, Juan probably didn't want to disappoint both the city and his wife, but it proved too much for him. The physician says he has done everything, but Juan's fever gets no better. Our son is too weak to fight."

The queen moaned. Her hands flailed out, her body writhing with no true purpose. She sounded and looked mad.

"Help me up – I must go to him." She attempted to right herself, pain distorting her face. Shutting her mouth and eyes, she slipped back upon the pillows and her moan became one of anguish. Beads of sweat ran down her forehead, over her closed eyes, dripping over the straight, thin line of mouth and slackening chin.

On the other side of her huge bed, the physician picked up her hand, checking her pulse. With considered gentleness, he placed her hand back on the bed and shook his head at the king. He gazed back at the queen with grave worry. "Your Highness, you're far too ill for travel. Going to the prince would only place your life in great jeopardy. I cannot in good conscience allow it."

From the shadows, Cardinal Cisneros stepped forward. He

stood by the physician's side. "My queen, think what's right for your kingdom."

Queen Isabel's agonised eyes flew open at the priest's words. Anger sparked a fiery renewal of her familiar majesty.

"Always I think what's right for my kingdom. That and only that has been my first concern from the time I first became queen." Raising her hand, she brushed tears from her eyes. "Sweet Jesús, I am a mother, too." The queen glared at her physician. "And pray tell me, little man, what gives you the right to say what I can or cannot do?"

The king dismissed the recoiling physician. He reached for the queen's hand. "Hearing his beloved mother is at her death door because she hurried to his side will not aid our son. I beg you, listen to reason and heed what I say. You're too ill to leave here, but I will go and act for us both in this, just as we have done for one another in the past. I can reach our son's side with greater speed if you remain here. With my best riders I make this vow to you. I will reach our son in less than a day."

Queen Isabel eyed her husband. As if passing all her remaining strength to him, she wilted against her pillows, her trembling hand spreading over the lower half of her face before dropping it to the bed's coverlet. The queen lifted her chin again, inhaling a ragged breath. "God speed, husband. God speed. Tell my son I love him. Tell him I pray only for good news of his recovery." She averted her face, tears trickling from her closed eyes. "Pray God strengthen me..." She spoke in a whisper, her quiet words pulsating in the room's uneasy, unearthly silence. "For I do not think I could withstand the loss of our boy. God – please God, if you love me, do not take him from me... do not take Juan, do not take my angel."

Dear Francisco,
I do not even want to put this down on paper. If I do
– I deny all hope of rumour, and rather confront
truth: word from Salamanca tells us that Prince Juan

is dying. Receiving the message from his son's physicians, King Ferdinand rode to the city that very day. We hear he rode all through the night and into the next day. The court waits, tottering on a dagger's point, for news.

One day. Two days. Three. Four. Five. Six. The long days drag from waking to sleeping – if any of us are fortunate to find sleep. All close to the queen live in hope of a messenger from Salamanca, living in fear of that message. When the messenger comes, the court hears the prince is better, and then worse, then better, but none tells the queen what we all pray to hear: that Prince Juan overcomes his illness and is well again.

It is now two agonising weeks since the king left for Salamanca. Two weeks of sorrow and helplessness. The queen is distraught. Princess Isabel, now the Queen of Portugal, walked like a sleep walker into her new marriage. Joyless, she wedded the King of Portugal loving life not at all, resigned to fulfil her duty. But I think only with her body – the queen's eldest daughter turns her gaze so much to the Kingdom of Heaven she cuts herself adrift from the mortal world.

Queen Isabel masked a brave face for her daughter's sake. She left her sickbed, calling upon all her powers of persuasion, convincing Isabel the right course of action meant she must go with her new husband as planned and wait in Portugal for news of her brother. Farewelled by the queen's court one more time in her life, Isabel departed yesterday for her husband's kingdom, not knowing whether her beloved brother would live or die. Her eldest daughter gone, Queen Isabel lives now for her husband's messages.

*My little infanta no longer enjoys her daily
lessons. All she wants is the comfort she finds in the
chapel when she prays with her mother...*

For days, the entirety of Beatriz's life seemed that of dark,
shuttered rooms and the strong smell of melting beeswax in the
chapel. But closed shutters did not shut out the sounds of the day.
Sunlight peeped into the chamber through every crack. Pulsing air
caused the lit candles to wisp with smoke. The crisp smell of
autumn awoke in Beatriz the desire to come away from the dark
oppressive air that lingered everywhere. One day Catalina refused
to consider doing anything other than pray. Unable to stay indoors
for one more moment, Beatriz asked for release and took herself
into one of the most beautiful courtyards of Alcántara. Once there
she sat by the pool, staring into the water, feeling as if swept into a
maelstrom. A sudden breeze blew loose strands of hair into her
eyes, forcing her to push it away.

An uncertain pale face wavered in the pool, breaking apart when
another gust of wind blew across the rippling surface. Beatriz
turned to see María beside her. No longer a child but still far from
womanhood, María looked more and more like her beautiful
mother. Beatriz sighed. And when time fulfilled that promise?
What then? Passing time would only steal beauty away again. Time
was as indefinable as the water passing through her trailing fingers.
Unable yet to trust her voice, Beatriz brushed away her tears.
Sorrow seemed to drub with every heartbeat – a painful cadence
echoing loudly in her ears.

A dragonfly flashed its shimmering, rainbow wings over the
silver, now still water. In the tree growing in the corner of the
garden, a bird trilled a short burst of song. Another bird answered,
and then another, until the air throbbed with birdsong. Comfort
settled upon her like the sun's mantle of autumn warmth. Her
heart swelled feeling, somehow, that this comfort came from the
prince.

Beatriz saw him in her mind's eye – lean and straight, fair and handsome, smiling his teasing and quirky smile at his sisters and María, who he always treated as another sister. She remembered the first time she had ever seen him playing upon his harp in his mother's chamber. Barely a youth he was already a skilled harpist. Whenever he plucked the strings of his harp or vihuela – whether as a boy, a youth or a man – he wove his passion for music into the melodies he played, melodies he composed from his loving, noble heart. They were memories that would stay with her forever. Not even death possessed the power to rob them from her.

Beatriz reached for María, putting her arm around her shoulders. A breeze teased the pool, rippling it alive and flecked with silver stars. The dragonfly winged close to them. The beauty of the moment left her breathless, aware of the sweetness of life. Surely nothing once loved is ever truly lost? Love, even if as brief in life as the ethereal, darting dance of a dragonfly flying across water, outlived time itself. Love held the pomegranate seeds of immortality.

Beatriz glanced at María, seeing her gaze down at her reflection.

"Avoid the mistake of Narcissus, child," Beatriz said automatically, then scolded herself for stupidity. María wasn't being vain, just contemplative, like she had been just seconds before. She wasn't surprised when she heard María's reply.

"I wasn't admiring myself, Latina. The whole world drifted away to nothingness. I felt at peace, like I was in a dream, looking down at my face in the pool."

Suddenly cold, Beatriz drew her mantle around her.

"What's wrong?" María whispered, her eyes frightened.

"Your words remind me of an old belief of the long ago Greeks." Beatriz took María's hand onto her lap, saying no more. Their faces wavered together in the water, sparking with diamonds of light.

"What old belief, Teacher?" María directed her question at Beatriz's reflection.

Beatriz considered the girl, biting her bottom lip.

"Tell me," María begged.

Beatriz turned, her fear widening its jaws. Once again scolding herself for stupidity, Beatriz held María's hand tighter, and inhaled deeply. "The Greeks once believed to dream seeing your reflection in water omened your death."

María sputtered out laughter. "Fear not, teacher. I daydreamed of what might one day befall me, all my hopes for a marriage like my mother's. There was no dream, daydream or otherwise, of my reflected face upon the tranquil water. Pray, don't worry about me. God willing, I don't plan to die, but to live a long, long life."

"No one plans to die." Beatriz cleared her throat, not daring to look at María. She tugged at her girdle, thinking of the prince. "Speak never thus aloud, for perchance we tempt fate."

The low shadows of autumn lengthened. Beatriz shivered, the sunlight no longer warming her, but thin like Lady Lent. Downy clouds gathered above, blocking out the sun, dulling the pool to burnished steel. She trembled again, unable to stop the flood of memories. So many, many precious memories of the prince, glittering jewels strewn along a beach stretching back for years and years. Without Prince Juan the court would be a place dark and bereft. Already the threat of losing him buffeted them without mercy, tossing them like a ship floundering on storm-swept seas. If the prince died, it diminished them all.

"I prayed for the prince," María said, lifting shining eyes.

Beatriz sighed. "We all are."

"Do you think God will hear us?"

Beatriz reached again for María's hand, shutting her eyes. "He hears us." Helplessly, she shrugged. "But, always, there's a time to be born and a time to die. Whether the time has come for Prince Juan we don't yet know..."

Beatriz gazed back at the pool. The wind blew gently on its surface, and moved the clouds away from the sun. Light danced upon the water. Swaying backward and forth, the shadows of the surrounding trees lengthened as time moved forward. She closed her eyes, her skin tingling in the cool air. Death did not belong here, not in this garden, and surely not with Prince Juan. The happiness of so many depended on his life.

The garden seemed an Eden untouched by death – all that

Beatriz loved safe within. The prince's death would mantle them with cause for sorrow until the end of their days. Like blind bats, her twirling thoughts and prayers circled in her mind without mercy. Her head pounded when María asked, "Why didn't the queen listen to the physicians?"

Beatriz stared at María, feeling the colour drain from her face. "What do you mean?"

"The prince was not well."

Beatriz swallowed. "All close to him saw that. The queen also owned it in her heart."

María grabbed her arm and shook. "If we all knew, why was nothing done?"

Beatriz lowered her head, retying her girdle. "María, 'tis hard to explain –"

"I beg you, tell me. I am no longer a child."

Beatriz found it hard to look María's way. "We are often blind when it comes to those we love. We only see what we want to see."

Beatriz thought over the last five months. The prince and princess's passion for one another resulted in disapproving and worried mutterings from many, not just the queen's physicians.

María shook her arm again. "I have learnt enough from you, Teacher, to recognise illness when I see it. The prince was not just frail... his recent malady was not the cause of this but just a small part."

"Si." Beatriz put her hand on her aching temple. "There was a translucent sheen to his skin; his eyes glowed with constant fever. He had lost much weight since his wedding."

María stirred in anger. "I do not understand. You've told me to use my eyes and instincts, and act on it. Did not the prince's physicians care enough? Why did no one do anything until now, perchance when 'tis too late? I am but a maid and of no importance, but the months since his wedding... Every time I looked on him, I felt anxious, scared for him. Passion did not cause this."

Beatriz played for time by tightening her girdle. She sniffed.

"No, you are right, my bright young student. There was another fire eating away at the prince. He fevered, not enough to bed him, but enough to drain away his strength."

"Then why did no one do anything to stop it? Why did no one take good care of him? Bar for lots of mutterings in corners and the few physicians brave enough to speak to the queen, everyone kept a conspiracy of silence about him. And now look at what has happened."

Beatriz bent her head and rubbed at her wet eyes. "You have known the prince since he was but a boy. You can answer this question just as easily as I."

Tears falling down her face, María stared across the expanse of water. A steady eddy of wind blew a few stray autumn leaves into the clear pool. They drifted towards them, their colours, red, gold and almost purple, brought to brilliant life again by water and the gloaming. Beatriz rubbed her eyes again, her sight blurring. She took a deep breath, trying to keep in control. If she started to weep, the tears would never stop.

Juan's fire of life had blazed bright alongside the bright light of his wife. Whereas Margot's fire ate to its content from a healthy body and spirit, the prince's stalwart spirit alone fed his. Others at the court saw this better and clearer than his family. They all wanted to believe the same as him and, God have pity, allowed Juan's pretence of health, his desire to be worthy of the love of his wife and not prove a disappointment to her, to his family, to blind them all. Love, or perchance the great fear of losing what they love, often stopped them from seeing what they should see. "What God joined together let no man rip asunder," the queen had said months ago. But what no man rips apart, death finds a way to do.

Almost two weeks passed, the queen still under strict instructions to rest in her chamber. Along with the infantas and María de Salinas, Beatriz was one of the few who daily attended her. Beatriz and the girls were with the queen when the king entered her chamber, unannounced. Before dropping to a low curtsey, Beatriz saw his defeated face. Her heart fluttered to her throat and seemed to strangle her. Watching him approach his wife, Beatriz wanted to disappear, to close her ears. His red-rimmed eyes told her his news before he said one word.

"Juan?" Queen Isabel attempted to lift herself out of her chair, but fell back, seeing the despair, the sorrow newly carved upon her husband's face. She stared at him, her mouth moving silently. All his attention on his wife, he strode to the chair facing her and sat before taking hold of her trembling hands. His bottom lip jutted over the top one, a muscle in his chin jerking, tightening. Tears welled and overflowed down his cheeks. The king's hollow voice echoed grief and hopelessness. "Our son is dead."

Beside Beatriz, Catalina gasped as if knifed, and the infanta María let loose an awful cry. *The prince dead? Prince Juan dead? Their golden prince, dead?* Beatriz found Catalina in her arms, not knowing how it came to be, no longer able to make sense of anything. Time and life tangled into a knot, tightening around her heart. Hugging Catalina to her, she knew she was not the only one in shock. It felt like a dream – a horrible, pitiless dream. The infanta María, her skirts gathered before her, sped from her mother's chamber, leaving the door wide open. Her gasping, broken sobs and stumbling footsteps petered away. Time remained still, and strangely at rest.

Queen Isabel, her high cheekbones splotched with unhealthy colour, the rest of her skin chalk-white, snatched her hands away. Recoiling in her high back chair, she gripped its carved armrests as if holding onto life itself. "No, no! It cannot be! Your last message said Juan was better."

The king muffled a ragged sigh with his hand. Hooding his eyes, he leaned against the back of the chair. Grief and exhaustion left him grey. More tears fell down his cheeks. Beatriz had now lived at court for over a decade. This was the first moment in all that time when she saw the man emerge from the king, a vulnerable man unashamedly exposing naked, raw emotions. He leant towards the queen, clasping her hands again.

"My love, I am your slave all my days... mine own beloved, I beg for your forgiveness and understanding. When I sent that message, our son was already prepared for his tomb. He died in my arms, on the Feast of Saint Francis."

The queen's eyes bulged, not focusing on anything, tears running down her face. Standing, she gripped the arms of her chair. Slowly enunciating each word as if she dipped them in venom, the queen asked, "My son... he died days ago, and you did not send word to me?"

The king clasped her clenched hand and bowed his head. His tears pattered like heavy raindrops upon their linked hands. Swallowing, he licked his chapped lips. Eyes swimming with more tears, he gazed at his wife. "Beloved, such news should not come other than from one able to grieve with you. I commanded no one to speak to you of our son's death until we could console one another."

Her eyes breaking from his, Queen Isabel swayed, fighting for breath. She raised her chin, breathing through her nose as if forcing back half-born sobs. Sitting back on her chair she shook her head, as if wanting to clear it, speaking in a voice hoarse with grief. "How did he..." Her trembling hand framed her face. Once again she shook her head. "How did my angel die? Did Juan... did he suffer?"

The king averted his face from his wife, a rapid pulse twitching the eyelid of his weak eye. Anger flared a flush of normal colour to his grey face. "We must give thanks to God." The king spoke bitterly. "He suffered but a little – and died confessed of all his sins."

Queen Isabel leaned closer, gripping his hands. "What is it, Ferdinand?"

The king's full, sensual mouth disappeared into one straight, hard and vicious line. Fearful, Beatriz recognised this look so well from the past – the need for the king to lash out at whatever stood in his way. "Juan resigned himself to death." His teeth gnawing at one side of his mouth, the king shook his head. "By the time I arrived, he had lost all heart. Juan fought a little harder knowing I was there, but I could do nothing but watch our son die." He glared at his wife. "I begged him to live. I reminded him of his wife, of his unborn child, the two kingdoms he would one day rule, joined together to their full glory. I do not understand why he gave up his battle for life so easily. He had so much to live for. Except for a too often frail body, he was the best of us..."

The king wiped the side of his hand under his dripping nose. "I cannot help remembering how we rejoiced at his birth, thanking God for him. Or how much I rejoiced knowing the man he grew to be and the strong kingdoms we were to pass to him. His death makes no sense to me – no sense at all. There's no purpose in it other than to destroy all our hopes. It mocks at everything we have worked so hard to do. 'Tis God Himself who mocks us."

The queen lowered her head. "Ferdinand, don't." Swallowing, she licked her chapped mouth. "You speak through grief. 'Tis pointless to go down that road, my husband." She lifted desperate eyes. "God gave him to us, and He has now taken him back. My angel is with God, amongst God's own angels."

The queen crumbled, her fragile bridge of comfort collapsing. Taking her hands from her husband's, she wound her arms tight across her chest. Bending forward, she wept.

King Ferdinand groaned. Violently shifting in his chair, he clunked his head against its back, bone against wood. Awash with tears, his eyes flew open. The king half stumbled, half tossed himself, kneeling beside his wife, gathering her in his rock-hard, muscular arms, befitting a soldier-king.

Man and woman sobbed, rocking together, united by mutual anguish, unaware of anyone or anything. Her arm around Catalina, Beatriz led her from the queen's chamber. In the long hallways outside, shock and sorrow weighed down both their steps. Beatriz wanted to wake from this awful dream. But it was too real to be a dream. Everywhere she looked she saw and heard the mirror and echo of despair, of sorrow.

Beatriz slept in the princess's chamber that night, knowing María out of her depths to comfort the Catalina. They prayed for the prince, prayed for God to comfort Juan's grieving wife and parents. They prayed for themselves, for God to give them strength to bear this loss – a loss that seemed so insurmountable. Well into the night, the three of them wept together until, exhausted, they fell asleep.

Dagger-sharp grief pierced Beatriz's dreams and she awoke to her tears chilling upon neck and face. Set close to the bed, the tall, guttering candle showed she had slept only perchance one hour or two. She wiped away her tears with the sleeve of her chemise. Still tears fell and fell. *Do I breathe only to weep? Our golden prince dead. Juan, dead... dead... dead...*

Half-rolling onto her back, she stared into the darkness, the awful nothingness above suffocating and oppressing her. Silently she railed at fate and the injustice of life. Like the king she hated, Beatriz did not understand God's purpose. Catalina and María both restless but still sleeping, she swung from the bed and lit another candle to leave at the door before going outside.

The inner doors of Catalina's chamber opened into the walled courtyard, shared with a few, fortunate others on the women's side of the royal chambers. Beatriz pushed open the heavy door, stepping into the black velvet night, seeking its embrace and comfort.

All her life, nature lifted her moments of sadness. The sudden trill and thread of birdsong, rain soughing after the heat of a summer's day, the gold-spun gloaming cast upon a garden. Nature renewed her and strengthened her faith, for in all such moments she felt God Himself holding her in his embrace.

Beatriz had never before doubted or questioned God, only owning the truth of human fallibility. But tonight her despair was such she entered a black valley of doubt, doubt leaving her tottering at its crumbling edge. Blinded by grief and anguish, she desperately sought for light to show her the way to step away from the edge.

Barefoot, almost welcoming the cold piercing the soles of her feet, she trod carefully on the night-damp, mossed-covered stone steps to the thick carpet of grass edging the courtyard's garden. She found herself in another world – a grey world lit by moonlight that, even so, was beautiful.

The huge full moon painted the stones of the palace's walls, grey by day, to luminous white and delineated the grove of tall poplars as if brushed white by an artist's hand. She halted on the steps, the moonlight pooling over her its scorn. How dare she recognise and acknowledge beauty with Prince Juan dead, and his young body food for worms?

"Latina!" Barefooted too, Catalina approached her, her mantle's hood settled upon her shoulders. Upon it, her unbound hair curled in heavy ringlets before disappearing down her back. Hair and mantle billowing out in a gust of strong wind, she moved towards Beatriz. Suddenly the bright moonlight outlined her naked, child-like form beneath her white shift. Beatriz was suddenly aware of freezing feet, and shivered. The thinness of her own shift offered no protection from the night.

Reaching Beatriz, Catalina took hold of her hand. She tutted, wrapping her thick mantle around them. "Latina – out here alone, on a cold night like this! You should know better. We need no more illness." Letting go of her attempt of maturity, Catalina lay her head upon her breast. Beatriz felt her chemise become wet with the infanta's tears.

Beatriz tightened her hold. "You're not alone in your sorrow. We all loved your brother."

Moonbeams cast Catalina in blue light, turning her into a living, moving statue of marble. "Why did he have to die?"

Beatriz sighed. Of all the questions Catalina had asked her since she was five, this one was the hardest to answer. "Mi chiquitina, who is not neustra chiquitina any more, I wish I had the words to comfort you. But 'tis a hard lesson we learn, so many times – life gives to take away."

Catalina shifted as if in anger. "Then life is cruel," she sobbed.

Beatriz kissed the top of her head. "Well and good, my child, you learn that at twelve. I learnt it long before that, before I could barely speak. But there's another side to life giving comfort. Surely all of us are richer for having had the prince in our lives, even if it means bearing his loss."

Catalina wiped her cheek on Beatriz's chemise. "That's no comfort, not when I will grieve for him for the rest of my days."

Beatriz let out a ragged sob. "You're such a young maid. Time will dull this grief until it becomes as distant as the moon that shines down on us tonight." She sighed. "I cannot say the same for the queen. Joy has left her forever. I am so worried for your mother."

"Father is broken-hearted, too"

"Si. The king too." Beatriz threaded her arm through Catalina's, leading her back up the steps to the royal chambers. "But he has other sons, all bastards, si, but soon this knowledge will console him. Shortly he returns to the battlefield. Action – dealing out life or death – will make him put aside his grief. But your poor mother... She has lost her only son... a son who died lacking his mother's final kiss. She was not even there when they laid his body in its tomb. I think we will find all her mortal joy lies entombed at Salamanca. Come, let us leave the chill of this sad, sad night."

28

Seeing as God made you without peer
In goodness of heart and goodness of speech,
Nor is your equal anywhere to be found,
My love, my lady, I hereby tell you:
Had God desired to ordain it so,
You would have made a great king.

~ King Dinis of Portugal of his wife Isabel, d. 1325

Dear love,

Pray come soon. I need your strength – and your
arms around me. I do not know how to bear these
sad days. The loss of Prince Juan strikes us all deep,
the sorrow for his death like a strangling winding
cloth on all our spirits, the family I serve most of all.
I so yearn for your comfort, Francisco...

Juan's heart-broken wife returned to court very changed from the
gay, vibrant princess farewelled at Salamanca. She came not only
bearing her own heavy, sorrow but also the hopes of Castilla and
Aragon in her swelling belly. Hopes too soon come to nought. Two
months after the prince's death, Margot's labour began.

Too early for the birth of a living child, the princess fought her
pangs of childbirth like a crazed woman. Helping the midwives in
the birthing chamber, when nothing more could be done to
prevent the inevitable, Beatriz turned her face and wept, hearing
the princess beg and plead, "Do anything!" she sobbed. "Oh God,
oh God! Don't take our child away too!"

On the morning of the third day, as dawn broke, Beatriz came to
the queen's chamber. Still spattered with blood, she wobbled an
exhausted curtsey. When she stood, she gripped her forearms,

trying to hold herself her together. The queen waved a hand towards the stool near her. Sitting, Beatriz met the queen's eyes.

"Speak, Beatriz."

"'Twas a girl-child, Your Grace..." Beatriz swallowed, realising how long it was since liquid had passed her lips. "My queen, there was never hope to bring forth a living child, not at six months. The babe's heartbeat stopped in the womb last night. We said nothing of this to Princess Margot, but she knew. The princess lost all heart and went into a stupor. It forced us to act for the princess's only chance for life this morning. We pulled the dead babe from her womb. God help and forgive us, 'twas the only thing we could do. My queen, if the princess survives and marries again, 'tis doubtful she will bear another child."

Sweet Francisco,

Will these dark days ever end? The loss of our princess's child was terrible enough, but it resulted in a dreadful power struggle, after the husband of Juana seized the opportunity to proclaim them both the queen's heirs. Such a despicable action of Philip the Fair – a man whose nickname seems more and more an ill-thought jest.

Queen Isabel summoned her daughter Isabel to come in person and ensure her rights of succession. Isabel was then five months gone with child, and it upset our queen greatly to have to beg her daughter to journey such a distance.

At Toledo, Queen Isabel's Cortes, the parliament of her nobility, proclaimed Isabel the heir to Castilla, but the Cortes of Aragon still stubbornly holds on to its desire for male ascension. To persuade them otherwise, the king and queen sent again for the young Queen of Portugal. King Ferdinand believed this was the only course of action to convince the Aragonese. How the queen hated to summon her daughter back to her court. Since Isabel's return to Portugal, the reports of her health have gone from bad to worse. Now the subjects of her father forced Isabel to endure yet another hard, long journey, this time to Zaragoza, far from the Portugal border, when all her physicians advise otherwise.

"My hija must conserve her strength. It would be more glorious and would cost me less to bring these people to the right by force of arms, rather than suffer their insolence," my queen fumed, her voice as cold as steel, to the kneeling Alonso de Fonseca, after he brought word from the king.

I saw Fonseca cross himself. His long, narrow face hardening, he lifted his chin and said: "Your Highness, if the Queen of Portugal wishes to be recognised as her father's heir, she must come. The Aragonese will prove constant to the monarch to which they swear."

We leave soon for Zaragoza, my love...

Two weeks later, Beatriz rode her mule behind the royal family to the Aljafería, leaving Margot behind in Sevilla. Still grieving for the loss of both husband and child, she had yet to find reason to regain her health after the birth. She was so unwell the queen and king put off all decisions regarding her future, not knowing if she would ever recover.

The summer alcázar of the kings of Aragon spread out its certain claim upon the highest hill in Zaragoza. Struggling up to reach it, Beatriz's tiring mule refused to lumber forward beyond what seemed a snail's pace. Exhausted too from the long journey and disinclined to use her whip on her poor beast, Beatriz studied the beautiful alcázar._Two circular greyish white towers at either side its entrance and similar round towers broke up the curve of strong walls. The alcázar seemed strong and impregnable, yet Christian victory had banished the Moors hundreds of years ago. On a far smaller a scale than other residences of the king and queen, this had once been the home of Saint Isabel. Eager to come to the end of her journey, Beatriz shivered, touched with forewarning.

Afternoon light crowning their veiled heads anew with gold, two black-robed queens walked arm-in-arm in the walled courtyard. Sunlight filtered through the decorative stone of the high arches and their filigree collars of lace, throwing out a dappled design of shadows upon the ground and into the building's interior.

Not long come from devotions in the tiny church belonging to the alcázar, once used as a mosque centuries ago, Beatriz sat with the infanta María, and her dueña on the stone bench sewing, while Catalina and María sat on another bench close by. The girls no longer even pretended to read the books selected for their study. Beatriz heard Catalina speak to María. "What do you think they're saying to one another?"

María shrugged, kicking the dead leaves in front of her, as if attempting to clear the paved footpath. "How would I know?" Putting out her leg, she rolled her ankle, looking at her new black slipper, its thin red ribbon criss-crossed her ankle before the final tie. Both slipper and ribbon made María's foot and ankle seem narrower, perchance even dainty. María eyed Catalina. "Whatever it is, they don't want us to overhear."

Catalina lifted her eyebrows as if surprised. Her eyebrows recently thinned like the older women at court, it gave her face a strange flicker of maturity. Beatriz finger followed the high arch of her own eyebrow, courtly camouflage veiled both youth and age.

"You were not the only one dismissed by my royal mother. Isabel is my sister and I have missed her every day since she left for Portugal. I have hardly spoken to her since she arrived."

Beatriz gazed at the two queens, their backs turned towards her. The paved, narrow footpath led around the courtyard's whole circumference as well between the twin rectangular gardens. Queen Isabel and her eldest daughter reached the other side, changing her view of them. Too far away to hear other than the murmur of their voices, Isabel's huge eyes locked on her mother. She nodded at something the queen said.

Beatriz worried again about Isabel's thinness. With the young queen so slender, her huge belly appeared grotesque. Chilled despite the warmth of this spring day, Beatriz returned her gaze to Catalina. Beside her María was kicking the leaves again.

Catalina shook María's arm. "What's wrong?"

María met her eyes, looking like she wanted to weep. The prince's death, soon followed by that of his child, swirled everyone's emotions too close to the surface. For months now they had struggle to reclaim and piece back together their lives after grief and more grief tore it into shreds. Beatriz sighed. *How many times is life's fabric undone?*

María stared at the ground. No leaves left for her to kick, she gazed back at Catalina. "I wish we were not here – anywhere, but here."

"But why? You've always liked it here!"

Perturbed, Beatriz wondered if María too had caught the same sense of impending disaster she had felt on coming here. She turned her attention to the courtyard. Sunlight slanted over the roof, deluging the small trees sculptured like huge globes. Losing none of its power, the afternoon light struck the water fountain at one side, sparkling the jets of water into crystals. Backed by a sapphire sky, a small bird, with a flutter of brown wings, hopped along the edge of the roof, stopping now and then to look around for foes, raking its beak upon stone. Nothing seemed to threaten them here. But Beatriz felt threatened. Day-by-day, she felt threat's shadow deepen and lengthen.

"Our ancestress haunts this place," María said. As if shocked at her own words, the girl's teeth clamped down upon her bottom lip.

"What's wrong with you today? You talk like a fool. And which ancestress do you speak of? So many of our family lived here."

"You should know. This courtyard was once hers, the place she spent her childhood. Always the queen has held Isabel, so long ago Queen of Portugal, up to you and your sisters. Always, it made me uneasy."

"Uneasy? Why uneasy about Isabel of Portugal? Surely a saint amongst our forebears is reason for pride. She would not haunt us. Why should she?"

María tossed back her head. "If she does not haunt you that does not mean she doesn't haunt someone else. You know as well as I, since her first husband's death, all Isabel has wanted was to be like this other Isabel..."

Catalina paled. Studying her older sister she shook her head.

"Maybe once, but you forget that our ancestor was an old woman when she took the veil, after her husband's death. Her children were grown. Now, thank God, my sister has the same chance to become a mother."

Beatriz also lifted her eyes to the young queen. Yet again, with her back towards her, she reminded her of a thin, straight stick. There was nothing to her but black robes and huge belly.

"Cannot you see?" María asked, holding her friend's hand. "Nothing really has changed for her. Too many times she smiles at us as if she is not really here, even to the queen, your mother. 'Tis as if she moves through life just to reach the day of death."

Catalina snatched her hand away. "Don't say that."

María lowered her head and shrugged. "You said you always want me to speak honestly to you. I know your sister almost as well as you. She has never hidden from us what is in her heart."

Catalina rubbed at her eyes. "There's the babe. When Isabel holds her child, she'll no longer think of death."

María clasped again Catalina's hand. Feeling cold, Beatriz sat in silence, left to the harsh mercy of her thoughts.

Am I a fool with all this disquiet about impending doom? Beatriz wondered the next day. For in the garden the young queen sat and smiled amongst them, busily sewing a baptism robe for her unborn infant. Talking about her new life in Portugal, she reminded Beatriz of the less dark-spirit Isabel at the onset of her first marriage to Alfonso. Her free hand resting on her swollen stomach, Isabel smiled tenderly. "My little son is restless. He knows his father will arrive here soon. Manuel will not miss our boy's birth."

Catalina and her sister María lounged against large cushions set upon a rug near Isabel. Beatriz sat with María de Salinas on the thick, lush grass. The infanta María reached over, plucking a few camomile daisies. Crushing the flowers in her hand, she brought them to her nose and closed her eyes.

Beatriz plucked a daisy too. Placing it face up on her palm, she spread out its petals, reminded of a golden sun, its centre gloriously yellow, rays white with heat. Hearing the infanta María's sudden bell of laughter, she raised her eyes. The girl knelt at Isabel's side, their heads close together, comparing the tiny baby clothes they made. Flowing free from under her black, unadorned roundlet, María's long blonde hair gleamed with red lights, contrasting vividly against her sister's black veils.

Seeing them close together always made Beatriz very aware of their similarities. Isabel's veils hid a similar glorious hair colour to her younger sister, and their eyes were of the same deep green/blue. Except for Juana, all the queen's daughters bore the strong physical stamp of their mother. As for the mental stamp... Beatriz thought again about the infanta María. Happy just to be and live, María never seemed to share the same stubborn fire of faith of her three sisters and her mother.

Catalina shifted, righting herself to her knees. Leaning closer to her older sister, she touched the swaddling clothes in Isabel's hand.

"They're so small, sister. You forget how little babes are until you ready garments for their birth." Catalina glanced at the blanket held in her hand. Hours of painstaking embroidery brought the coat of arms of Portugal nearer to completion, a red shield with yellow castles all around, set in the midst of a yellow circle. Now she sewed the final smaller blue shields upon the white shield in the centre. "Would it matter so much if your child is female? I would welcome a niece as much as a nephew."

Isabel laughed, shadows deepening the hollows of her face. "You would be singing a different tune if you were the one awaiting childbirth. I would not be too pleased to go through all this trouble, all the days of illness, just to bring forth a girl-child. Especially remembering how much trouble being a girl-child brought me. Being female is not something I would ever wish for my child."

María narrowed her eyes against the light. "You seem so certain the child will be a boy. Surely, 'tis not for us to know the sex of our children before birth, and girls must be born, no matter our desire."

Isabel considered María, drumming fingers against the side of her taut gown. "You're right, girls must be born. But I feel certain I bear within me a son. I have felt like this ever since I first felt the child quicken with life." She laughed a little. "You know I am rarely wrong."

Catalina laughed the gruff laugh so alike her mother's. Peering at her sister, she smiled mischievously. "And the times you were wrong, our Isabel? I remember not so long ago you said you would never be happy again, yet here you are today, making merry with your sisters. It gives me joy to see you thus."

Isabel drooped forward over her big belly like a flower pushed forward in the wind. She sighed. "Mi chiquitina, I know now we are fools if we don't take joy when it is offered and revel in happiness while we may."

Isabel became silent, spreading out her baby's robe upon her lap. She lifted shining eyes. "I have done much soul-searching ever since our brother died. It took his death, rather than all the years Juan tried so hard to comfort me, to awake me from the darkness of my half-life, never seeing the woman I so sinfully allowed myself to become.

"I caged myself in my grief, selfishly shutting out all those who loved me. When Juan died, in my mind I heard his voice encouraging me to seek out joy... I felt again the warmth of his love that I often turned from while he lived.

"I know now my self-pity cost me much, years and years when I could have been a better sister, not only for you, María and Juana, but also for him. Juan hated the thought of being king, yet few he trusted with the burden of this knowledge. He trusted me – tried to talk to me about his fears of not being the king our parents hoped and wanted of him. I will regret to my death how I failed him. I should have listened to him rather than wallow in self-pity." Brushing away her tears, Isabel smiled, looking at the sunlit garden. "But I try hard not to fail him now. I have had enough of unhappiness."

Catalina and María gazed at one another. Without a word, the sisters knelt on either side of Isabel, nestling in close, each taking one of their sister's hands. Despite their smiles, grief marked their faces. The months since the tragedy of the prince's passing had not lessened the gaping hole of loss. Beatriz brushed away tears. Her heart ached too. She doubted time would ever heal the loss of their golden prince.

As predicted by his wife, Queen Isabel's court was soon joined by the King of Portugal. Arriving with little fanfare, none knew of his presence until he burst into the garden, looking for his wife. "Isabel," he cried, his unhidden anxiety turning into joy.

Surprised to see him race to his wife's side like a boy, Beatriz stood and then curtseyed with the infantas and the other attendants. The king did not notice. He dropped to his knees, threw his arms around Isabel, laying his head on her breast.

Kissing the top of her husband's dark head, Isabel laughed. "I fear your son must learn courtesy. Our boy has kicked you."

Hands on Isabel's belly, the young king hooted out a laugh that made all smile. His eyes alight, the adoration he showed during their wedding celebrations had not changed since the months of marriage. He rose to kiss his wife. Beatriz smiled. It seemed their months of marriage had only served to increase his love. Isabel too lifted to him shining eyes. Whilst they blazed not with the deep, first love she once showed to Alfonso, they still glowed with something near.

The final weeks of her pregnancy passed slowly. Soon, Isabel's belly became so large she needed the assistance of those around her to help her rise from sitting to standing. Her husband was often the first one to help. Bringing out his harp to make music while she sewed the baptism gown for their child, the king spent all his free time with his wife enjoying the lovely spring days in the garden.

Two weeks after King Manuel's arrival, Beatriz knelt on the grass in the courtyard, picking camomile daisies to make a soothing tea for the queen. Lessons over for the day, Catalina was again with her mother, playing chess with María. No doubt the girls were talking about the latest communications from England. The English king grew more and more impatient for Catalina's arrival.

Feeling too warm, Beatriz righted herself, her eyes drawn to the beautiful staircase leading to the royal chambers. A coffered ceiling overtopped the staircase. On one side, the interior of the alcázar opened up. She leaned against the Corinthian column that formed one end of an arch, looking up at the ceiling. The throne room also possessed a ceiling worthy of note, an over-ornate carved and painted artesonado ceiling, the rich wooden panels very alike to that of a ceiling at the Alhambra. All feasted the eye.

Heavy footsteps crunched gravel. Beatriz looked through a crack between wall and the jutting Corinthian column hiding her from view in the garden. The young queen and her husband walked along the garden path, talking animatedly to one another, but as yet too far away to hear.

Beatriz gazed at Isabel's husband. The complicated web often spun out by kinship, especially that of royal kinship, very little suggested the blood ties between this short, slight man and his nephew, the long-dead Alfonso. King Manuel's much older sister was Alfonso's mother. Isabel's distressed voice stopped her thoughts. Through the crack she saw Isabel push her husband away. She spun around, facing the path leading in Beatriz's direction. Her eyes blind and wide with horror, she ran awkwardly. The short distance left her gasping for breath.

Beatriz stood and stepped back, tight against the wall, keeping herself out of sight. King Manuel reached his wife and took her arm. His black eyes beseeched Isabel. "My love, forgive me. I thought it wisest to keep this from you, but how could I when we vowed to speak truth to one another? Now we are here... a voice from the grave does not give me any peace. You needed to know, my Isabel."

"You lie," she sobbed. Hiccupping through her tears, she sagged against him. "Why do you tell me this? Why now? Manuel, why now?"

His face the colour of ash he lifted his chin, the angles of his face sharpening in his finely drawn face. "Love, believe me only fear for our child moved me to speak. I would not have told you this for the world, but my cousin João would never have spoken to me of such matters unless he thought it true."

Isabel pulled away from him and stood rigid, her hands tight fists at her sides. "My father is not a murderer!"

Beatriz's heart stopped, freezing her to absolute stillness.

King Manuel reached out to Isabel, dropping his hands to his sides at what he saw in her face. "Forgive me. Put it from your mind, my Isabel. I promised your mother our son can be raised at her court. I know he will be safe with her."

Isabel stared at her husband. "Our son... remain in Mother's care? When was this arranged? Why am I the last to know that my child is to be taken from me?"

The king took hold of her shoulders before slipping his arms around her. "Sweet love, my own sweet love. This is why I had to tell you. Treachery has been my companion all my life. I smell it, as if I smell a decaying corpse. My love, that smell follows your father, wherever he goes. Marrying you, I never wanted to believe what my cousin told me, but if our child is a son... I cannot risk his life by acting blind and deaf. Placing our boy in your mother's care ensures him of life. I believe that. And your father will not rid himself of a grandson he comes to love or trains to be king after him. I have to believe that, have to believe he'll grow to forgive our boy my blood."

Isabel slumped into his arms, holding onto him for support. She stared up, breathing heavily. "Manuel..." All life drained from her face. "You truly believe my father murdered Alfonso?"

The king groaned and tightened his arms around her. "Love, you must know political expediency is your father's only catch-cry. For years he has pushed the English king to do what he would have done years ago, rid himself of a harmless, imprisoned man, just because his blood makes him too close a claimant for the throne."

Isabel shook her head. "No, no – you do my father grave injustice." Her hand gripping her throat, she swallowed. "To say such things about my father... As for Warwick, he just wants to make England safer for my sister when she's queen."

King Manuel's face became ugly. "Si, safer for your sister. All should have such fathers..."

"Is it wrong that he cares about my sister's safety?"

He stared over her head. "I don't believe it is just for your sister's safety, but rather looking to the future and ensuring she becomes queen and stays queen. Power means all to your father.

"With Alfonso, your father feared your mother's worsening health would bring Juan to her throne too soon. Your brother was untried and often unwell, when Castilla needs a ruler with a strong hand. With you married to the heir of Portugal and next in line to your mother's crown, your father worried João might be tempted to reach for the apple itself. Many in Castilla respected my cousin João, knowing him a strong king with a strong son.

"Your father hates us. The turd Portuguese he calls us behind our backs. I don't think he cares over-much that his insults come back to me. He did not trust the uneasy peace your marriage to Alfonso brought with it. Your father never wanted your marriage, but the queen, your mother, knew you loved Alfonso. What she can do for you she does, even at the cost to herself."

Isabel's fingers squeezed her husband's hands, as once before on a beach at sunset, before the beginning of so much grief, she held onto her brother, begging release from the fetters of duty. "My mother... does she know?"

The king shook his head. "No, no, my love. João was certain it was your father's hand that set in motion Alfonso's death. Remember, it came at a time when your hopes of bearing Alfonso's child had just come to nought, followed by the fire that almost cost your mother her life. A short time afterward, Alfonso received a gift from your father, the stallion that took his life."

Her mouth open, Isabel stared. "But it was an accident."

Manuel shook his head. "Made to look like an accident. My cousin learnt later that the horse hated the touch of man and was easily spooked. And if that was not enough, a Castilian groom was Alfonso's only companion that night. Who knows what really happened that evening."

"King João went to his grave believing the tragedy was no accident. It bore too much the wily, underhanded stamp of King Ferdinand. He believed that after the camp fire your father decided to take no more chances of Portugal threatening the smooth succession of your brother. He wanted Juan to assume the throne without any threatening him."

Her face wet with tears, Isabel shook her head and hiccupped. "Father killed Alfonso." She stared up at him. "You are certain my mother does not know?"

The king tightened his arms around her. "Your mother loves God too much to ever design to kill the beloved husband of her daughter, whom she loves more than life itself. But my love, when I spoke to her about our child... Isabel, my heart tells me she suspects your father, but is too loving a wife to ever voice these suspicions."

As quietly as possible, Beatriz stole away in the direction of the staircase and, once up them, to her chamber. She closed her door and sat on the closest stool. She wished she had never been in the garden. Now she possessed knowledge of such magnitude it could have her killed. She gazed towards the fireplace. The hearth black and dead, yet she felt she stared into Hell. She knew the king was capable of murder, but whether he had Alfonso's blood on his hands she did not want to know.

Her husband's suspicions destroyed Isabel. She no longer sat with her sisters in the garden, enjoying the warm days of spring, but remained in a darkened chamber, waiting for her baby to be born, waiting to die. Blaming himself and increasingly desperate, despairing, King Manuel only left her chamber to walk around the garden.

Isabel told her mother she no longer wished to live. She wanted to be with Alfonso and Juan, where nothing and no one would hurt her again. Whether she told the queen the reason why, Beatriz did not know. But she suspected she did. Queen Isabel, when she emerged from her daughter's chamber, seemed an utterly broken woman.

All day long, hour by hour, back and forth, her confessor, her mother and her husband visited Isabel in her darkened chamber. None turned her from her quest to seize death in childbirth. Thus, Beatriz joined the midwives, preparing to battle for her life.

Catalina could not understand why her sister no longer wanted life. Listening to her, consoling her, Beatriz locked her awful knowledge away, praying to God for the strength to always keep it from her. Catalina loved her father. It would not help her to know the truth of the shallowness of his love for her, that her happiness meant nothing to him before his ambitions.

Spring no longer ruled their days. The knowledge Isabel turned her face from life darkened everything. They prayed and prayed, but Beatriz knew in her heart of hearts that Isabel's last chance for life died when Manuel told her the truth behind Alfonso's death.

King Ferdinand returned from his discussions with his Cortes on the day Isabel began her labour. Still unhappy with the thought of a woman ruler, his grandees asked to delay their decision until the birth of Isabel's child. They hoped a son would solve the problem of succession. The king never realised his daughter no longer cared who ruled Aragon, or Castilla.

Isabel gave birth to her boy, held him for a moment, and died. Beatriz brought the news to Queen Isabel, leaving the midwives to deal with the weak infant.

Beatriz entered the queen's chamber and the queen rose from her chair, hands gripping tight the armrests, her face so bone-white and ill-looking Beatriz feared for her life too. The king stepped out of the shadows, standing next to his wife. Beatriz couldn't speak but shook her head, holding out her hands in defeat.

As if she defended herself against life, against grief, Catalina bolted up from the cushion beside the queen's chair. She whispered, "Mother –" Beatriz did not know whether Catalina cried for help for herself or in worry for Queen Isabel. She wound her arm around the now weeping girl.

"Isabel's son lives," Beatriz said, desperate to say something of hope.

"Our hija has left a son," the king repeated.

Queen Isabel stared at him, her mouth snapping shut. She groaned, falling to her knees, arms tight around her body, chest heaving, rocking to and fro. Blinking back tears, Beatriz winced. The queen moaned and moaned like a woman in the throes of agonising childbirth. The king gazed at her with distaste, and then searched the room as if seeking escape. He heaved a shuddering breath, pain and grief carving deeper lines on his face. Straightening his shoulders, he strode over to his wife's side.

"My Isabel –" He tried to pull her up from the ground. Again, he gazed around the room, this time at the queen's weeping attendants. Pulling once more at his wife's arm, King Ferdinand gathered back to him the guise of a king. "Let us go your bedchamber, and grieve in privacy."

She shook off his hand. "Don't touch me!"

The king took her arm again, speaking so softly that only those close enough to him could hear. "Wife, remember where you are.

I say again, let's us go to your rooms together and there grieve for our daughter."

The queen shook her head, refusing to meet his eyes. "I don't want you here. Leave me. Please, please, leave me alone."

Bewildered, his mouth trembling, he stared at her. The king almost appeared like a child suddenly abandoned by his mother. "Isabel. Isabel –"

"Ferdinand –" The torments of Hell blazed out of the queen's eyes.

Beatriz licked her dry lips. *Dear God. Pray, this latest tragedy does not drive the queen to madness like her mother.*

"Leave me now if you don't want our love destroyed."

Fear alight in his eyes, the king stared at his wife. He bowed, backed away, and left the queen to her women.

Beatriz thought, *She knows! She knows everything.* Next to her, Catalina began to weep. Murmuring, "I am here," Beatriz led the shocked girl into the courtyard. Spring still embraced the season, but it seemed the bleakness of winter chilled all their hearts.

My love,

You are away from me too long – how I look forward to the day when I welcome your return. I received a letter from Josefa yesterday. She tells me our son is well and happy, and invites us to stay with her when our duties allow.

The queen is sadly changed from the woman we knew years ago. Her sorrows weigh her down until she almost drowns under their weight. She closets herself with her priest for the hours and worries about dying well. Since her daughter's death, she has placed her house in order and paid many debts.

The infanta María is now married to the King of Portugal. With his daughter Isabel securing the succession of Aragon by the birth of a son, the king was happy to see another of his daughters become a consort to a king. The queen told me that it was seeing the tenderness and devotion of Manuel for her Isabel that swayed her to marry him to María. Pray to God, may María have the happiness denied to her poor sister...

That tragic spring frittered away to autumn, to winter and then another spring. Spring restored verdant life to the land, but not to the spirit of Queen Isabel. Fighting her own battle against despair, Beatriz felt bereft of any words offering any real meaning as the increasingly fragile queen spiralled deeper where none could help her. But she tried to talk to her, tried to get her to open her heart to her. One day, she was more fortunate than on others.

"God's wounds, Beatriz," the queen said to her. "There isn't one day or night when I do not doubt. Every day my doubts pull me down like hunting wolves in winter."

"My queen, doubt is a part of life."

"Part of life... Once life was not the dark world I find myself in now. Once, doubt never ruled me. Once, with all my heart, I believed I had to ensure the succession of a strong kingdom for my son. I believed I did it for God. I believed I did it for my son. Juan's death showed me the error of that belief. What I believed came from God was but the drub of my own desire, my own fear and lack of true faith. Was it all for nought, Beatriz? The last few years have seen me like Job."

"Your Grace, your losses would test the strength of saints. But cannot you think your hard trials prove God's love for you? Suffering turns us to God and the truth of our existence. The labour pains of our Earthly life birth us into Heaven. Remember, sorrow comes in order to test faith."

The queen sputtered a grim, bitter laugh. "You speak like my confessor. Perchance on another lighter day I'd give your words better credence. Today I am just too tired, too heart-sore. I have tried my upmost to be a just queen. I never wanted to be called a tyrant. I came to the throne believing with all my heart that

Castilla was mine, that the deaths of my two brothers left me the rightful heir to our father's crown. I never wanted to see Castilla endangered by passing to the rule of a foreign lineage. God, I truly believed, placed me in this royal state as rightful queen. All I thought was to do right by God and my country, to bring my subjects peace after years of so much evil and destruction."

"And so you have, your Grace. You are a good queen."

"I remember well the times you told me otherwise – if not in words, then a look I could not fail to understand. You were right. I made too many mistakes thinking I acted for God when it wasn't that way at all. I only listened to myself, or my husband. I wasn't listening to God at all."

"My queen, please don't torment yourself. We all make mistakes. We are human, after all."

Queen Isabel laughed bitterly. "My husband assures me queens and kings do not make mistakes... But I have made them, Beatriz. I vowed to bring peace and prosperity to Castilla, only to bring the harbingers of death and destruction. I lie awake at night and think that the loss of Isabel and Juan is more God's punishment for the evil of my mistakes. Remember, Abravanel promised divine punishment if I expelled the Jews. Perchance that's the root for all my grief.

"My thoughts at night suck me into a black void of nothingness. I wonder then if this is Hell, for all my days seem Hell already."

Her heart heavy, Beatriz thought, *Was the victory of the Holy War paid in sorrow? Did the queen reach for glory, only to find it hollow and worthless?*

"Isabel, how I wish I knew the words to comfort you. If I was a priest, I'd probably say 'tis not for us to question the way of the Lord."

"Those words do not help, Beatriz."

"Then let me speak of what's in my heart. Life means more than simply waiting for death. I believe everything in life happens for a purpose. I believe we are here to learn – and the lessons are so often hard. Sometimes, it would be far easier to let ourselves go under than keep on fighting. Yet this is what we must do. It is the only thing we can do."

24

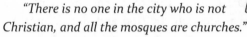

"There is no one in the city who is not
Christian, and all the mosques are churches."
~ Cisneros

In the Hall of the Two Sisters, the overhead cupola tempered forth a muted light – a light birthing another day, a light that conjured the imaginings of wide awake dreams. Beatriz wrote beside Catalina. The girl read *The City of Women*, while Beatriz wrote notes concerning her favourite tract of Aristotle.

María plucked notes on her vihuela, singing a slow song of love, betrayal and death. Catalina put her book down and rose from the bench. She began to dance, her movements flourishing the song's lyrics with measured movements. Catalina was still tiny, but she danced in perfect harmony with her height.

Beatriz sighed. The girls were now thirteen and no longer children. Their bodies took on womanly forms and flowered to the promise of spring. Already small apple breasts pushed against their chemises, waists nipped in, widened hips boded fertility.

Months ago the queen had wept when Doña Teresa Manrigue murmured of the start of Catalina's courses. Discussions then became frequent about the right time for her to leave her mother's court for England and make a true marriage. While the queen conceded these talks to the English, all knew she would not let her youngest child leave her court for some time yet, not only because Catalina was just thirteen. Queen Isabel needed her youngest child at her side.

Si, both her girls were no longer children. The presence of Doña Eliva Manuel, elected the dueña who would one day go with the princess to England, now became a constant shadow on their day.

Overly efficient in her duties she strived to please Catalina, even biting back in the presence of the princess her dislike and jealousy of Beatriz. This morning Catalina escaped her watchful eye by asking her to oversee the selection of gowns for the expected arrival of English diplomats.

Lifting her head, María closed her eyes. Her beautiful voice soared and throbbed like the notes of her vihuela, touching Beatriz's heart. The page she wrote on blurred, and she saw Francisco in her mind. They rode together on his horse from the abundant, colour rich gardens banked against the walls of the Alhambra. The river of Darro wound before her eyes, like a thin ribbon of silver, alive, pulsing, glittering and glinting, as if the morning light jewelled it with countless diamonds. The hills and plains of Granada stretched out as far as the sight of an eagle in flight. Sunlight seeped into the very air itself. The brown, flower-rich land swelled with life and passion, a land feeding and nourishing heart and soul.

Astride, mantle-less, skirts tucked up high, thighs pressed tight against the sides of the mount, Beatriz wound her arms around Francisco's lean waist. Her long black hair streamed loose in the wind. Like Adam and Eve, they were the only man and woman in an innocent world. A world untouched by sorrow.

A string broke and woke Beatriz from her trance and daydream, desire firing her heart and coursing in her veins. She gazed at María. Still an awkward maid, the girl was like Catalina, protected from the gaze and touch of man. The girl looked bewildered, as if her song had stirred her too. Beatriz knew from their conversations that María yearned for adulthood, but feared it, too. Catalina also seemed disturbed, breathing hard from her dance, hands planted on her hips, she shook her head, as if shaking away the remnants of a dream.

Beatriz smiled and clapped her hands. "Your song goes well, María. It is finished, si?"

The girl blushed, her fingers strummed the unbroken strings, they made a jarring noise. "My infanta thinks it finished. But I'm not certain."

Beatriz laughed. "In all the time I have been your teacher I have never seen you entirely satisfied with what you do. That makes me content because I know you'll always strive to climb higher. All teachers should have such students."

"And me?" Catalina asked. Standing beside her friend, a wide smile spread on her face.

Beatriz reached for the bowl next to her with pieces of dry apricot. Taking a piece, she put it in her mouth and chewed, thinking out her answer. "I never hide from you the great delight you give me. Often I regret I cannot train you to take my place as professor at Salamanca. You have so many skills and talents, just like the queen."

Catalina bit at her bottom lip and blushed. "If I am just a little like my mother, I'll be content."

Her eyes staying on Catalina, Beatriz pulled her earlobe. "Infanta, don't mistake my meaning. You bear the seeds of great promise, but they are different seeds to that of our noble queen. You are unique, we all are. If life teaches us anything it is to know ourselves, our strengths and weaknesses. Do not fall into the trap of yearning to be someone else. We praise God for much, but our greatest praise to Him must be to gift Him with our true selves.

"Be thankful, my princess, that God has given you the learning the queen lacked as a young girl. Most importantly, God places you where you can observe a woman ruler able to rule men. No lesson I could teach you has as much value as that."

Another day, another sweet, pure voice sang another song:

> *For ever there remains with me one longing,*
> *Ceaselessly, day and night, at every hour,*
> *Tormenting me so I would gladly die,*
> *For my life is nothing but a pining,*
> *And in the end I'll have to die of it.*
>
> *I thought myself quite sure against misfortune*
> *When that accursed longing in which I dwell*

Overtook me, intent that I should die,
For my life is nothing but a pining,
And in the end I'll have to die of it:
For ever.

Margot's fingers plucked the final note. "For ever," she repeated. The young woman stared as if at nothing, her tears dripping onto Juan's vihuela. Beatriz met the miserable eyes of Catalina and María. What comfort can be given to one so full of grief, especially when you too share that grief?

María turned, rubbing at her eyes. The girl had grown up watching Juan play his harp or vihuela, his beautiful voice wooing her from childhood to a sadder and more uncertain time. It was no wonder his wife begged the instrument from his mother. María probably wished she had the same right to ask for something, anything, once belonging to Juan. She had only the vihuel he gave her in childhood. She had nothing else of him but the memories they all shared. Somehow that thought comforted Beatriz. She gazed around so certain of Juan's presence.

Despite the tears lighting her eyes, Margot seemed comforted too. "The queen and king have given me many gifts to take home, but none is more precious than this."

"You will write, my sister?" Catalina asked.

Fresh pain thickened Margot's voice. "I cannot promise you that, mi chiquitina."

Catalina turned a face furrowed by distress. "But why?"

Margot got up, placing the vihuela carefully on the stool's cushion. She sat next to Catalina and wound her arm around her.

"Not because I don't love you. Never think that. I will always love you. But you forget, I go back to be a pawn again. My father hates your father – and so does my brother. I do not believe we will be allowed the consolation of letters." She gazed sadly at the vihuela. "Perchance that is for the best. I must stop myself from looking behind, otherwise my poems will come true and I'll die of grief." She rested her head on Catalina's shoulder. "Juan..." Margot swallowed hard. "My sweet Juan would not want me to pine my life away."

273

There was one more royal death during these dark years. Writing of it to her husband, Beatriz recalled the gossamer-winged dragonfly she had seen, just days before knowing Prince Juan was lost to them forever in this life. Across the water it darted, in an eye-blink of time, its shimmering, rainbow-hued wings flashing over the water's surface before clouds blocked out the sun. A moment of beauty gone forever, but even though grief tore once more at Beatriz, she held onto the one thing she believed with all her heart: you cannot really lose what you love, for loving renders eternity.

Two years of life was more than enough time for love to bridge eternity. And how could any not love a little bright-eyed boy so filled with joy? Every day of his short life, he stretched out his arms for his family's embrace. How could any ever think of him as a promise never fulfilled, a flower pushing through the winter snow to never bloom?

The boy made his grandmother smile again, sitting on her lap, one hand patting her face and the other playing with the heavy chain of her crucifix, chattering a mixture of real words and ones he made up in his attempt to tell one of those he loved the great story of his small life. The little one gave them the delight of hearing the queen laugh once more.

If not in his grandmother's arms he was in the arms of those who attended her. Not a day passed after Isabel's death when Catalina and María did not hold him, kiss him, play with him. Before they knew it, he grew from tiny infant to active child, wriggling out of arms, demanding to be let down, wanting to toddle around his world in his impatience to seize it.

Dark-haired like his father but with his mother's sea-blue eyes, in his tiny palm he captured so many hearts during his brief life. With great pride, he spoke his first full, clear sentences the day the fever struck. Death again stole away the darting dragonfly of beauty and left them bereft once more. But that was not the end of grief.

Beatriz sat with Francisco by the hearth. Leaping flames of a famished fire flickered its reflections on the polished wood of his vihuela. His fingers plucked the strings, the ruby in his heavy gold ring flashing in the firelight with each note. "Time for one more song before we go to bed?"

Her hand going to rub her throat, Beatriz laughed. "I think you said that about the last song. I am likely to be hoarse if I sing any more."

Francisco laid his hand over her hand. "Sing for me. You don't know how much I dream of evenings like this when I'm away from you. I hate and curse these unending skirmishes. I hate and curse those Moors who refuse to admit defeat. I resent anything that keeps me from your side. I'm an old, weary warhorse who only wants to be put out to pasture."

Beatriz shook her head. Taking her hand from his, she placed a finger across his mouth. "Shhh – not old – never that. We can only pray that soon all the fighting will come to an end."

Francisco averted his face and gazed at the fire. He sighed. "Don't waste your prayers on something that never will happen. I have lived long enough to know to talk of peace and men is but a children's fable."

Beatriz clasped his hand. "Remember – we promised to speak of only happy things tonight, and all the nights we have together before you must leave me again."

Francisco grinned at her like a young man. "So we did. And for me to play my vihuela and for you to sing."

Beatriz laughed at him. "All right – one last song. What will it be?"

Francisco brushed his fingers against the strings of his vihuela and a familiar chord took shape.

Beatriz laughed again. "Will you sing it with me?"

Francisco leaned across and kissed her lips tenderly. "I am so happy," he murmured.

Beatriz stroked his face, her finger tracing around his mouth. "While you are with me, love, so am I."

Beatriz cleared her throat, and sang with her husband:

"I am so happy!"
All of the birds of the world of love were singing;
It was my love and yours that they had in mind.
"I am so happy!"
All of the birds of the world of love were chanting;
It was my love and yours that they were naming.
"I am so happy!"

In the school-room the next day, her own father also soldiering again, María hounded Beatriz mercilessly with her questions, trying to understand why her father must again go forth into battle when she knew he had so hoped to go home. Loud rumours at court blamed the most recent rebellion on the queen's new confessor.

"You must know the Franciscan Cisneros is a man of deep convictions," Beatriz at last answered. She bent over her desk, sorting through a thick pile of untidy papers.

"My princess tells me he once lived a hermit life in a wooden hut he built himself. He did not want to be confessor to the queen."

Still searching amongst her papers she glanced up, relieved María was now thinking about other things. "Si. The dying Cardinal Mendoza thought Cisneros the right man to take his place." She shrugged and tried to laugh. "Cisneros had his own doubts about this. He believed being the queen's confessor would only bring him in too much contact with worldly matters. Cisneros understood confessor to the queen also meant political advisor. He did a great deal of soul-searching before accepting."

"You mean Cardinal Cisneros ran away." María giggled. "Remember when Cardinal Mendoza died? The queen wanted Cisneros to take upon the now vacant Archdiocese of Toledo? He raced from her chambers as if in fear for his life. The guards had to bring him back to the queen to accept."

Beatriz placed one heap of papers to the side of the table, her hand weighing down the greater pile. She eyed María. "I'm not sure I blame him for doing so. The archdiocese brought with it the office of chancellor to the kingdom and all that entailed."

Returning to their conversation about the new battle, María blurted out, "The king believes the cardinal is at fault at this latest rising at Granada."

Beatriz cried out in delight, unfolding a paper and laying it flat on the table. It was a recipe to treat burns, something she wanted to give to Francisco before he left again. Francisco commanded another team of men in these last days of Queen Isabel's Holy War, helping douse out the last flaring fires of resistance.

"The king is likely right. I also thought Talavera's gentle approach wisest, and said as much to the queen. Talavera believed time, education and example would solve the problem of conversion. But when Cisneros joined him, all his work went to ruin. Cisneros forced Moors to convert, not only lapsed Christians. Can you imagine how the Moors must have felt when Cisneros burned countless and priceless manuscripts?" Biting back her own anger, Beatriz shook her head. "What utter stupidity – books we will never be able to replace. Thank God he didn't burn books important to our knowledge of medicine."

A recent memory flashed into Beatriz's mind. The king, revealing again his dark side, had rounded on the queen and snarled, "What do you think, Lady, of the situation your archbishop has put us in? What our kings, our forebears, won with so much zeal and blood, we have now lost in an hour because of him."

"Is this the reason for the rebellion?" María asked.

"No..." Beatriz sighed. "Cisneros believes force necessary, if it means gaining converts for God. He imprisoned a Moorish leader, placing him in chains until he yielded to conversion. Before we knew it, all hell's let loose, and rebels besiege the cardinal's residence. Cisneros refuses to leave for the safety of the Alhambra.

That's why your father finds himself wielding his sword again, and my husband must again serve the queen in war."

María punched the air. "'Tis not fair – none of it is. Not fair for us, nor the queen. The king is as furious at her as he is at Cisneros."

Beatriz picked up her paper. "María, the king is very jealous of the power the queen has given to her new confessor. She struggles to keep the peace between them."

Beatriz recalled the queen's reply to the king: "My lord husband, I beg you, give him the benefit of the doubt and do not listen to rumour until we have all the facts before us and hear what he has to say. Let's wait until we know the full story before we point fingers of blame."

Thus, before the end of another week María's father and Beatriz's husband accompanied the king to put out the fire of this new rebellion.

The sky still streaked with the colours of dawn, Beatriz and María stood close together, watching them go. María's father hurried after his lord, King Ferdinand, his long, black hair now streaked by grey. Years of soldiering out in the field bronzed his skin to dark leather, etching deep and permanent lines upon his face, but still he strode to his waiting horse with all the loose-limbed grace of a far younger man.

But Beatriz really had eyes only for one man. From their vantage point, Francisco seemed little changed from the handsome man she had fallen in love with years ago. Wise when she first met him, time only deepened that well while gently changing his physical shell. Her forever merry husband appeared to possess not one worry in the world, taking charge of his men with power, energy and confidence.

Seeing his brown hand on his sword, Beatriz thought of his long, calloused fingers making music and touching her with love. Her heart started to hurt. She heard him saying again, "I'm an old, weary warhorse who only wants to be put out to pasture." But there was no other choice for him. The passing of years only made Francisco more devoted to the queen, and more expert with gunpowder. While the queen needed his skills, he would never ask for release from her service.

Francisco took the reins of his horse from one of his waiting men. It was his favourite stallion he rode that day. Later, much later, Beatriz was glad of that. A man going unknowingly and so nobly to his death should have with him at least one thing he loved. Placing his hand on the saddle, he effortlessly bounded onto his horse's back.

Astride, Francisco half-twisted towards her, a wide smile stretching across his face. The steady wind ruffling his greying hair, he flung out his arm wide in farewell. Beatriz would never forget the pride in his eyes, the pride that seemed to shine brighter than the sun. How could she forget? That day, for the last time, she saw his pride in her.

Beatriz lifted her own arm in farewell. Francisco wheeled his horse. Half-rearing, it neighed, as if welcoming the coming battle, and galloped away, out of sight. For a long while Beatriz stood with María until they could watch no longer, and then went back to the royal chambers. Before that week's end, both of them would have reason to comfort the other.

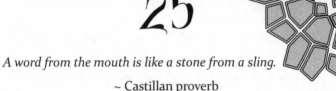

25

A word from the mouth is like a stone from a sling.

~ Castillan proverb

The king backed Beatriz against the wall, tearing off her widow veils, roughly dragging down her bodice to bare her breasts. His other hand disappeared under her skirts, his arm levering up her gown. A beam of light struck the naked skin of her legs as he elbowed them apart.

"No, please, no. I beg you, my lord... my Lord King, please! I am in mourning."

The king kissed her hard, all the while loosening the drawstrings of his black leggings, ramming her against the wall with his soldier's strength. Helpless to fight back, Beatriz put out her hands on either side of her, feeling like one crucified.

"Mourning? I'm sick of mourning, Beatriz. Sick of women who mourn. Sick, do you hear? I want to forget grief and what better way than this. Beg again, my dear, I like women who beg..."

With a violent movement, he pushed her legs apart, wider. He ground into her, one hand squeezing her breast and the other beneath her buttocks. He grunted and grunted to rhythmical movements, while Beatriz crumbled against him, beaten by pain, defeated by life, and turned her face away. She wept. Birds chirped to the sound of his heavy breathing. She wept. The king's awful animal sounds went on and on, assaulting her almost much as the physical assault. She wept and wept.

How could she let this happen, couldn't she have done something to stop him? Why now? Why again? She wanted to die.

Selecting her book from the pile on the table, Beatriz sat there, leaving it unopened before her. It was still unopened when Catalina turned from her half-filled parchment to resharpen her quill.

"Thinking of your husband?" she asked.

Beatriz shrugged. "I will always think of him." She rubbed her wet eyes. "My books give me little joy today."

Her face empty of expression, Catalina gazed at her quill. "Do you want to talk about it?"

Beatriz bent her head. "Is life a jest that God plays on us?"

Catalina bent forward with widening eyes. "Teacher!" she gazed all around, as if wanting to ensure they remained alone. "What has happened for you to say such a thing?"

Unable to look at her, Beatriz put her head in her hands and wept. She felt the warmth of Catalina's hand, touching her head. "Forgive me," she sputtered. "I am just raw today."

Before her marriage, Beatriz had sometimes thought it would be far easier to die by her own hand, like the Roman Lucretia, rather than live with dishonour. Marriage to one of his favoured men had protected her from the king's lust. In her first years at court, she had believed his threats – that he would take almost everything she valued away from her. She could not bear the thought of not teaching, but then she had found herself in a mire almost impossible to get out of – the more she tried, the deeper she sunk. Only marriage to Francisco had saved her. Now she wondered how she would bear it for it all to start again. She lifted her head and tried to smile at her princess. She had to tell the queen, no matter the consequences. She could not live like this again.

"You asked to speak to me, Latina?"

Beatriz rose from her curtsey and lifted her eyes. Seated by the open window, Queen Isabel bent her head over her embroidery, the harsh afternoon sun showed all the lines on her face. She looked so much older than her years. But was that surprising? The last years had been grief after grief.

Beatriz licked at her dry mouth. All her life she had never struggled to begin a conversation. She thought of words as stones – things she used to build, not to destroy. Now? Now she was terrified of what her words could do to her queen.

"Beatriz?" Queen Isabel waved a hand towards a nearby stool. "Pray, sit. I have seen that look too many times over the years to not recognise trouble."

Sitting on the stool, Beatriz took a deep breath. "Your Majesty – what I have to come to say is painful – not just for me, but for you."

Queen Isabel blinked. Cocking her head to one side, she narrowed her eyes. "Painful? My friend, pray come to the crux of the matter."

"You called me friend, my queen. Do you really see me that way?"

"Beatriz – I have never known you to make no sense. Of course we are friends. Good friends. How can we not be, after all these years... you are one person who I thank for stopping me from going mad. Never doubt my friendship – never doubt you can speak to me about anything."

Beatriz swallowed. It was the opening she wanted. This was the moment when she would discover the truth of their relationship. "Pray, I must talk to you about the king."

"The king?" Queen Isabel stared at her. "You say the king?"

"Oh, Isabel, I must call you Isabel or I cannot speak of this." She swallowed again. "Your husband..." She bent forward, her head between her hands. "Oh, God, dear God. I cannot say it..."

Beatriz wiped the tears from her face, aware of the other woman's silence – a silence that seemed endless. She raised her head, rubbing her wet eyes. Isabel sat very still, her white face averted to the window. At last she turned, breathed deeply through her nose, and looked sadly at Beatriz.

"I think I know what you cannot say. I think I have always known. My husband hates you, my friend. When he hates, he acts on it." Isabel placed her arm on the armrest of her chair and cradled her chin in her hand. She pursed her lips. "How long?"

"For years – but never often. And never while I was wife to Francisco. But it has started again..."

Isabel lowered her head, placing her embroidery on her lap. "You should have told me, Beatriz. To suffer in silence for so long – my friend, did you not think to come to me?"

"Not when it began. I did not know you then, not as a friend. All I knew were the king's threats, and his promise to see me removed as tutor to your children and teacher at the university if I refused him. I am no longer a young woman. I believed I was no longer in danger of the king's unwanted attention. But now, to my great shame, I know otherwise."

Turning again, Isabel looked at the window. A lush green pomegranate tree grew close by – its branches heavily laden with unpicked fruit, so heavy, the luscious red fruits weighed down the branches. Bright green leaves and bright red fruit against bright blue sky – the tree was a reminder that spring was almost at an end.

Isabel heaved in a long breath and let it out. "The shame is not yours, Beatriz. Do not think that. It is not my place to beg you to forgive him, but we can guess what lies at the root of his actions. He is a man with a powerful wife, a wife far more powerful than him. All the years of our marriage I have tried so hard to not remind him of this. But I am Queen of Castilla. Sometimes, Aragon must remember its place. I make my husband very angry when that happens.

"He knows I love you. By hurting you, he hurts me. This does not excuse him. And in this instance, I am glad I have the power to remind my husband how much he needs my partnership... even if it is but the wealth of Castilla he needs. This is why you are here? You want me to speak to him?"

"Isabel – please. I know I ask of you a great boon, but I cannot remain at court if I am forever avoiding the king."

"You'll not leave the court. I say this selfishly. I do not want to lose my friend. I will speak to him tonight and warn him. If he touches you again, do not fear to come and speak to me again. I promise you, my husband will live to regret it."

Another year wore on, a far, far kinder year. The queen kept her promise. She never told Beatriz what she said to the king, but he avoided her from that time. Just when she started to believe they had finally emerged from the years of darkness, Beatriz found Catalina sitting on her clothes chest, weeping. Hands planted on either side of her, she held herself straight, taking quick breaths as if in shock.

Beatriz sat beside her "What is it?" she asked, her heart in her throat. Whatever upset her must be dreadful. No longer a girl who wept easily, Catalina was a maid who knew well the burden of grief.

"He's dead," she whispered.

Beatriz's heart missed a beat. "Who?" *Death had smitten again a man or boy in their close circle – someone to give Catalina cause for sorrow?* Only her father was left for her to grieve over. Beatriz had gone the other way when she saw him, hale and vigorous, coming out of the queen's chamber less than one hour ago.

Catalina wiped her pale face with the sleeve of her chemise. Several times, she inhaled and exhaled deeply. "Forgive me. The news has come of Warwick's execution. He tried to escape with the traitor Warbeck – and now they are both dead." Catalina took another long breath. When she spoke again, Beatriz could almost hear the voice of the queen. "It is for the best. Henry Tudor has done right by his kingdom. There's now one less cause for rebellion. I shouldn't let it disturb me."

Beatriz swallowed, clasping Catalina's hand. The girl had dreaded this news for years. "It is not your fault," she said.

Startled, Catalina stared up. Fresh tears fell down her white face. "Not my fault? How can you say that? Our ambassador told King Henry in great secrecy my parents would not let me go to England until Warwick was dead. Latina, they killed him for me."

Tightening her grip on Catalina's hand, Beatriz leaned closer. "Listen to me – I say again it is not your fault." *What to say – what can I say to her to chase the demons away?* She swallowed again.

"Terrible things happen in this world..." She shook her head. "Evil things, Catalina. But think, my princess – Warwick was a catalyst for greater evil –" Seeing Catalina about to speak, Beatriz placed a finger on the girl's lips. "Let me finish. Yes – Warwick was not evil, only a young man whose great tragedy was his birth. But by allowing him life, others would have been tempted to use him for evil – and start another English civil war." *Oh – the emptiness of my words.* She took a deep breath. "We live in a world where it is wiser to enact a lesser evil to prevent a greater. Dear God, Catalina –" Beatriz cradled the side of her head. "It is not your fault, but the world we live in. All we can do is strive to change the world by our own lives, and to remember we never come to the Kingdom of Heaven but by troubles."

Too full of thoughts to desire company, once again Beatriz sat alone in the courtyard where, years ago, she had spoken to Admiral Colón. Then, as now, early morning sunlight hazed forth the verdancy of spring and countless butterflies dappled her with their fluttering shadows as they danced in mid-air. She gazed at the sky. Blue and cloudless, it mattered little when the departure of her princess and María loomed like storm clouds on the horizon of her life. Thinking about all she would soon lose, and all she had already lost, Beatriz thanked God for the intertwining of good with bad. The constant flare of Moorish rebellion close to Granada ensured the king and queen remained at the Alhambra beyond just one summer season. Content to stay at their favourite royal place of all, they still dwelled there when time approached for Catalina to start her long journey overland to the ships that would take her to England.

Days kept them busy with making and packing, ensuring the dowry chests the princess took with her included everything she needed to begin a new life in a new land. And, likewise, her attendants, those the queen chose to accompany her daughter, prepared for their new lives, too.

These busy days of preparation brought María's mother to court for a rare visit. Not yet forty, once constant childbearing softened and rounded her form. Now a year and more had passed since her husband's death. Sorrow left her thinner whilst not lessening her attractiveness. The last months had cried rumour of another grandee wooing her, desiring not only the great wealth she inherited after her mother's death, but also her mature beauty and proven fecundity. She soon sent her suitors away. Josefa refused to consider another marriage. In truth, while no other man ever threatened her husband's place in her heart, nine hard childbirths, and one that of twins, would leave few women lusting for more.

Even so, Josefa was lonely, a palpable loneliness that Beatriz knew too well.

When María told her mother she wished she could find some other man to love, Josefa had smiled at her daughter. "My María," she answered. "There's no reason for you to feel pity for me. Few in life experience the love I knew with your father. Hija, 'tis a love bridging between life and death, me on one side and your father on the other. How could I marry again feeling like that? I'm content to wait for the sake of our children, knowing when I cross that bridge, I return to his side, this time forever. I know your father waits for me."

Her way of dealing with his loss meant leaving herself with not one idle moment from dawn to dusk. María's twin brothers, now seven, as well as Beatriz's growing son, came more and more under her older brother's guidance, and her two older sisters were married to well-placed grandees. María's baby brother, the child her mother bore four months after her father's death, seemed to live with her two sisters and their children as much as he lived with his mother.

Si, Josefa was a grandmother now, but like her own mother before her she refused to just sit and sew or weave by the fire. Be that as it may, María's mother still sewed and weaved. In the school-room, Josefa threw over her daughter's shoulders a deep red woollen mantle.

"Red suits you." She drew it around María, pulling the hood over her head and straightening its folds. "I dyed it until I got the colour right. Others wanted to help me with it, but I refused. Every stitch is from my own needle. It will last you many years."

Gazing wordlessly at her mother, María gathered its thick, soft folds against her chest. From another full saddlebag, Josefa took out a tied canvas bag. "Take these too."

Standing next to them, Beatriz breathed in the smell of earth and glanced inside the bag at the small brown bulbs. There were too many to count.

"What are they?" María asked.

"Saffron. Look after them and keep them safe from frost. That's certain to kill them and prevent them flowering. They take a lot out of the earth when they grow. Take the bulbs out every year or so after they have done with flowering, then feed the earth before you plant the bulbs back again. Do this and they will multiply and give you much cause for pleasure. You know their many uses?"

Holding the precious bag to her chest, María beamed. "Gracia, Mamá, si. I shall find a place in England to plant them." The girl glanced at the bundles already piled high on the bed – amongst them apricot and peach kernels and apple seeds from her mother's best trees. María bit her lower lip. "As I will do with the other seeds from home."

Josefa fixed her gaze on her daughter. "When you're married, I'll send you more. I will also send you young saplings from our orchards by ship."

María offered her mother a trembling smile. "Mamá, I am grateful." She touched her mother's hand.

Beatriz thought Josefa somehow diminished. Beside her towering husband, her friend's huge spirit more than made up for her tiny size. Somehow, Beatriz felt as if Josefa's inner core of strength had passed from her to her daughter, like the mantle she had placed over her shoulders. Beatriz heaved a deep sigh.

"But it might be best to send them for my princess's wedding, not mine. Who knows when I will marry," María said.

Alarmed, Josefa blinked. "The princess will find you a good husband."

Turning to her mother's distress, María clasped her hand. "Si, Mamá."

Beatriz studied the girl. María was likely wise to keep silent about Catalina's promise to let her first seek out her own. The knowledge would worry her mother.

Gazing at Josefa in her widow's weeds, Beatriz remembered her in her husband's arms. Like her and Francisco, Josefa and Martin's love blazed dazzling white-gold like a well-stacked fire. She did not blame María for wanting the same as her parents, for wanting abiding love and passion, a true marriage, not a sham. Josefa's eyes drowned in tears, running down her aging cheeks. Beatriz touched her loosening cheek. *Si. Like mine.*

Josefa cradled María's face between her hands. "Promise to write?" Her voice choked. "If you send your letters home with the princess's letters, the queen will ensure I get them."

Beatriz thought she could be strong, now watching her friend weep showed this only make-believe. A tidal wave swelled within her, and she rubbed at her wet eyes.

"Mamá mine, I vow to you, I shall write. As many letters as I am able." María wrapped her arms around her mother and kissed her. The girl seemed to be breathing in her mother's smell. "Mamá, if the letters come slowly, please remember I will pray to God every day of my life to keep you and my brothers and sisters safe."

Josefa smiled, reaching to give María her kiss and blessing. The girl crumbled in her mother's arms and wept, holding her tight.

"Dear one, I am here. I am here. Always," Josefa comforted.

Beatriz rubbed at her eyes. Soon María would never hear again those words from her mother's lips.

Beatriz witnessed another farewell, this time in the royal baths at the Alhambra. Both now finished bathing and in their dry shifts, Queen Isabel stood behind her seated daughter and brushed Catalina's hair before a body-length mirror propped against the tiled wall. Beatriz leaned back against the marble bath, going deeper in the hot water. The white shift she wore billowed. She lifted a hand and studied her wet, water-shrivelled fingers. She wondered if she should get out of the baths too, but it was so pleasant to just be at rest and linger in the heated water. Overhead, light beamed down from the star-shaped skylights of the cupola and created a constellation of twinkling stars around her in the water. She raised her head when she heard the queen say, "Mi chiquitina…"

Catalina glanced at her mother, then lowered her gaze to her lap. Queen Isabel straightened her stance, not missing one brush stroke.

"I shall write to you every moment I can. My letters to you will make you feel you are with me and never, ever lonely for my love. I tell you true, love makes of distance nothing. Nothing, I tell you." The queen swallowed, shaking her head. She sniffed. "Catalina, I am a good judge of character, si?"

Catalina lifted her grey/blue eyes again, glistening bright in candlelight. The mirror reflected her mother's sorrowful smile. From her earliest years, Queen Isabel told Catalina her English great-grandmother and namesake possessed such eyes. Beatriz inwardly shrugged. Catalina of Lancaster was the daughter of John of Gaunt – also the ancestor of Henry VII of England. Queen Isabel regarded the English king as kin, but she was a crowned queen, the daughter of a crowned king. King Henry's background was like a shabby, half-made blanket compared to the gold-cloth of her queen's.

Catalina chewed her upper lip and cleared her throat. "Si, Mamá."

"Mi chiquitina, you know letters have gone from me to Elizabeth of York since her firstborn wore swaddling cloths. The queen is a good, wise woman and devoted to her children. She will care for you as one of her own. Always listen, Catalina, to her. Her husband, the king... Hija, I am not as certain of him."

The chamber became so quiet Beatriz counted the strokes of the brush, so many it transmuted Catalina's hair into what seemed liquid gold. The queen's eyes fell upon her daughter's reflection.

"Hija, I believe King Henry to be like most men – desiring his women to make him believe himself better than other men. I have not enjoyed the marriage negotiations he has forced on us. Our arguments over your dowry have made me feel like a shopkeeper. But to be fair to him, he is a man who has learnt the hard way to value gold. Never forget he is a king not long secure in his crown."

Catalina blinked. "But he has been England's king for sixteen years."

The queen paused, tightening her lips. She lost the vibrancy sometimes making her seem ageless. "Si. More than your whole lifetime. I understand it seems a long time to you." She bent her head, and began brushing again. "But sixteen years is nothing for a king such as Henry Tudor... and an English king..."

Her hands stilled. "There are those in England with blood more deserving of England's crown. Henry won his throne by killing in battle England's last king. In truth, King Henry, descended from bastard, albeit royal blood, only became king through the ancient right of conquest." The queen glanced and smiled at Beatriz. "I know your teacher has told you this."

Catalina's eyes narrowed, a line puckering deep between her eyebrows. The queen rested a hand on her daughter's shoulder.

"Your father and I have watched the English king closely. Never would we send you to marry his son if, for one moment, we harboured any doubts of Henry Tudor's capability to stay upon his country's throne. Just know my assurance, mi chiquitina, all you need do is enjoy your wedding day and be Prince Arthur's good wife and consort."

Placing the brush aside, the queen lifted Catalina's thick hair, now gleaming with red-gold lights, away from her neck. The long minutes of brushing had chased away most of its natural wave. Queen Isabel took up a tendril, curling it around a swollen finger.

She sighed, patting the curl back in place, smoothing the brushed hair behind her daughter's ear. The flowing hair fell like a silken, golden-lit mantle down Catalina's back, reaching beyond the seat of the stool.

Fingertips touching the sides of her daughter's head, the queen spoke again. "As a girl my hair too was thus. You are my true daughter. My heart knew this from the first moment I held you after your birth." The queen inhaled a deep breath. "All last night I found myself thinking of that time at Alcala de Henares, you in my arms, your sisters and brother by my bed. You made Juan annoyed, child, by being another sister, but Isabel took you from me and fussed over you like she was your mother. At fifteen she wanted to be a wife and mother very much." She heaved another sigh. "Your birth was such a happy time – all my children close to me, the blessing of a new hija."

The queen lifted Catalina's chin. "You are strong, strong and brave and intelligent. There's a great queen in you, a true lioness. How you'll surprise men with your roar. You'll make them quake, just as I do. How could you not, my hija, born in the middle of a Holy War? Catalina, you make me proud. Every day of your life you've made me proud. The English do not know yet what I send to them, but they soon will. One of my greatest, and most precious jewels." Queen Isabel rested her hands on Catalina's shoulders. She gazed with her daughter into the mirror– a picture of hopeful youth and sorrowing maturity shining together in the amber glow of candlelight.

Queen Isabel bit her lower lip, leaving behind the mark of teeth. When next she spoke, her deep voice trembled. "Always, always remember this: drink nothing without first seeing it tasted by someone else; sign nothing without reading it thoroughly. Be careful where you give your trust." She swallowed, gazing at Beatriz. "Latina would give her life for me, and my heart tells me this is also true of our María for you. But other than María... Hija, I know you like and trust Geraldini, who I send with you as your confessor. He will also keep you company in your studies. But even with confessors you must be very careful. Only trust the good God."

The queen gently caressed Catalina's cheek, heaving a deep sigh. "Hija, always remember the mask we wear when the doors open from our private chambers to the court. That's your armour behind which you hide your heart. Reveal that, and you give a weapon into the hands of your enemies. You will have those, and many. Our place in the world makes it so. But you're my child. You'll know what to do. I have won countless enemies to me, and do not doubt you can too."

The queen's arms slipped around Catalina's neck, her chin resting on her head. Beatriz huddled deeper into the shadows of the pool, her presence forgotten, feeling like an intruder.

"Next week, you shall leave us. Next week, my letters to you shall begin. Every free moment I shall write to you. I vow this as the mother who loves you."

"I promise too, Mamá." Catalina's eyes glowed brighter, brimming with liquid gold.

The queen gently shook her. "Mi chiquitina, you promised me. You are a princess and one day will be queen. There have been enough tears in recent years... Your marriage gives us reason to rejoice."

Catalina blinked, nodding.

Sitting far from them, Beatriz remembered Catalina's daily prayers. She so wished to postpone this departure for the sake of her ailing mother.

The queen reached for her cloak. From inside its deep, hidden pocket, she pulled out a chain with a heavy gold cross. "Take this with you."

Catalina stared. "Mamá! Your fragment of the true cross?"

Queen Isabel smiled, passing the golden chain over her daughter's head. "I always planned to give this to you. I have another gift too." Again she reached into the pocket, drawing out a small gold book. "I had this made for you, mi chiquitina – a private parting gift from me to you."

Catalina took the book from her mother. She turned the pages.

Beatriz saw her swallow hard, gazing with tear-bright eyes at her mother. "Gracia. 'Tis beautiful, Mamá."

"I agree, child. I wanted you to have an hour book like the Flemish one I treasure. The painter did well with it. This annunciation scene – he made our good Virgin look somewhat like you, si?"

With a wry smile Catalina gazed down at the book. "She's very pretty."

The queen laughed a little. "You're just as pretty. When I saw the red-gold hair and grey eyes of this young Madonna, I realised what had happened. The painter, knowing it was for you, looked to you for his inspiration. He painted it with love, Catalina. Mi chiquitina, so many love you. Mark my words – the English will love you, too."

A week later, at dawn, Beatriz stood with Catalina and María on the terraced roof of the Tower of Comares. Rivulets of white gold streamed through feathery clouds, the deluge of light from a rising sun turning the snowy top of Sierra Nevanda aflame, continuing to the near fortress hill. On the last morning with her girls at the Alhambra, the scent of oranges and pomegranates, and a silver morning wove together a vivid design of poignant farewell.

Morning light struck the paved, narrow, winding streets and buildings of Granada, dawn's light gilding red stone gold. Gardens hugged the stone walls of the city, forming a lush, green belt, spreading out wide to the near valley of the Darro. The morning breeze wafted a heady perfume of summer flowers from the gardens. In the valley, crops of grains began to yellow, ripening for the harvest. The same breezes caressing their bare skin on the tower's roof also played a gentle game of back, forth, and back again through the tops of the long green stalks. Stretched out as far as their feasting eyes could see, fruit orchards and mulberry trees rendered a canvas of vivid colour. Festooning vines climbed as if from tree to tree, their yet unripe grapes hanging in plump, glistening clusters.

Beatriz inhaled a deep breath. The aroma of nearby orange groves invigorated and soaked into her soul. She straightened her shoulders, almost feeling the presence of her ancestor Samuel Ibn Nagrela. Unable to take her eyes away from the view, she wondered if he had once stood here, just like the three of them, to greet a new day. Perhaps this was the place that had inspired him to write:

Hurry and give me drink,
Before the rise of dawn,
Of spice wine and juice of pomegranate,
In a cup held by the perfumed hand of a young maid,
Who will sing to me of many things
Both life giving and death dealing.

As if in answer to her thoughts, Catalina's voice returned Beatriz to the waking city. "Of all the places I've lived, I love here the best. 'Tis my heart's true home."

Beatriz squeezed her hand. "All will be well."

"I pray to God that it will be so." She gazed towards the palace. "How will my mother be with the last of us gone?"

Letting go of her hand, Beatriz listened to the bells calling to morning mass. María folded her arms on the top of the wall, glancing at the tiles near their feet. Sun rays spilled through the delicate stonework etching its lace design upon the ground.

Turning to Catalina, María sighed. "God will give the queen strength, as He does for us all, my prima hermana."

Catalina moved closer to her friend. "All her strength comes from God. Her faith is all the certainty she has left now." She lifted her chin, eyes welling with sorrow. "I don't want to leave her, not while she needs me."

Beatriz looked over the city. So far away it appeared so tiny, and almost dreamlike. A loaded wagon headed slowly towards the gates. Time moved them closer to when it would be the girls' turn to follow the same route. Her girls. How she wanted to weep.

"The king says there have been too many excuses, too many

delays. You know when the king speaks thus your mother bows to his will," María said.

Tears shimmered gold in Catalina's eyes before she blinked them away. "Why can't he see how much she needs me?"

Beatriz clasped her hand again. "The king sees that every new day you remain makes it more difficult for the queen. Perchance he does only what he thinks right. I promise you, I will never leave your mother. I can never replace you, but you know my devotion to the queen."

The girl rubbed her face. "That gives me some comfort, my teacher." She sighed. "Mother tells me she will not journey with us. She says she will not say goodbye. She cannot." Catalina looked at the sky. "Will England have dawns as beautiful as this? I want to imprint it on my memory so I never forget. There is so much to say goodbye to. Too much." One tear and then another tracked down her cheek. "I told Mother I shall take the pomegranate as my token." Her eyes looked first at María, and then at Beatriz. "Do you want to know why?"

Beatriz gazed down at the city, the well-paved, winding, narrow streets, its golden domed alcázars, the close-placed homes of the city dwellers, some like the rich grandees, but on a far smaller scale, designed for beauty as well as homes in which to live. Courtyards, festooned with flowering vines and water-singing fountains, pomegranate trees with turning leaves of red, already laden and pregnant with fruit. Joyful bells – north, south, east and west – they rang out this fair city's abundant life and vitality.

"An easy riddle, my scholar." Beatriz waved her hand over the city. "Granada, the pomegranate itself. Your parents laboured long for its conquest."

Catalina smiled tenderly at the clouds. No longer wisps of feathers sweeping across the sky, they reminded Beatriz of the latticed stone at her fingertips.

"You guess wrong, my teacher, you who is so rarely wrong. I chose it because of the legend of Proserpina... it is what I want my mother to remember and keep always in her heart. One day I shall return to her, as Proserpina did for her mother." Catalina's gaze lifted to the morning sky. "One day, in Heaven, she and I shall be together, but with no more sorrow and with no more farewells."

Beatriz rested her eyes again on the city. Birdsong scored the bright morning, twittering whistles answered by the warble of bolder birds in an unshaped, musical concert. Carried high and thin in the wind, a cockerel crowed and crowed its pride and delight at the new morn, brooking no rebuttal. Someone on a balcony below plucked the strings of a vihuela. A young boy and girl laughed and tossed a ball, playing with their dog. Heading to the city gates with little hurry, a straight-back, broad-shouldered grandee rode his white stallion as if he owned the world.

The splendour of the morning strummed her like a harp. Wind, light and the warmth of morning sun resonating deep within her, her whole body throbbed with the sweetness of life. She gloried in the day, her whole spirit singing like a bird its own sweet ode. Beatriz squeezed Catalina's hand. "Remember to take joy in life too. Remember, there always will be light, even in the darkest days." She smiled through her tears at her girls. "The love you two share is one such light. It will guide you both through all your days. While you can, live and be happy."

THE END

WRITING FALLING POMEGRANATE SEEDS

First published at *www.tudorsdynasty.com*

A footnote. Sometimes it takes just a footnote to set my imagination alight. Years ago, I found such a footnote, in Isabel la Católica, Queen of Castile: critical essays, a book of academic essays about the times, influence and mythology of Isabel of Castile[1], the mother of Katherine of Aragon. Katherine, of course, was Henry VIII's wife, and went to her grave calling herself that. Really, that's not surprising considering that she was a devout Catholic, and had been married to Henry for over twenty years, and let's not forget their five dead babies and one living daughter, before he decided to replace her with Anne Boleyn. But back to my footnote.

This footnote introduced me to Doña Beatriz Galindo (1465/75? -1534)- a woman who taught not only Katherine of Aragon, but also Latin to Queen Isabel herself. Latin was the necessary language of Medieval diplomacy for the Christian world, but, because she was 'female' and an unforeseen successor to her half brother's throne, Isabel was not schooled or expected to learn this language in her childhood and early youth. As a mother, Isabel remembered how her own education did not prepare her for her future life. She ensured her five children received the best education possible by employing the best teachers for them.

When I decided to explore in *Falling Pomegranate Seeds* the forces that originally shaped Katherine of Aragon (or Catalina as she was known to her family) during her time at the court of her mother, I turned to Beatriz Galindo to tell this fictionalised story of Katherine's early years. Beatriz was a perfect subject for me as a writer of fiction. I could only find the barest bones of her life story, which offered me a huge gap to fill with the use of my imagination; but what fascinating bones I had to play with. Beatriz was a scholar, a poet – sadly, like so many talented women of the past, her work is lost to us – and such a gifted Latin teacher that she lectured at the University of Salamanca. She also lectured on

Aristotle, medicine and rhetoric. And did I mention she was a wife and mother as well?

I felt in awe of Beatriz when I started writing Falling Pomegranate Seeds. I could not help wondering how it must have been for her – a woman who lived a life denied to most women in the Medieval period. Did it come at a personal cost? That question opened up a lot of 'what if' questions that acted as midwives to my imagination.

My imagination constructed Beatriz as a woman who lived a life that challenged the status quo. In a male dominated society, Beatriz somehow, and extraordinarily so, rewrote her life story. She appeared to have both worked with and resisted a society that could have easily prevented her from reaching her true potential.

A recognised scholar and a respected advisor to Queen Isabel, wife of King Ferdinand of Aragon, a kingdom of lesser importance than Castile, Beatriz lived in a time of great change and upheaval - accompanying her Queen during the 'Holy War', Queen Isabel's campaign to 'cleanse' her country of the Moors, which closed the door upon hundreds of years of Islamic influence in Castile. Beatriz Galindo was also a personal friend to the Queen. As a member of Queen Isabel's court, she frequently accompanied the queen in her court's peripatetic journey around her kingdom while employed as Katherine of Aragon's tutor, and likely the tutor to Katherine's three sisters.

Beatriz Galindo seems almost forgotten by world history, yet she deserves to be remembered. Her one and only biography, written in Spanish, is still untranslated and thus unavailable to the English-speaking world. As a tutor of Katherine of Aragon, a woman known and respected for her intelligence and learning, I believe we can say that Beatriz's influence continued into the reign of Henry VIII of England and beyond.

History tells us that Beatriz Galindo was a scholar of the Greek philosopher Aristotle. This philosopher spoke loud and clear his views concerning women who he saw as "unfinished men" and vessels simply designed for childbearing. It intrigued me that

Beatriz Galindo studied Aristotle and wrote commentaries about him. Did her resistance to and questioning of his beliefs result in her own empowerment and reshaping her life to one that allowed fulfilment? I could not help thinking about how such a teacher could have influenced Katherine of Aragon.

Falling Pomegranate Seeds is set during the time that saw Cristóbal Colón discovering the "New World" and Isabel and her husband Ferdinand engaged in their Holy War. Married to Francisco Ramírez, master of the King Ferdinand's artillery, Beatriz Galindo was an eyewitness to the fall of Granada. Later, she saw Isabel send into exile her Jewish subjects, after giving them an ultimatum to convert to Christianity. With her passion for learning and knowledge of medicine, I suspect the expulsion the Moors and Jews would have shaken Beatriz's identity to the core, as would have had a later happening: the burning of countless and priceless Islamic manuscripts, which erased knowledge that had come down the centuries.

Envisioning Beatriz made me wonder what it may have cost her to claim her own life. My imagination posed one possible scenario. My imagination also opened the door to Katherine of Aragon, as both child and girl. Katherine was a woman who loved books and learning. As England's very loved Queen, she was the patron of scholars and of the arts. It is not hard to imagine her then as a child who loved to learn. It is not hard to imagine that she would have loved her tutor, Beatriz. The youngest child of five children, Katherine suffered sorrow after sorrow before she left England to begin her life of exile. But she came to England trained and ready to be a queen. *Falling Pomegranate Seeds* imagines how that happened.

REFERENCES

Boruchoff, D. A. 2003, *Isabel la Católica, Queen of Castile: critical essays*, Palgrave Macmillan, New York.

Denzin, N. K. and Y. S. Lincoln 2003 *Collecting and interpreting qualitative materials*. Thousand Oaks, Calif., Sage.

[1] Studying that book is also the reason why I call Isabel of Castile Isabel rather than Isabella. One of the essays strongly suggests that Isabella originated as a form of belittlement of this strong Queen - who was referred to as 'King' during her long and world changing reign.

ACKNOWLEDGEMENTS

First and foremost, I want to acknowledge my dear husband for supporting my writing obsession. I sincerely thank him for putting up with our very untidy house and for financing a research trip for this novel. He is often forced to push aside a pile of books to get into bed at night, helpfully locating my missing pens when he tries to sleep on them. Despite everything, he has always encouraged me to pursue my dreams.

Writers need people to believe in their writing. I'm lucky there too. Glenice Whitting, author of the award-winning *Pickle to Pie*, and a darling and long-time friend, never let me forget about this novel. One of my important beta readers, I thank Glenice for always believing in me. I also thank my dear friends Valerie Clukaj and Kristie Dean for their encouragement.

The first version of this work saw Cindy Vallar giving my work the benefit of her red pen and her talents as a gifted editor. This overhauled and reworked version benefited from the red pen of another gifted editor: Rachel Le Rossignol. I express my sincere thanks to you both.

I also want to thank Jan Crosby, who has also read this work in its early life. I am also grateful to Sandra Worth, C. W. Gortner, Barbara Denvil, Nerina Jones, Eloise Faichney, Helen Barnes, Professor Josie Arnold and Adrienne Dillard for their willingness to read and offer feedback on *Falling Pomegranate Seeds* – whether it was years ago for the first version, or this completely reworked version. I also wish to express my gratitude to Dr Carolyn Beasley – who does so much to support me in so many ways.

One lovely memory I have of writing the first version *Falling Pomegranate Seeds* involves my youngest son, David, who was then still a child. As I wrote in bed, David would nestle up beside me and ask for the latest word-count. I will never forget the light of pride in his eyes as the novel grew and grew. That light of pride kept me writing.

Thank you all!

READING GROUP QUESTIONS

Thank you for taking the time to read my novel. As with all novels, there are a number of themes which run through the narrative. I hope that you enjoyed the book and that the following questions help you to get a deeper understanding of the novel.

1. Falling Pomegranate Seeds takes place in Spain as Isabel and Ferdinand finally capture the regions still occupied by the Moors. What did you discover about Spain at this time?

2. Who were the major players in the book, and what were their motivations?

3. How does Beatriz find herself conflicted in her role as tutor to Catalina?

4. Some of the story revolves around the Alhambra palace in Granada. Have you been to the Alhambra or seen pictures of the Nasrid Palace? Even by today's standards, it is a beautiful place. What do you think it must have been like to live in or leave such a place?

5. Beatriz hides some secrets of her own. What are they? Do you understand and agree with why she kept them secret?

6. What does Beatriz's character tell us about the role of a woman at this time in history?

7. We know that Catalina eventually becomes Katherine of Aragon, the first wife of Henry VIII of England. Do you think that she was prepared for such an important role by her upbringing?

8. Do you think that court life was easy for Isabel, Ferdinand and their children or were the pressures of being a royal family very great indeed?

9. Was life different for the king and queen compared to those who surrounded them?

10. How much did the attempt on Ferdinand's life change Catalina? Was this a key moment in her life or just something she accepted?

11. I have described this book as "a tale of mothers and daughters, power, intrigue, death, love, and redemption, in the end, Falling Pomegranate Seeds sings a song of friendship and life." Do you think this is a good description of the themes running through the book? Which theme is the strongest within the book?

12. Who was your favourite character in the book, and why?

13. Are there any characters you particularly admire or dislike, and why?

14. There are strong emotions throughout the book. Can you pick out a passage that you found particularly profound or interesting? Did it make you think about your own life?

If you enjoyed *Falling Pomegranate Seeds: The Duty of Daughters*, please consider leaving a review at Goodreads or the place where you purchased the book. I read every review left online and really appreciate the time you have taken to read the book and comment on it.

WENDY J. DUNN

THE ALHAMBRA

I decided to first visit Spain in 2007 after writing a scene in the first draft of *Falling Pomegranate Seeds: The Duty of Daughters*. The scene set in The Alhambra of my imagination, I had a vision of white butterflies, countless white butterflies, fluttering a graceful dance in a garden where sunlight flittered through pomegranate, orange and cypress trees. I had no idea if the vision had any similarity to the reality of the gardens of The Alhambra, although an internet search reassured me that butterflies are indeed a part of the natural environment of The Alhambra. In fact, The Alhambra is famed for its butterflies.

My problem with imagining places still in existence today is that I begin to yearn to see them with my own eyes. I live in Australia, but my imagination has never really latched onto the history of my beautiful homeland. My ancestry is British. My children, born and raised in a multicultural country, have always declared their British ancestry as "boring". Two years ago, for my birthday, they gave me a DNA test, hoping to discover ancestral lines far more interesting than those belonging to the British Isles. Alas, my DNA results proved I am more British than the average Brit. For many years now, I have wondered about ancestral memory – and if that may explain why my imagination is so fixated on England. I have in my lifetime somehow managed five trips to the United Kingdom, three of them including time in Europe. One of those times saw me on a tour of Spain for seventeen days. At that time, I was working on my first vision of Falling Pomegranate Seeds: The Duty of Daughters, and had fallen in love with the descriptions of Spain through my research. I wanted to see for myself the places important to the early life of Catalina of Aragon.

My time in Spain enriched and fed my imagination. I saw in my mind Beatriz Galindo sitting and talking with Catalina and María de Salinas, in sunlit courtyards edged by well kept gardens and shaded by cypress and orange trees. I closed my eyes and smelled the perfume of flowers and heard in my mind the song of water cascading into stone water fountains. My then eleven-year-old son, who accompanied me on this wonderful adventure, was so impressed with all the water fountains we saw on our travels he was determined to convince his father to build one in our small front garden back in Australia. Alas, that never happened.

What did happen is I fell in love in Spain – not with a person, but with a place; it is a love I share with many. I only had one day at the The Alhambra back in 2007. I remember well the grey sky, and my anxiety that my long awaited day would be spoiled by a downpour of rain. The rain held off until we left – long enough for The Alhambra to soak into my heart and psyche.

Once again, water fountains delighted my son, especially the stone lion protected fountain, which aptly named its courtyard: The Courtyard of the Lions. For myself, I delighted in Moorish architecture, water features and gardens designed to feast the eye.

The Alhambra was built by Badis ibn Habus, the Berber King of Granada, in the 11th century. There is a romantic legend that The Alhambra, meaning 'red castle', was built at night, under torchlight. The family of Catalina of Aragon took possession of it from the Moors in 1492, and her parents Isabel and Ferdinand used it for their royal court. It was home to Catalina from the time she was seven to fifteen.

Strolling in the gardens, it was very easy to imagine Catalina there, growing up in this place of great beauty, until the day came when she would leave her parents for ever. My time at The Alhambra helped me describe the palace and its surrounds in Falling Pomegranate Seeds: The Duty of Daughters. To my eye, the stone interior and exterior seemed like delicate lace work – allowing light to filter in and out, dappling over floor and wall. The architecture of *The Alhambra* is married to water and gardens. One water feature is very famous, and has been the subject of countless photographs of tourists and the inspiration for artists. A long rectangular pool mirrors the arches of the Partal façade in the Patio de los Arrayanes, or the court of the myrtles.

I was at The Alhambra for only about five hours. It did not feel long enough, but it was long enough to embrace The Alhambra in my heart for ever as one of my favourite places on Earth. I will never forget my time there, or its unbelievable beauties. It was also long enough to fire my imagination. I saw Catalina and María practicing their dancing steps in The Courtyard of the Lion. I imagined them bathing together in the bath of the Comares Palace, under a small stone dome cut with stars to let the light flicker on the water. I saw them in the garden with Beatriz Galindo, sitting at her feet as she read them stories. I saw them preparing to say their final farewells before they started their long journey to England.

Leaving The Alhambra, I promised to return one day. I was lucky enough to do that this year – and I hope one day to make another return.

FALLING POMEGRANATE SEEDS:
ALL MANNER OF THINGS

The final part of the story of Katherine of Aragon.

Winter, 1539: María de Salinas is dying. Long widowed of her beloved husband, all María wants in her last days is to know she is no longer estranged from the daughter she loves. Too ill to travel, she writes a letter to her daughter Katherine, the young duchess of Suffolk. A letter telling of her life: a life intertwined with her friend and cousin Catalina of Aragon, the youngest child of Isabel of Castile. It is a letter to help her daughter understand the choices she has made in her life, beginning from the time she keeps her vow to Catalina to share her life of exile in England.

Friendship, betrayal, hatred, forgiveness – *All Manner of Things* tells a story of how love wins out in the end.

Pre-publication praise for *All Manner of Things*

A moving account of one woman's strength and courage against impossible odds. Seen through the eyes of her friend Maria, Catalina/Katherine of Aragon grows from a young, powerless girl to become a queen England will remember for ever. A timeless story of friendship and love, which will stay with the reader long after the last page is turned, *All Manner of Things is Wendy* J. Dunn's best novel yet. ~ Lauren Chater, author of *The Lace Weavers* and *Gulliver's Wife*.

To read this book is like tasting a succulent pomegranate that swells and ripens and reveals the luscious fruit. ~ Glenice Whitting, author of *Pickle to a Pie* and *What Time is it There?*

A sensitive and inspiring portrait of faith and friendship, framed around the devotion inspired by a remarkable queen. Wendy J. Dunn has written another gem of a novel for Tudor enthusiasts! ~ Gareth Russell, author of *Young and Damned and Fair: The Life of Catherine Howard, Fifth Wife of King Henry VIII* (US title) (2017) *The Darksome Bounds of a Failing World: The Sinking of the Titanic and the End of the Edwardian Era* (2019), plus others.

All Manner of Things is an evocative retelling of the life of Katherine of Aragon from her arrival in England. This is a story ripe with passion and rich in historical detail. *All Manner of Things* draws the reader deep into the heart of Henry's Tudor court, with its machinations, betrayals and very human stories of love and loss. ~ Rachel Nightingale, author of *The Tales of Tarya* series.

A finely wrought tale that resurrects the indomitable spirit of Katherine of Aragon, breathing new life into her oft-told story. Maria's voice is fresh and engaging – a perspective sorely needed in novels of this era. You can't help but rage and grieve alongside her as her beloved Catalina's fate races towards its inevitable and heartbreaking conclusion. Yet another spellbinding novel from Wendy J Dunn! – Adrienne Dillard, author of *Cor Rotto* and *The Raven's Widow*.

"I'm so fussy about historical fiction, but Wendy J. Dunn never fails to please. Dunn breathes life into Catalina and Maria in this celebration of true friendship. Their story seemed to reach through the ages to truly touch me. Beautiful, just beautiful." – Claire Ridgway, author of *The Fall of Anne Boleyn: A Countdown*.

Lightning Source UK Ltd.
Milton Keynes UK
UKHW042355100522
402764UK00015B/462